D1557420

Nietzsche

contra Democracy

FREDRICK *Appel*

CORNELL UNIVERSITY PRESS *Ithaca and London*

Nietzsche
contra
Democracy

First published 1999 by Cornell University Press

Printed in the United States
of America

Cornell University Press strives to use
environmentally responsible suppliers
and materials to the fullest extent possible in the publishing of its books.
Such materials include vegetable-
based, low-VOC inks and acid-free pa-
pers that are also recycled, totally
chlorine free, or partly composed of
nonwood fibers.

Cloth
printing   10 9 8 7 6 5 4 3 2 1

Library of Congress
Cataloging-in-Publication Data
Appel, Fredrick.
    Nietzsche contra democracy /
Fredrick Appel.
        p.   cm.
    Includes bibliographical refer-
ences and index.
    ISBN 0-8014-3424-6 (alk. paper)
    1. Nietzsche, Friedrich Wilhelm,
1844–1900—Contributions in
political science. 2. Democracy.
I. Title.
JC233.N52A66   1998
320′.092—dc21   98-27125

To the memory of my father,
LARRY MORRIS APPEL

contents

acknowledgments

Many of the ideas in this book have been presented over the last few years at annual meetings of the American Political Science Association, the Midwest Political Science Association, the Northeastern Political Science Association, the American Philosophical Association (Eastern and Pacific Divisions), the North American Nietzsche Society, and the Canadian Political Science Association. I thank all of my respondents, especially Maudemarie Clark, Christoph Cox, and Leon Craig. My gratitude also extends to the fine scholars who commented on or challenged the arguments made in various parts of this book: Peter Berkowitz, Monique Deveaux, Jeremy Goldman, David Kahane, Brian Leiter, Pratap Mehta, Louis Miller, David Owen, Mark T. Reinhardt, Alan Ryan, James Tully, Brian Walker, and Bernard Yack. While I have not learned as much from them as I should have, their advice has made this a better book.

I also acknowledge the inspiration (both professional and personal) received during my postgraduate years from Charles Taylor. His strong encouragement of this project came at an especially crucial juncture. A special word of appreciation is due to my friend, colleague, and sometime collaborator Ruth Abbey, who has been uncommonly generous with her time and comments and who graciously allowed me to include a revised version of our joint essay as Chapter 6. The reader will note the pervasive influence of her important work on Nietzsche in what follows.

I acknowledge the financial assistance of the Social Sciences and Humanities Research Council of Canada during the years in which this book was first conceived and researched. Because of a postdoctoral fellowship awarded by the Quebec government's Fonds pour les chercheurs et l'aide à la recherche, I had the privilege of revising the manuscript in the congenial and stimulating atmosphere of Harvard University. I am grateful to Kenneth A. Shepsle, chair of the Department of Government, and Charles S. Maier, director of the Minda de Gunzburg Center for European Studies, for their kind hospitality.

Without the strong support of Roger M. Haydon at Cornell University Press, this book might never have been published. As a young author I could not have wished for a more patient, thoughtful, engaged—and engaging—editor. I am also grateful to Priscilla Hurdle, managing editor, Nancy J. Winemiller, manuscript editor, and to Liz Holmes and John LeRoy for their fine copyediting.

Finally, a word of heartfelt thanks to my immediate family. More than anyone else, my wife, Marilyn Besner, made this book possible with her magnanimous understanding, love, and support. The birth of our older daughter, Lottie, coincided with the start of this project, and Martine joined our complement as it entered its final phase. I have no doubt that the great joy they have all brought to my life has touched this book—indeed, all of my endeavors—in ways I can scarcely imagine.

• • •

Portions of Chapter 1 have appeared in my articles "The Objective Viewpoint: A Nietzschean Account," *History of Philosophy Quar-*

terly 13, 4 (October 1996): 483–502, and "Nietzsche's Natural Hier-archy," *International Studies in Philosophy* 29, 3 (1997): 49–62. Chap-ter 4 contains material published in "The *Übermensch*'s Consort: Nietzsche and the 'Eternal Feminine,'" *History of Political Thought* 18, 3 (1997), 512–530, copyright © Imprint Academic, Exeter, U.K. Much of Chapter 6 appeared in a slightly different form as "Nietz-sche's Will to Politics," an article coauthored with Ruth Abbey in the *Review of Politics*, 60, 1 (Winter 1998): 83–114. I thank the publishers of these journals for giving me permission to reproduce this work here.

F. A.

notes on the use
of primary sources

References to Nietzsche's writings are documented parenthetically in the text, with the exception of references to Nietzsche's personal correspondence, which are cited in standard note style. Translations are by Walter Kaufmann and/or R. J. Hollingdale, with the exception of *The Birth of Tragedy*, translated by Shaun Whiteside, and the *Selected Letters of Friedrich Nietzsche*, translated by Christopher Middleton. I use the following abbreviations of translated works:

A   "The Antichrist," published with TI (see below).

AOM   *Assorted Opinions and Maxims*, in HAH, vol. 2 (see below).

BGE   *Beyond Good and Evil*, trans. R. J. Hollingdale (Harmondsworth: Penguin, 1990).

BT   *The Birth of Tragedy*, trans. Shaun Whiteside (Harmondsworth: Penguin, 1993). (The 1886 preface to this 1872 text, the seven-part "Attempt at Self-Criticism," is referred to as "BT Preface.")

D   *Daybreak: Thoughts on the Prejudices of Morality*, trans. R. J. Hollingdale (Cambridge: Cambridge University Press, 1982).

EH   *Ecce Homo*, trans. R. J. Hollingdale (Harmondsworth: Penguin, 1992).

GM   *The Genealogy of Morals*, trans. Walter Kaufmann and R. J. Hollingdale (New York: Vintage, 1969). Also referred to in the text as *The Genealogy*.

GS   *The Gay Science*, trans. Walter Kaufmann (New York: Vintage, 1974).

HAH   *Human, All Too Human: A Book for Free Spirits*, trans. R. J. Hollingdale (Cambridge: Cambridge University Press, 1986). (All references with this abbreviation concern vol. 1, except for references to the Preface of vol. 2).

HC   "Homer's Contest," in *The Portable Nietzsche*, trans. and ed. Walter Kaufmann (Harmondsworth: Penguin, 1982), pp. 32–39.

SE   "Schopenhauer as Educator," the third of Nietzsche's *Untimely Meditations*, trans. R. J. Hollingdale (Cambridge: Cambridge University Press, 1983), pp. 127–194.

TI   "Twilight of the Idols," published with A (see above) in *Twilight of the Idols and The Antichrist*, trans. R. J. Hollingdale (Harmondsworth: Penguin, 1990).

UD   "On the Uses and Disadvantages of History for Life," the third of Nietzsche's *Untimely Mediations*, trans. R. J. Hollingdale (Cambridge: Cambridge University Press, 1983), pp. 59–123.

WP   *The Will to Power*, trans. Walter Kaufmann and R. J. Hollingdale (New York: Vintage, 1968).

WS   *The Wanderer and His Shadow*, in HAH, vol. 2 (see above).

Z   *Thus Spoke Zarathustra*, trans. R. J. Hollingdale (Harmondsworth: Penguin, 1969). Also referred to in the text as *Zarathustra*.

When referring to the German original, I rely on the standard *Werk: Kritische Gesamtausgabe*, ed. Giorgio Colli and Mazzino Montinari (Berlin: de Gruyter, 1967–1978).

Roman numerals refer to major divisions or parts in Nietzsche's books; Arabic numerals refer to sections and subsections, not pages. So, for example, (WP 300) refers to *The Will to Power*, section 300, and (Z III, 11, 1) refers to *Thus Spoke Zarathustra*, part III, section 11 ("Of the Spirit of Gravity"), subsection 1. Unless otherwise indicated, all emphases are Nietzsche's own.

A brief explanation is warranted for my routine departure in this book from the accepted practice of gender-neutral language. A book on Nietzsche that scrupulously avoids the use of sexual stereotypes and sexist language would obscure, rather than highlight, Nietzsche's own sexism. Hence my repeated use of phrases such as "higher men" rather than "higher human beings." As I argue in Chapter 4, Nietzsche believes that only a certain type of *man* is capable of the highest levels of human achievement. I hope it will be clear in what follows that I wish to highlight, rather than endorse, this Nietzschean view.

Introduction

Friedrich Nietzsche's great concern is for the flourishing of those few whom he considers exemplary of the human species. He believes that we can—and should—make qualitative distinctions between higher, admirable modes of human existence and lower, contemptible ones, and that these distinctions should compel his target readership to foster higher forms of human life at whatever cost to the many who cannot aspire thereto.

Such a project, he fears, has become increasingly difficult in the modern world because the dominant social, political, and ethical thrust of modernity is undermining the very possibility of human greatness. Christian and post-Christian ethical and spiritual ideals have attained hegemonic status in the Western world and are effectively indoctrinating superior human beings into a leveling, egalitarian ethos that, if unchecked, may eradicate human excellence. Nietzsche sees his project as nothing less than the rescue of the species from this degradation, and he initiates it by appealing to the deepest instincts of those superior specimens of humanity now in the grips of "herd morality." By attempting to help them wean themselves from values that are manifestly bad for them, Nietzsche sees himself as laying the foundation for a new, aristocratic political order in Europe in which the herdlike majority and its preferred values are put in their proper place: under the control of a self-absorbed master caste whose only concern is for the cultivation of its own excellence.

It would be a gross understatement to say that this picture of Nietzsche's project is not often encountered in the contemporary Anglo-American world of letters. Political theorists and moral philosophers who consider themselves radical democrats have grown accustomed to viewing Nietzsche as a useful resource in their efforts to champion the interests and concerns of those who are disadvantaged and marginalized. As efforts to draft Nietzsche's thought into the service of radical democracy have multiplied, his popular association with emancipation and "progressivism" has become ever more entrenched and his patently inegalitarian political project ignored or summarily dismissed.

This book challenges this popular, "progressive" reading of Nietzsche. More specifically, it takes issue with a claim being made with increasing confidence and frequency, namely that an embrace of Nietzsche's emancipatory message is easily reconcilable with a steadfast commitment to egalitarian ideals. Although Nietzsche claims in a late work to develop his own, superior brand of "philanthropy" [*Menschenliebe*] (A 2), this book argues that his work is best understood as an uncompromising repudiation of both the ethic of benevolence and the notion of the equality of persons in the name of a radically aristocratic commitment to human excellence.[1] Nietzsche's critique of modern democratic sensibilities and practices is as central

1. The first to refer to Nietzsche as an aristocratic radical was a contemporary of Nietzsche's, the Danish critic Georg Brandes. In a letter to Brandes dated 2 December 1887, Nietzsche endorses this characterization, saying that it is "the shrewdest remark that I have read about myself till now." *Selected Letters of Friedrich Nietzsche*, ed. and trans. Christopher Middleton (Indianapolis: Hackett, 1996), p. 279. Although my approach differs from that of Bruce Detwiler in some important respects, I find the title of his book apt: *Nietzsche and the Politics of Aristocratic Radicalism* (Chicago: University of Chicago Press, 1990).

to his commitment to excellence as his seemingly less objectionable evocations of self-overcoming.

The objections and dismissals that will greet this book have already been rehearsed many times. Many will claim that Nietzsche is a "protean" thinker whose writings can be (and have been) twisted in innumerable ways.[2] It may be conceded—with varying degrees of readiness or reluctance—that textual evidence can be found in the Nietzschean corpus for the reading proposed here. But, so the argument goes, any suggestion that it is the "right" interpretation is spurious; indeed, any project attempting to "get Nietzsche right" is sterile and a colossal waste of time.

Partisans of this view tend to be enthusiastic followers of Foucault's cavalier approach to the interpretation of texts. His suggestion that "the only valid tribute to [Nietzsche's] thought . . . is precisely to use it, to deform it, to make it groan and protest" provides convenient cover for those wishing hastily to proclaim the irrelevance of Nietzsche's illiberalism and antiegalitarianism.[3] Thus William Connolly cautions democrats against responding too single-mindedly to Nietzsche's antidemocratic remarks, for such a reaction "represses dimensions in those same formulations that speak critically to the democrat as a democrat."[4]

---

2. See, for example, William E. Connolly, *Identity\Difference: Democratic Negotiations of Political Paradox* (Ithaca: Cornell University Press, 1991), p. 185. Cf. his more recent *The Ethos of Pluralization* (Minneapolis: University of Minnesota Press, 1995), pp. 26, 206.

3. Michel Foucault, *Power/Knowledge: Selected Interviews and Other Writings, 1972–1977* (New York: Pantheon, 1980), pp. 53–54. Connolly, for one, does not always adhere consistently to this "protean Nietzsche" line. For example, he criticizes Charles Taylor's "selective reading" of "the Nietzschean stance" for, among other things, "underplay[ing] the role of *amor fati* in Nietzsche's thought" (*Ethos of Pluralization*, p. 15). In this passage it seems that getting Nietzsche right *matters*. Bonnie Honig similarly suggests that a democratic appropriation of Nietzsche produces a truer reading. When Honig speaks of "radicalizing" Nietzsche's thought "in ways suggested by Nietzsche's own texts," the implication seems to be that her interpretation is better than rival accounts because it follows or highlights the logic of Nietzsche's position more rigorously or fully than a less radical rival. Honig, *Political Theory and the Displacement of Politics* (Ithaca: Cornell University Press, 1993), p. 65.

4. Connolly, *Identity\Difference*, p. 191.

With the infinite malleability of Nietzsche's writings conveniently assumed as a point of departure, postmodern theorists of democracy approach Nietzsche with the following question in mind: to what purpose can and should we use (or abuse) his work in the pursuit of our ends? Since we happen to be interested in radicalizing democratic theory and making a more pluralistic democratic practice conceivable (so their reasoning goes), we should focus on those elements of his opus that seem especially conducive to radical democracy and jettison the rest as retrograde and unusable.[5]

Just which element to begin with is a matter of some disagreement among those determined to fashion a Nietzschean pedigree for their radically egalitarian and pluralist visions of liberal (or social) democracy. Romand Coles's point of departure is a particular reading of Zarathustra's "gift-giving virtue,"[6] whereas Mark Warren privileges Nietzsche's conception of agency, which is said to undergird a "positive political vision" that "include[s] the values of individuation, communal intersubjectivity, egalitarianism, and pluralism."[7] Bonnie Honig, for her part, joins with Connolly in lauding Nietzsche's celebration of agonistic conflict and contest, which she claims is exemplary of a *virtù* politics that fosters the contestability of concepts and identities and valorizes dissonance, resistance, and disruption.[8] David Owen similarly prizes Nietzsche's agonistic politics and claims that one of the most useful elements of Nietzsche's philosophy is his

5. In this spirit, Mark Warren speaks of a postmodern "gentle Nietzsche" alongside a "bloody Nietzsche" and of the need to dispose of the latter in order to recover the former. Warren, *Nietzsche and Political Thought* (Cambridge: MIT Press, 1988), p. 211. See also David Owen, *Nietzsche, Politics, and Modernity* (London: Sage, 1995), p. 171. Richard Rorty, a self-declared postmodern liberal, is not as interested in radicalizing democratic theory, but he remains similarly confident that we can safely dismiss Nietzsche's darker musings as "mad" while profiting from Nietzschean notions of self-overcoming. See "The Priority of Democracy to Philosophy," in *Objectivity, Relativism, and Truth* (Cambridge: Cambridge University Press, 1991), p. 187. I have more to say about Rorty's argument in the concluding chapter.

6. Romand Coles, "Liberty, Equality, Receptive Generosity: Neo-Nietzschean Reflections on the Ethics and Politics of Coalition," *American Political Science Review* 90, 2 (June 1996): 375–388.

7. Warren, *Nietzsche and Political Thought*, p. 247; cf. p. 157.

8. Honig, *Political Theory*. Both Honig and Connolly attempt to democratize Nietzsche by seeing the *Übermensch* as part of all selves rather than a particular elite.

development of a "perspectivist" epistemology with emancipatory potential that is easily detached from Nietzsche's embarrassingly elitist rantings (which he may not have meant seriously, in any case).[9] Indeed, to draw attention to the latter is not only wrong-headed but also (we are told) politically suspect. As Tracy Strong seems to suggest, only "Straussians" and others with right-wing political agendas would be interested in treating seriously Nietzsche's attraction to notions of rank and hierarchy.[10]

One obvious objection to this "progressive" reading readily comes to mind. Let us put aside the considerable textual evidence against it for the moment and assume that Nietzsche is indeed a protean thinker whose work, with some creative bending and twisting, can be appropriated in limitless ways. Why, then, would anyone interested in radical democratic theory want to expend the considerable amount of creative energy required to adapt Nietzschean thought for democratic purposes? Why bother making Nietzsche's work "groan" and "protest" when there are so many other thinkers past and present with less dubious credentials who could provide ready inspiration? If all of this bending and twisting turns the end-product— call it "Nietzsche"—into a mirror image of one's own convictions, it is hard to imagine the point of such an endeavor. A Nietzsche thus sanitized or domesticated can teach nothing that could not be learned directly from dozens of contemporary writers.[11]

There is another, deeper objection to the progressive appropriation which I develop in the course of this book. One of my central claims is that Nietzsche's radically aristocratic commitments pervade every aspect of his project, making any egalitarian appropriation of his work exceedingly problematic. Thus my intention is not simply to point out how fervently Nietzsche wished to be understood as an advocate for illiberal and inegalitarian ideals. (If this were the extent

9. Owen, *Nietzsche, Politics, and Modernity*. For other recent book-length treatments in this vein, see Alan White, *Within Nietzsche's Labyrinth* (New York: Routledge, 1990); and Daniel W. Conway, *Nietzsche and the Political* (New York: Routledge, 1996).

10. Tracy B. Strong, "Nietzsche's Political Misappropriation," in *The Cambridge Companion to Nietzsche*, ed. Bernd Magnus and Kathleen M. Higgins (Cambridge: Cambridge University Press, 1996), pp. 128–129.

11. This point was suggested to me by Bernard Yack.

of my argument, the Foucaultian critic could readily concede my point and blithely reply that evidence of Nietzsche's authorial intentions need not restrict *our* interpretive freedom. Why shouldn't we ignore his intentions, the critic will suggest, and mine his work for nuggets that would prove useful to a project that he himself shunned?) Instead, I intend to argue for the all-encompassing nature of Nietzsche's elitist predilections.

I show in the coming chapters, for example, how assumptions of rank order among human beings undergird not simply his political stance but also his epistemology and his understanding of concepts such as nature. Nietzsche claims to perceive the existence of different types of human nature that represent higher and lower orders of human existence. Only higher-order human beings (such as himself) can sense the truth of this normative ranking and courageously, joyfully embrace the "hard truths" that science provides us of a contingent life without God. Only members of the tiny minority that embodies truly noble instincts are, in Nietzsche's view, "natural" in the fullest, finest sense, that is, creators who impose meaning and order on chaos and who thus serve as paradigms for the species as a whole.

Nietzsche aims at persuading these noble types—those for whom his books are written—to reorient their views toward a greater respect for their own visceral instincts and drives. The idea is not to attempt a nostalgic return to the "blond beast" of antiquity but rather to learn the lessons of this distant ancestor's downfall in order to propel a new, modern nobility into political and cultural ascendancy in Europe. By revealing his own trials and tribulations at the hands of mediocre sensibilities and by weaving a genealogical narrative that places his own suffering in context—that is, in the context of a panhistorical struggle between master and slave moralities—Nietzsche hopes to jar his readers out of their lethargy into a healthier, greater form of existence.

I also examine how his celebration of contestation (agonism) is bound up with a warrior ethos that legitimates both a quasi-deification of those fit to compete and an easy contempt for—and dehumanization of—those unworthy of the contest. Nietzsche's version of *noblesse oblige* or magnanimity, highly touted by those who would reclaim him for egalitarian thought, will be revealed as a highly uncertain safeguard against the Dionysian excesses of his highest human beings. I argue that Nietzschean magnanimity refers ultimately to nothing more than a sense of good taste and to the higher man's obligation to himself (rather than to others). Nietzsche, as we shall see, recognizes no duty to (inferior) others based upon any inalienable right to personal security, respect, or dignity. The studied indifference that passes for merciful forbearance in his thought may dissuade the noble type from lording it over his inferiors in a vulgar fashion, but it is not meant to halt any unintended harm that results from innocent acts of creative self-assertion. In Nietzsche's view, the benefits of such self-assertion far outweigh any accidental, destructive by-products of the creative process.

Postmodern theorists attracted to the notion of agonistic democracy would do well to examine more deeply what a politics given over to unlimited agonistic struggle might entail. The best way to begin this task, in my view, is to revisit Nietzsche's politics without dressing it up (tacitly or otherwise) with our liberal democratic scruples. Herein lies what may well be the real importance of Nietzsche for those of us who subscribe to the broad egalitarian consensus.[12] Nietzsche's usefulness to contemporary democratic theory may derive, paradoxically, from his uncompromising antiegalitarianism. An engagement with his "untimely meditations" about rank, domination, and nobility can enliven the sensibilities of egalitarians of all stripes by forcing them to account for and defend those convictions he holds in contempt: concern for the weak, belief in the equal moral

12. Following Will Kymlicka, I assume that all contemporary political and moral philosophy, whether of a liberal, libertarian, utilitarian, socialist, feminist, or other bent, works on an "egalitarian plateau" where it is agreed (a) that all human beings are of equal moral worth and are equal bearers of certain basic rights and (b) that one of the main tasks of the political community is the defense and promotion of these rights. How these rights are conceived and adjudicated is of course highly contested; but the conviction that we all share them (or should share them) is not. See Kymlicka, *Contemporary Political Philosophy: An Introduction* (New York: Oxford University Press, 1990), pp. 4–5, 49. The notion of a broad consensus on equality is also discussed by Ronald Dworkin in *Law's Empire* (Cambridge: Harvard University Press, 1986); and Amartya Sen, *Inequality Reexamined* (Cambridge: Harvard University Press, 1992).

worth of all human beings and the desire to preserve and promote liberal institutions.[13]

The view that alien ideas have these salutary antidotal benefits is one Nietzsche himself occasionally professes, and it underlies his famous claim that "what does not destroy us makes us stronger" as well as his repeated insistence upon the value of enemies.[14] This view, incidentally, is no stranger to the liberal tradition: one of John Stuart Mill's defenses of free speech is that when a view is silenced, even those who oppose it suffer because they lose "the clearer perception and livelier impression of truth produced by its collision with error."[15] Ironically, by drawing attention away from the illiberal and inegalitarian elements of Nietzsche's project and thereby sheltering contemporary democracy from the full force of his critique, radical democratic theorists may be doing their fellow democrats a disservice.

Nietzsche's Anglo-American Reception

The construction of an essentially benign, emancipatory Nietzsche in the collective imagination of the Anglo-American academy can be traced back to Walter Kaufmann, whose role as Nietzsche's foremost English-language translator and as author of an oft-cited study can scarcely be overestimated.[16] In his now-classic 1950 book and throughout the lengthy and ubiquitous editorial comments in his

13. As Laurence Lampert puts it, "Nietzsche's politics broadens the political perspective instead of shrinking itself into some modern option." *Nietzsche and Modern Times: A Study of Bacon, Descartes, and Nietzsche* (New Haven: Yale University Press, 1993), p. 431.

14. The claim can be found in WP 934 and TI I, 8; cf. D 507, GS 19. On the value of enemies, see AOM 191; GM I, 11; Z I, 22, 3; EH I, 7; EH II, 6; and TI V, 3.

15. This citation is from chapter 2 of "On Liberty." See John Stuart Mill, *On Liberty and Other Essays*, ed. John Gray (Oxford: Oxford University Press, 1991), p. 21. Nietzsche's faith in the antidotal value of opposing ideas and forces can be added to the convergences between him and Mill identified by Gerald Mara and Suzanne Dovi in their "Mill, Nietzsche, and the Identity of Postmodern Liberalism," *Journal of Politics* 57, 1 (February 1995): 1–23.

16. Walter Kaufmann, *Nietzsche: Philosopher, Psychologist, AntiChrist*, 4th ed. (Princeton: Princeton University Press, 1974).

translations, Kaufmann's main concern was to counter the prevailing postwar view of Nietzsche as a proto-Nazi, a view that had been encouraged by Elisabeth Föster-Nietzsche's selective editing of her brother's unpublished work and by the Nazis' own embrace of this doctored product. By highlighting Nietzsche's contempt for conventional anti-Semitism, for nineteenth-century racism, and for German chauvinism, Kaufmann provided us with a valuable corrective. In trying to bring his subject into line with prevailing liberal sensibilities, however, his gesture ironically mirrored that of Nietzsche's sister. Kaufmann's Nietzsche, a heroic figure aligned with other luminaries of the Western canon such as Socrates, Christ, and the Enlightenment *philosophes*, turned out to be scarcely more accurate a depiction than the Nazis' Aryan version (albeit from a much more palatable perspective).

A decided shift in Nietzsche scholarship began in the 1970s and accelerated in the 1980s, when an important part of Kaufmann's legacy was called into question. Under the influence of Jacques Derrida, Michel Foucault, and other representatives of French postmodern or poststructuralist thought, a "new Nietzsche" appeared on the Anglo-American intellectual scene, one who turned from torch-bearer to gravedigger of the Western philosophical tradition.[17] In this enthusiastic *nouvelle vague* of French postmodern influence, Nietzsche was pictured as a playful debunker of all ethical-normative language and conceptions of truth. Ironically, this repudiation of one part of Kaufmann's reading served to solidify another part of the Kaufmannian legacy: namely, his picture of Nietzsche as an essentially benign, admirable figure. For the postmod-

---

17. *The New Nietzsche* is the title of an influential collection of articles on Nietzsche in English translation, ed. David B. Allison (1977; Cambridge: MIT Press, 1985). The French-language work that inspired this collection included book-length studies by Gilles Deleuze, *Nietzsche and Philosophy*, trans. Hugh Tomlinson (1962; New York: Columbia University Press, 1983); Sarah Kofman, *Nietzsche and Metaphor*, trans. Duncan Lange (1972; London: Athlone Press, 1993); and a few short pieces by Michel Foucault (in, e.g., *Power/Knowledge*). See also Jacques Derrida, *Spurs: Nietzsche's Styles*, trans. Barbara Harlow (Chicago: University of Chicago Press, 1979); and, more recently, Eric Blondel, *Nietzsche, the Body, and Culture: Philosophy as Philological Genealogy*, trans. Sean Hand (Stanford: Stanford University Press, 1991).

ernists held that Nietzschean thought is emancipatory in its laying bare of the oppressive, stultifying dogmatism of all philosophical categories or grand narratives, especially those dealing with "morality" and "truth."[18]

Seen through the lens of a Derrida or a Foucault (or, in the anglicized version, an Alexander Nehamas or Rorty), Nietzschean "perspectivism" came to represent a dizzying, radical type of freedom from all traditional forms of thought and practice. As Peter Berkowitz has recently noted, it became standard practice to follow Foucault's concern with "regimes of truth" into the assumption that Nietzsche's main significance—indeed the source of his emancipatory potential—lay in his critical treatment (or deconstruction) of epistemology.[19] Even philosophers out of sympathy with postmodernism, such as Allan Bloom, Alasdair MacIntyre, and Alain Renaut, routinely associate Nietzsche with the epistemic and value relativism of his postmodern champions.[20]

18. Among the more prominent works in this line are Arthur Danto, *Nietzsche as Philosopher* (New York: Columbia University Press, 1980); Bernd Magnus et al., *Nietzsche's Case: Philosophy as/and Literature* (New York: Routledge, 1993); Alexander Nehamas, *Nietzsche: Life as Literature* (Cambridge: Harvard University Press, 1985); and Tracy B. Strong, *Friedrich Nietzsche and the Politics of Transfiguration*, expanded ed. (Berkeley: University of California Press, 1988). Among philosophers not generally known as Nietzsche scholars, Rorty has been particularly influential in promoting this view. See the reference in note 5 along with his *Contingency, Irony, Solidarity* (Cambridge: Cambridge University Press, 1989).

19. Peter Berkowitz, *Nietzsche: The Ethics of an Immoralist* (Cambridge: Harvard University Press, 1995). It is indeed strange that Foucault, after resolutely deflecting attention from Nietzsche's ethical and political concerns, revealed his own normative concerns more clearly near the end of his career, in the context of his work on Hellenistic conceptions of "care of the self." See Foucault, "The Ethic of Care for the Self as a Practice of Freedom," interview with Paul Fornet-Betancourt et al., trans. J. D. Gautier, in *The Final Foucault*, ed. J. Bernauer and D. Rasmussen (Cambridge: MIT Press, 1988). It seems that Foucault did not come to his interest in this aspect of ancient philosophy through Nietzsche, nor (to my knowledge) did he acknowledge that Nietzsche shared in this interest.

20. See Allan Bloom, *The Closing of the American Mind: How Higher Education Has Failed Democracy and Impoverished the Souls of Today's Students* (New York: Simon and Schuster, 1988); Alasdair MacIntyre, *After Virtue: A Study in Moral Theory* (Notre Dame: University of Notre Dame Press, 1984), especially chapter 9; and Alain Renaut, *The Era of the Individual: A Contribution to a History of Subjectivity*, trans. M. B.

Fortunately, the vogue of forcing Nietzsche into a triad with Foucault and Derrida has diminished markedly in more recent years, thanks to the appearance of fine studies that have effectively challenged many aspects of the postmodernist reading. On the epistemological front, recent studies have argued convincingly that the Nietzschean critique of conventional morality is undergirded by serious appeals to a notion of truth. According to these scholars, Nietzsche understood that the implausibility of positivism and Platonic realism need not impel us into an embrace of relativism. Nietzsche is described as carving out a position for himself in that vast middle ground between these two extremes.[21]

Recent authors have also begun to unearth the strong ethical-normative component in Nietzsche's project. Its identification becomes easier once we employ something like Bernard Williams's distinction between "ethics" and "morality."[22] Nietzsche's repeated self-description as an amoralist—indeed, an *im*moralist—and his repudiation of "morality" are best understood in light of his own alternative conception of human flourishing: his (Nietzschean) ethical standpoint.[23] And alongside this salutary shift toward the normative dimension of Nietzsche's thought, it is now increasingly accepted

---

DeBevoise and Franklin Philip (Princeton: Princeton University Press, 1997), chapter 5. See my review of Renaut in the *Boston Book Review* 4, 10 (December 1997): 14.

21. See, for example, Richard Schacht, *Nietzsche* (London: Routledge and Kegan Paul, 1983); Maudemarie Clark, *Nietzsche on Truth and Philosophy* (Cambridge: Cambridge University Press, 1990); and Brian Leiter, "Nietzsche and Aestheticism," *Journal of the History of Philosophy* 30, 2 (April 1992): 275–290. Cf. Leiter, "Perspectivism in Nietzsche's Genealogy of Morals," in *Nietzsche, Genealogy, Morality: Essays on Nietzsche's "On the Genealogy of Morals,"* ed. Richard Schacht (Berkeley: University of California Press, 1994), pp. 334–357; and his "Nietzsche and the Critique of Morality: Philosophical Naturalism in Nietzsche's Theory of Value" (Ph.D. diss., University of Michigan, 1995).

22. Bernard Williams, *Ethics and the Limits of Philosophy* (Cambridge: Harvard University Press, 1985), pp. 6–7.

23. For some recent attempts at exploring Nietzsche's normative dimension, see Lester Hunt, *Nietzsche and the Origin of Virtue* (London: Routledge, 1991); Ophelia Schutte, *Beyond Nihilism: Nietzsche without Masks* (Chicago: University of Chicago Press, 1984); and Berkowitz, whose 1995 book *Nietzsche* reflects Williams's distinction in its canny subtitle, *The Ethics of an Immoralist.*

that Nietzsche saw himself as an educator of sorts and wished to share his ethical-normative vision with others.[24]

All of this recent work represents an undeniable advance. Yet with very few exceptions, the Kaufmann legacy of tidying up Nietzsche for contemporary (liberal- or social-democratic) sensibilities remains the rule in the Anglo-American academy.[25] The consensus around the picture of Nietzsche as an essentially benign figure is rarely challenged and underlies many of the scholarly skirmishes that invoke Nietzsche's name and spirit. It is shared even by those who disagree over the political significance of his writings.

Nietzsche and Politics

For some, Nietzsche is a thinker wholly uninterested in or contemptuous of politics. Kaufmann's shadow looms particularly large here, for he was the first to adopt the now-familiar strategy of exonerating Nietzsche from the charge of proto-Nazism by dismissing or downplaying the political content of his writings. Kaufmann's claim that "the *leitmotif* of Nietzsche's life and thought [was] the theme of the antipolitical individual who seeks self-perfection far from the modern world" has resonated through many approaches to Nietzsche's

24. See, for example, Richard Schacht, "Zarathustra/Zarathustra as Educator," in *Nietzsche: A Critical Reader*, ed. Peter R. Sedgwick (Oxford: Blackwell, 1995), pp. 222–249; and Laurence Lampert, *Nietzsche's Teaching: An Interpretation of "Thus Spoke Zarathustra"* (New Haven: Yale University Press, 1987).

25. Exceptions include Berkowitz, *Nietzsche: The Ethics of an Immoralist*; Schutte, *Beyond Nihilism*; Stanley Rosen, *The Mask of Enlightenment: Nietzsche's Zarathustra* (Cambridge: Cambridge University Press, 1995); and J. P. Stern, *A Study of Nietzsche* (Cambridge: Cambridge University Press, 1979). Charles Taylor also evokes a less than comforting Nietzsche in his *Sources of the Self: The Making of Modern Identity* (Cambridge: Harvard University Press, 1989), pp. 444–455, 516–520. In France, meanwhile, a younger cohort of moral and political philosophers has for the last decade been engaged in a serious reexamination of the Nietzsche who had been trumpeted by the generation of Deleuze, Derrida, and Foucault. See, for example, the essays in *Why We Are Not Nietzscheans*, ed. Luc Ferry and Alain Renaut, trans. Robert de Loaiza (Chicago: University of Chicago Press, 1997), and my review of this book in the *Boston Book Review* 4, 9 (November 1997): 26–27.

thought, even those rejecting other aspects of Kaufmann's interpretation.[26] Nietzsche's focus on himself and his own experiences, his stress on individuality, his contempt for egalitarian collectivism, his disdain for the "petty politics" of his day, and his abhorrence at the idea of providing others with blueprints and prescriptions all seem to obviate (in this view) any substantive political vision for the future.

For others, this equation of Nietzsche's criticism of modern politics with an opposition to politics in general is tendentious. Alongside his castigation of petty politics, Nietzsche is said to gesture toward what he considers a different, grander type of politics.[27] In what follows I endorse this position—although, as noted above, I think there are grave difficulties with the widespread "left-wing" variant—and attempt to show how Nietzsche's politics emerge out of his concern for the flourishing of the "higher," "stronger" type of human being. I take up his aesthetic approach to political action and explore some of the qualities he believes future rulers would need and the mechanisms they could use to exercise and legitimate their power in a revitalized European political and cultural order.

To call for political and cultural revitalization is, of course, to embrace some vision of sociability, for politics cannot be a solitary affair. Here we encounter one of the deepest tensions in Nietzsche. I argue that he is genuinely torn between two competing ideals: a stoic notion of autarchy and an Aristotelian sense of our dependence on the right sort of company for the fullest cultivation of our virtue. Both in

26. Kaufmann, *Nietzsche: Philosopher, Psychologist, AntiChrist*, p. 418. More recent antipolitical readings that come readily to mind include the aforementioned works of Magnus, Nehamas, and Schacht, as well as Ted Sadler, *Nietzsche: Truth and Redemption* (London: Athlone, 1995); and Leslie Paul Thiele, *Friedrich Nietzsche and the Politics of the Soul: A Study of Heroic Individualism* (Princeton: Princeton University Press, 1990). Although he acknowledges passages that suggest otherwise, Berkowitz similarly concludes that Nietzsche "radically denigrates" political life. See his *Nietzsche: The Ethics of an Immoralist*, pp. 2, 19, 91, 102, 123, 148, 151, 161, 166, 238, and 246–247.

27. Among those alive to the political dimension of Nietzsche's thought are Detwiler, *Nietzsche and the Politics of Aristocratic Radicalism*; Nancy Love, *Marx, Nietzsche, and Modernity* (New York: Columbia University Press, 1986); Keith Ansell-Pearson, *An Introduction to Nietzsche as Political Thinker* (Cambridge: Cambridge University Press, 1994); and Lampert, *Nietzsche and Modern Times*.

his own voice and in that of his literary creation, Zarathustra, Nietzsche urges his readers to take on a higher, noble "selfishness" by escaping their stifling proximity to the majority and fleeing into a spiritually cleansing solitude.[28] As I argue below, however, he is also concerned that the indefinite maintenance of this initially salutary, healing isolation might eventually harm rather than foster nobility. My examination of his agonistic type of friendship and his views on gender relations, family, and "breeding" strongly suggests that his embrace of an aristocratic form of sociability mitigates (but does not completely subsume) his more extreme position on individual self-sufficency. The latter retains its most telling expression in the so-called eternal return of the same, which, as we shall see, functions in Nietzsche's thought as both a daunting thought experiment and a healing epiphany.

It is often noted, rightly, that Nietzsche abhors strict blueprints and does not provide us with a draft constitution for a new society ruled by *Übermenschen*. If one believes that the appellation "political philosopher" ought to be reserved exclusively for those with such blueprints in hand, he clearly would not fit the bill. But to hold this view is to opt for an exceedingly narrow conception of political philosophy. Under such rigid criteria even Plato would find his credentials as a political philosopher called into question, for his *Republic*

28. The question of just how seriously to take the title character of *Thus Spoke Zarathustra* is far from settled. It would be foolish to deny the ironic elements in the text. Indeed, in an 1886 preface to *The Gay Science* Nietzsche himself alerts his readers to the many elements of "wicked and malicious" parody in *Zarathustra* (GS Pref. 1). I am unconvinced, however, by Robert Pippin's argument that the redemptive message of this work is entirely undermined by irony. See Pippin, "Irony and Affirmation in Nietzsche's *Thus Spoke Zarathustra*," in *Nietzsche's New Seas: Explorations in Philosophy, Aesthetics, and Politics*, ed. Michael Allen Gillespie and Tracy B. Strong (Chicago: University of Chicago Press, 1988), pp. 45–71. Nietzsche explains in his personal correspondence that "behind all the plain and strange words" of *Zarathustra* "stand my deepest seriousness and my whole philosophy. It is the beginning of my disclosure of myself." Letter to Carl von Gersdorff, 28 June 1883, in *Selected Letters of Friedrich Nietzsche*, p. 213. Other professions of the profound seriousness undergirding *Zarathustra* can be found in EH Foreword 4 and EH XI. More generally, Nietzsche suggests that free-spirited types who engage in all sorts of mockery "are at bottom grave and serious human beings" (GS 107; cf. BGE 94, 232).

contains no such nuts-and-bolts analysis.[29] Nietzsche deserves his place in the canon of political philosophy not because he provides a detailed institutional account of the optimal type of polity, but rather because his sweeping denunciation of liberalism, democracy, social-ism, feminism, and other offshoots of modernity leads him to formu-late (albeit in a sketchy and unsystematic manner) an alternative, rad-ically aristocratic model of politics that bears serious examination.

29. I am indebted to Leon Craig for this point. (Admittedly, in his *Laws* Plato did get around to the more detailed policy prescriptions lacking in *The Republic*.)

o n e   **Science, Nature,**

and Nietzschean Ethics

The Hardest Service

It is sometimes argued that Nietzsche's embrace of the language of scientific rigor and method extends no further than his supposedly uncritical, science-worshipping "positivist" period of the late 1870s. After this time he is said to have adopted a resolutely skeptical view of modern science and to have prized unbounded artistic creativity over scientific discovery.[1] While this view seems to

1. See, for example, Arthur Danto, *Nietzsche as Philosopher* (New York: Columbia University Press, 1980); and Alexander Nehamas, *Nietzsche: Life as Literature* (Cam-

be suggested in a few passages of Nietzsche's later writings, where he appears to many commentators to be offering a picture of science as mere subjective projection of the desires of the scientist onto the world, I think it is mistaken. Whatever one may think of the scientific pedigree of Nietzsche's view of the human condition—and there is much that is tendentious and disputable in his "scientific" account of reality in general and humankind in particular—he bestows a central role upon science in his politico-philosophic enterprise. The finest human beings, claims Nietzsche, celebrate science as "the wisdom of the world" (A 47; cf. GS 335; WP 442, 443). He speaks in glowing terms of a new type of philosopher who would be "hardened by the discipline of science" and decries traditional beliefs and practices for their ignorance of and/or contempt for scientific method (BGE 230).[2]

The acerbic treatment of positivist notions of science in the later works is all too often mistaken for a generalized skepticism toward the very possibility of science. In his criticisms of positivism, however, Nietzsche professes support for an empiricist principle characteristic of modern science: namely, the importance of sense experience to the generation of all genuine knowledge.[3] As he proffers in *Beyond Good and Evil*, "all credibility, all good conscience, all evidence of truth comes only from the senses [*Sinnen*]" (BGE 134; cf. TI III, 3). Rightly exercised by those with the proper instincts (see below) and correct "breeding," sense perception allows for the attainment of *real*—as opposed to bogus, positivistic—scientific objectivity. The Nietzschean free spirit has the capacity for "delineat[ing]

bridge: Harvard University Press, 1985). For a more recent articulation of this view, see Leslie Paul Thiele, *Friedrich Nietzsche and the Politics of the Soul: A Study of Heroic Individualism* (Princeton: Princeton University Press, 1990), pp. 103–118.

2. See, for example, the derision directed at priests who claim to be "above" scientific knowledge (A 8, 12) and Nietzsche's condemnation of religious faith for its "*veto against science*" (A 47; cf. A 48, 49).

3. Brian Leiter, "Perspectivism in Nietzsche's Genealogy of Morals," in *Nietzsche, Genealogy, Morality: Essays on Nietzsche's "On the Genealogy of Morals,"* ed. Richard Schacht (Berkeley: University of California Press, 1994), pp. 336–337. Laurence Lampert also notes that Nietzsche rejects the nineteenth century's reigning scientific paradigm in the name of science. *Nietzsche and Modern Times: A Study of Bacon, Descartes, and Nietzsche* (New Haven: Yale University Press, 1993), p. 301.

reality *as it is*" (EH XIV, 5) and, like the good philologist, learns the art "of being able to read off a fact *without* falsifying it by interpretation" (A 52).

Nietzsche castigates positivism not for its goal of uncovering the true nature of reality—this is a goal he shares—but rather for an account of scientific objectivity that is both naïve and cowardly. (I deal with its supposed naïveté here and take up Nietzsche's charge of cowardice below.) It is naïve because of its implausible view that an accurate account of the facts is possible only after the observer becomes "impartial" by purging himself of all "bias," that is, all affective, normative, and/or theoretical orientation to the object in question. In a passage often echoed in contemporary philosophy, Nietzsche claims that the positivist conception presupposes "an eye that is completely unthinkable, an eye turned in no particular direction, in which the active and interpreting forces, through which alone seeing becomes seeing *something*, are supposed to be lacking " (GM III, 12).

In proposing a completely unmediated, neutral grasp of reality, positivists presume that the attainment of knowledge and truth depends on privileged access to an unearthly, disembodied realm—a "real" world which then serves as the Archimedean point for judgment in the imperfect, "apparent" world of embodied feelings, opinions, and other corrupting biases. Thus positivists unwittingly replicate the metaphysical realism of Plato and Platonic Christianity.[4] Whereas positivists claim to have banished the Platonic philosopher's eternal Forms, the Judeo-Christian God, and Kant's *Ding-an-*

---

4. One should keep Nietzsche's repudiation of allegedly "higher," more real realms of existence in mind when reading passages such as the following: "In the 'in-itself' there is nothing of 'causal connection,' of 'necessity'. . . ; there 'the effect' *does not* 'follow the cause,' there no 'law' rules. It is *we* alone who have fabricated causes" (BGE 21). The target of this critique is not causation as such but rather the bogus causation that is part of the equally bogus realm of the "in-itself." Once we refrain from speaking of higher realms and focus our attention on *this* (the only) world, we can make use of that "sound conception of cause and effect" he associates with science (A 49). See Brian Leiter, "Nietzsche and the Critique of Morality: Philosophical Naturalism in Nietzsche's Theory of Value," (Ph.D. diss., University of Michigan, 1995), p. 177; and Maudemarie Clark, *Nietzsche on Truth and Philosophy* (Cambridge: Cambridge University Press, 1990), p. 217.

sich from legitimate scientific discourse, their talk of an unbiased, unmediated access to "the facts" simply replicates this same metaphysical gesture (cf. WP 481).[5]

Nietzsche claims that one of the "hardest" truths to embrace is the existence of only one world. There is no escape, no transcendent appeal from our embodied, natural world of sense, instinct, and thought to a more "real" world. Although the universe may be governed by scientifically discernible natural laws, it is not governed by supra-human ethical law; apart from (or before) human intervention, nothing is good or bad, right or wrong. "Let us beware," he announces in *The Gay Science*,

> of attributing to [nature] heartlessness and unreason or their opposites: it is neither perfect nor beautiful, nor noble, nor does it wish to become any of these things; it does not by any means strive to imitate man. None of our aesthetic and moral judgments apply to it. . . . Let us beware of saying that there are laws in nature. There are only necessities: there is nobody who commands, nobody who obeys, nobody who trespasses. (GS 109; cf. WP 708, 711)[6]

The supposed truth of this proposition, which essentially relegates traditional religious and philosophical notions of transcendence to fairy-tale status, is deemed "hard" or "terrible" because very few people are said to be constitutionally equipped to willingly and joyfully embrace what it implies. Because "the service of truth is the hardest service," it remains within the purview of a minority (A 50; cf. Z III, 12, 7).

Repudiating the tenets of metaphysical realism and limiting oneself to earthly forms of transcendence—to what Zarathustra refers to as "the humanly-conceivable, the humanly-evident, the humanly-

---

5. Nietzsche does credit positivism, however, for making an initial attempt to break with traditional metaphysical frameworks. See, for example, his reference to the dawning of a new age of knowledge as "the cock crow of positivism" in TI IV, 4.

6. As I read this passage, the "laws in nature" against which Nietzsche warns are those of explicitly normative content, for example, the supposed "natural laws" (of self-preservation, duty to others, etc.) forming the basis of seventeenth-century social contract theories, or Romanticism's claim to be in tune with Nature's "voice" (cf. Z II, 16). His further claim that "there are only necessities" is perfectly compatible with the modern scientific notion that all natural phenomena obey the "laws" of physics.

palpable"—is a tall order (Z II, 2). Historically, we are told, humankind has always projected its own normative preoccupations and obsessions onto the natural world (D 17). To come to see this as projection, to see "life" scientifically, as neither moral nor immoral but rather "essentially amoral," is a fearsome prospect (BT Preface 5). But as Zarathustra says of himself and those like him, "*fear*—is the exception with us" (Z IV, 15).

This is why Nietzsche charges those who subscribe to any form of metaphysical realism not merely with error and naïveté but with cowardice. In his view, the majority (including most of those who call themselves scientists) cling to the metaphysical realist framework out of fear.[7] To face up to the reality of what Max Weber would later describe as a disenchanted universe would drive lesser sorts of men "to nausea and suicide" (GS 107). This truth would produce profound disillusionment in such individuals, who would be "crushed beneath the weight of contempt" for a life that would be seen as bereft of value or meaning (BT Preface 5). Hence the recourse to mendacious religious and philosophical worldviews that closed the door to "suicidal nihilism" by providing a supposedly externally grounded interpretation for human existence and suffering and the hope of redemption (GM III, 28). This embrace of error is said to be due to cowardice rather than to mistaken but easily correctable reasoning: "Error (—belief in the ideal—) is not blindness, error is *cowardice* [*Irrtum ist Feigheit*] . . . Every acquisition, every step forward in knowledge is the *result* of courage " (EH Foreword 3; cf. EH XIV, 3).

Why do some people need to believe in such lies, while others do not? Whence the cowardice of those "who take flight in face of reality" (EH XIV, 3) and the intellectual integrity and courage of those who can face it unblinkingly? Nietzsche's characteristic response is to trace the intellectual and normative stances of individuals back to what he sees as their fundamental character or disposition—back, in other words, to the "type" of person they really are. And human

7. Even as Nietzsche trumpets the scientific nature of his own approach, he derides the positivist "scientificality" [*Wissenschaftlichkeit*] and the "average man of science" of his day as the embodiment of a fearful flight from truth. See, for example, BT Preface 1; EH X, 2; EH III, 1; BGE 204, 206, 211; GM III, 25; and WP 120, 420. Scholars who consider Nietzsche a debunker of science tend to refer to passages such as these.

"types," as they are presented in Nietzsche's brand of science, are ranked according to different sorts of instinct.

The Primacy of Instinct

Nietzsche's many and varied accounts of human comportment are punctuated with affirmations of our inescapably embodied condition as animals. Zarathustra claims, for example, that "the enlightened man" refuses to repudiate his animality and instead refers to the human being as "the animal with red cheeks" (Z II, 3). Nietzsche has no patience for the belief he associates (perhaps unfairly) with the Platonic and Christian traditions, namely that the only way to exalt the human species is to help it transcend its bodily, animalistic instincts. "We philosophers," he declares, "are not free to divide body from soul as the people do," presumably because "we" have grasped the scientific truth that our entire being is inescapably corporeal (GS Preface 3). Zarathustra's enlightened man insists that he is "body entirely [*Leib bin ich ganz und gar*], and nothing beside; and soul is only a word for something in the body" (Z I, 4; cf. Z I, 3; WP 229). As unwilling as he is to attribute an independent existence to the soul [*Seele*], Nietzsche is no more prepared to make concessions to the idea of a disembodied "spirit" [*Geist*]. Zarathustra is prepared to talk of spirit only in a figurative sense after coming to know the body better (Z II, 17).[8]

As human animals, our conduct is said to be shaped by certain primal instincts or drives [*Triebe*] rooted in our bodies, whether we are aware of this or not. Casting aside all notions of a disembodied form of transcendence, Nietzsche claims that "we can rise or sink to no other 'reality' than the reality of our drives" (BGE 36). He maintains

8. And yet Nietzsche also claims that the value of a human life is measured by how much truth a "spirit" can bear (EH Foreword 3). Peter Berkowitz rightly notes Nietzsche's propensity for appropriating terms—such as "spirit," "soul," and "virtue"—that also seem to be attacked and discarded in other passages. Berkowitz, *Nietzsche: The Ethics of an Immoralist* (Cambridge: Harvard University Press, 1995), pp. 5–6. In attempting to describe his notion of embodied agency, Nietzsche repeatedly makes use of traditional terms with unmistakably metaphysical connotations.

into his late period the view formulated earlier in his career that our intellect "is only the blind instrument [*das blinde Werkzeug*] of *another drive*" (D 109). Reason should be seen not as an independent faculty but as "a system of relations between various passions and desires" (WP 387). The philosophers' claim that reasoning is independent of instincts is merely a "misunderstanding of the body," and any attempt to repudiate one's bodily affects in the name of Reason can only result, paradoxically, in a deformation of one's ability to think clearly (Z I, 3).

In a crucial passage early in the *Zarathustra* narrative, Nietzsche underscores this primacy of instinct thesis through a distinction between "the Self" [*das Selbst*] as creative body and "the Ego" [*das Ich*] as conscious thought and feeling. The latter, though proud of its imaginative leapings and prone to vainglorious celebration of its allegedly independent power, is portrayed as the former's handmaid: "Your Self laughs at your Ego and its proud leapings. 'What are these leapings and flights of thought to me?' it says to itself. 'A by-way to my goal. I am the Ego's leading-string and I prompt its conceptions'" (Z I, 4). In this section the Ego is described as a "little intelligence" [*kleine Vernunft*] that is, in fact, "an instrument of your body, a little instrument and toy of your great intelligence [*großen Vernunft*]." Nietzsche suggests elsewhere that to think of oneself as exercising free will over and against this embodied self is a form of hubristic temerity characteristic of the "half-educated" (BGE 21).[9] Against the proponents of metaphysical realism, who insist in various ways on the possibility of rising above instincts, desires, and interests into a higher realm of knowledge and Truth, Nietzsche claims that the pursuit of knowledge is both intertwined with and driven by these same instincts, desires, and interests.

But what is the status of his primacy of instinct thesis? Is it meant to be a value-neutral, scientific account of the way the natural world

9. Thirty years later Sigmund Freud would echo this view in his criticism of the "human megalomania" that clings to "a deeply rooted faith in undetermined psychical events and in free will." Freud, *Introductory Lectures on Psycho-Analysis*, trans. and ed. James Strachey (New York: W. W. Norton, 1966), pp. 353, 130. On the relation between Nietzsche and Freud, see Paul Laurent Assoun, *Freud et Nietzsche* (Paris: Presses Universitaires de France, 1980).

works from a perspective wholly outside the realm of ethics? Certain textual passages seem to support this reading. When, for example, Nietzsche declares that "every table of values, every 'thou shalt' known to history or ethnology" ought to be subject to the critical assessment of "medical science," he seems to be looking upon all forms of ethical discourse with the same detached, scientific manner; all sets of values are determined by the same natural laws and processes and are to be distinguished (rather than ranked) according to various types of physiology (GM I, 17). According to this reading, Nietzsche distances himself from all forms of ethical valuation and tells a scientific causal story about how and why values (including his own) are held and asserted.[10] This reading has the merit of logical coherence, but is it a sufficient account of Nietzsche's view?

Bodily Knowledge, Bodily Ignorance

I do not think this interpretation can withstand the weighty textual evidence suggesting something quite the contrary: namely, that a normative vision of human flourishing is driving Nietzsche's "science" and that the rhetoric of science is invoked primarily to infuse that vision with added respectability. Nietzsche is indeed proposing a story about the causal impact of instinct on human thought and action, but the story does not end there. He goes much further in advancing an ambitious truth-claim for his *ranking* of different types of human instincts and, concomitantly, for the superiority of certain types of human being over others.

Nietzsche slides effortlessly and almost imperceptably from an ostensibly value-neutral, "scientific" account of instincts to a normative *prise de position* in favor of certain types of instinct over others. According to the laws of what he refers to as rank order [*Rangordnung*], each living species is divided generally into "different kinds of life" and more specifically into "ascending" and "decaying" forms of the species in question (WP 592, 857). Human beings are no different, as he suggests by his repeated mention of an "unalterable innate or-

10. This, as I understand it, is Leiter's position (see notes 3 and 4 above).

der of rank between man and man" (BGE 263; cf. BGE 228).[11] Nietzsche regards every human being as first and foremost a "physiological representative" or "carrier" [*Träger*] of one of the two types of existence—strong/healthy/ascending and weak/unhealthy/declining—and therefore "may be regarded as representing the ascending or descending line of life" (TI IX, 33; cf. TI VI, 2; WP 287).

This rank order, he insists, is not merely his own way of looking at the human world (although of course he does not deny, and indeed goes out of his way to confirm, that it is his view); on the contrary, Nietzsche claims that his proposed account would be apparent to any healthy, well-bred individual capable of grasping the "hard" truths of the natural world. Our place in the "order of castes [*Die Ordnung der Kasten*] . . . is only the sanctioning of a *natural order*, a natural law of the first rank over which no arbitrary caprice, no 'modern idea' has any power" (A 57). Anyone capable of examining reality without illusion can grasp the truth that the representatives of "a *higher, brighter* humanity" are "very small in number (for everything outstanding is by its nature rare)," while those who represent degeneration and weakness are many: "Among men, as among every other species, there is a surplus of failures [*Mißratenen*], of the sick [*Kranken*], the degenerate [*Entartenden*], the fragile [*Gebrechlichen*], of those who are bound to suffer; the successful cases are, among men too, always the exception" (WP 993; BGE 62; cf. BGE 29, 126; EH III, 1; WP 420).

Given Nietzsche's repeated insistence that all of us are driven by visceral, "animal" instinct, it is clear that the key difference between strong and weak persons cannot lie in the former's ability to transcend animality. Whereas both human types evince an animal nature, the issue is the *type* of animality, or (what is for Nietzsche the same thing) the quality of the instincts and drives in the individual in question. Nietzsche never fails to underline the importance of this ad hominem ability to discriminate among different types of instinct and people; indeed, he thinks it takes priority over any independent

11. Passages such as this, where Nietzsche identifies *Rangordnung* as an intrinsic part of human existence, create difficulty for Strong's suggestion that Nietzsche rejects the existence of any "necessary and permanent characteristics of a so-called human condition." Tracy B. Strong, *Friedrich Nietzsche and the Politics of Transfiguration*, expanded ed. (Berkeley: University of California Press, 1988), p. 26; cf. p. 37.

assessment of action as such: "An action is perfectly devoid of value: it all depends on *who* performs it" (WP 292).[12] The value of an action, feeling, or sentiment can be assessed only with reference to the value of the actor—that is, the value of that person's character and instincts. A backward inference must always be made "from the deed to the doer, from the ideal to those who *need it*" (GS 370; cf. BGE 221; WP 675).

So, for example, someone who can grasp the true nature of the universe and reject any notion of a "higher," "real" world of Being embodies strong, healthy instincts, whereas an "instinct of life-weariness" leads weaker human types to mendacious beliefs in the "other [higher] world" (WP 586c). Those who claim that their penchant for metaphysical transcendence is driven by something infinitely higher than instinct—faith, for instance, or reason—are simply deluding themselves. Religious faith is but "a cloak, a pretext, a *screen*, behind which the instincts played their game—a shrewd *blindness* to the dominance of *certain* instincts . . . [O]ne has always *spoken* of faith, one has always *acted* from instinct" (A 39). Whereas religious ascetics may sincerely believe themselves to have transcended their bodily instincts, close observation reveals that these same (morbid) instincts are at play in their efforts to flee earthly reality. For all their transcendental longing, the "afterworldsmen" gain an almost sensual pleasure from their flights of fantasy, thereby exposing the lie at the core of all metaphysical realist frameworks: "To what do they owe the convulsion and joy of their transport?" asks Zarathustra. The answer is categorical: "To their bodies and to this earth" (Z I, 3; cf. Z II, 15; Z III, 12, 17).

Whether one can come to recognize and affirm these truths—of the primacy of bodily instinct and the rank order of human beings—depends very much on where one is situated in the rank order. Whereas (as we shall see in the next chapter) the prudential interests and instincts of lower-order human beings lead them to deny the very existence of the *Rangordnung* and to affirm instead the menda-

12. Robert Solomon has recently drawn attention to Nietzsche's ad hominem style in "Nietzsche *ad hominem*: Perspectivism, Personality, and Ressentiment," in *The Cambridge Companion to Nietzsche*, ed. Bernd Magnus and Kathleen Higgins (Cambridge: Cambridge University Press), pp. 180–222.

cious notion of human equality, it is at least potentially within the reach of all "higher" or "stronger" persons to understand and rejoice in their superiority to the "weak."

Nietzsche claims to possess a superior, discriminating sense of this sort.[13] In speaking of his innate "psychological antennae" that allow him to identify the essential servility of those who attempt to "white-wash" the "dirt" at the bottom of their natures with book learning, Nietzsche describes a type of discriminating knowledge that is less self-consciously rational than instinctive and visceral. In this context he sings the praises of his senses (EH I, 8). The nose of a higher type of human being is described as an organ of which "no philosopher has ever spoken with due respect" yet which is "the most delicate scientific [*physikalisch*] instrument in existence" (WP 461). "My genius is in my nostrils," he declares in *Ecce Homo*, lauding his ability to "perceive physiologically—*smell*—the proximity or . . . the innermost parts, the 'entrails' of every soul" (EH XIV, 1; EH I, 8). Similarly, in *The Genealogy* Nietzsche confesses that he finds "utterly unen-durable" the smell of "the entrails of some ill-constituted soul" (GM I, 12; cf. TI IX, 20). "Where the people eat and drink," we are in-formed, "even where it worships, there is usually a stink. One should not go into churches if one wants to breathe pure air" (BGE 30).

Nietzsche makes use of the metaphor of taste just as often as that of smell when discussing the human rank order and his lofty place in it. The finest human beings, Zarathustra teaches us, are not those who know how to "taste" everything. On the contrary, they have the most "obstinate, fastidious tongues and stomachs" (Z III, 11, 2). Wanting to be in agreement with the many is taken as a sign of bad taste, for the simple fact of the matter is that the "average man" is uninterested in that which most stimulates every "higher nature and more refined and fastidious taste" (BGE 43, 220).

13. It might be objected that Nietzsche claims to be "experienced" in "questions of *décadence*" and thus denies holding any superior view (EH I, 1). But this confession of decadent tendencies is crucially mitigated by his assertion in the same work that he is "*summa summarum* . . . healthy" (EH II, 2). To have a decadent streak, for Nietzsche, is not the same thing as being part of the mediocre majority. I argue below that he sees the "master" or "strong" types of his era as both decadent (in the sense of misguided as to their true interests and deepest inclinations) and (at least potentially) redeemable.

Thus, to reiterate, Nietzsche claims that the rank order in things and persons is discernible only to those of higher rank and superior sensibility. Only good taste can recognize the distinction between good and bad taste. This is why the basic question of whether to prefer the cultivation of lower or higher men is "at bottom a question of taste and aesthetics" (WP 353; cf. WP 878). But here my suggestion that Nietzsche makes a partisan entry into the domain of *ethical* valuation might seem to be compromised. Does this emphasis on *taste* not suggest that his perceptions and valuations are matters of mere subjective preference?

It would seem so only if Nietzsche's use of the notion of taste corresponds to our typical usage. In everyday language the qualifier "mere" is often placed in front of "taste" to highlight the latter's supposedly idiosyncratic nature—when, for example, someone claims that her preference for Hollywood movies over opera is "merely" a matter of her personal taste. If Nietzsche shares our habitual association of taste with idiosyncratic preference—or if he subscribes to something like Weber's view that aesthetics has become an autonomous value sphere in the modern world, wholly distinct from ethics and science—the aforementioned passages could be read simply as assertions of his own subjective preference for certain types of people over others. But Nietzsche does not in fact subscribe to the common, subjectivist view of taste. By insisting on the normative and cognitive significance of judgments rooted in taste, he rejects the Weberian notion that the aesthetic, the moral, and the scientific operate according to separate, mutually exclusive logics.

Of course, Nietzsche's incessant highlighting of the intensely personal nature of his predilections can easily be mistaken for a deliberate attempt to undercut their objective truth-value. In *Ecce Homo*, for example, he refers twice to "his" morality, and in *Beyond Good and Evil* he "grants" that his will to power thesis (discussed below) is "only interpretation" (EH II, 1; EH III, 5; BGE 22). Rather than see in these constructions an attempt to relativize or otherwise mitigate his own views, however, I think they are most profitably looked upon as rhetorical devices aimed at distinguishing his (accurate) evocation of truth from the lies that historically have monopolized the language of truth. Against those who insist upon the impersonal nature of truth, who claim that objectivity involves attaining an Archimedean point denuded of all perspective, Nietzsche insists that there is no contradiction between the deeply personal, embodied perspective of a superior, perspicacious human being and objective truth. Claims to truth and objectivity can be made only from an inescapably personal point of view (GM III, 12; BT Preface 5; GS 374; HAH I Preface 6).[14]

When Zarathustra describes the body as a "great intelligence" [großen Vernunft] and declares that to the "discerning man [Erkennenden] all instincts are holy," it appears that bodily instinct is being credited with something more than simply reflecting subjective preferences (Z I, 4; Z I, 22, 2). "Of all forms of intelligence [allen Arten von Intelligenz] discovered hitherto," Nietzsche proffers elsewhere, "'instinct' is the most intelligent" (BGE 218). We learn that there is a cognitive element in our passions, that every passion contains "its quantum of reason" (WP 387; cf. Z IV, 13, 9). What Nietzsche seems to be suggesting in these passages is that the embodied inclinations of exceptional human beings can result in a form of knowledge or wisdom rather than simply a manifestation of subjective preference.[15] This is the reasoning that forms the background to Zarathustra's coupling of subjective perception and knowledge claim: "There is wisdom in the fact that much in the world smells ill" (Z III, 12, 14).

Nietzsche repeatedly insists on the incommunicability of this "bodily knowledge" to most people. The "goodness" [Gut] that his imagined higher caste embodies can never become a "common good"

14. This, in my view, is how Nietzsche's celebrated "perspectivism" should be read. A fuller discussion of Nietzsche's attempt to reconcile the ubiquity of perspective with the possibility of objective truth is found in my "The Objective Viewpoint: A Nietzschean Account," History of Philosophy Quarterly 13, 4 (October 1996): 483–502. The popular association of Nietzschean perspectivism with pure subjectivism owes a great deal to Nehamas's Nietzsche: Life as Literature. For an effective critique of Nehamas's reading, see Brian Leiter, "Nietzsche and Aestheticism," Journal of the History of Philosophy 30, 2 (April 1992): 275–290.

15. Even though Jürgen Habermas acknowledges that Nietzsche "enthrones" taste as an "organ of knowledge," he ignores Nietzsche's insistence on its cognitive and normative import when he refers to it as "beyond true and false, beyond good and evil." Habermas thereby joins those who see Nietzsche as a purveyor of nothing more than a subjectivistic l'art pour l'art. Habermas, The Philosophical Discourse of Modernity: Twelve Lectures, trans. Frederick Lawrence (Cambridge: MIT Press, 1987), p. 96.

["*Gemeingut*"], the very notion of which is "a self-contradiction: [for] what can be common has ever but little value" (BGE 43). It would be sheer folly to attempt to teach the many about rank order and self-overcoming, as Zarathustra discovers early in his odyssey.[16] By parts II and III of this work, Nietzsche's alter ego has concluded that one should not attempt to be physician to the "incurable" (Z III, 12, 17). All speech is in vain among them because they represent a fundamentally different human type and possess instincts foreign to the superior man, whose teachings cannot possibly elicit a sympathetic, knowing response (Z III, 9; cf. Z IV, 13, 9; Z III, 8, 1; WS 131).

Thus Nietzsche writes only for those whom he considers "most select" (EH Foreword 4). Like Christ, both Nietzsche and his literary creation describe themselves as "fishers of men," but with one crucial difference: in rejecting Christianity's universalizing message, Nietzsche/Zarathustra claim to be much more discriminating in their choice of fishing hole and catch (EH X, 1). Unlike those who cast their fishing rods into swamps "where there are no fish," Zarathustra seeks "the fairest human fish" (Z III, 8, 2; Z IV, 1). Instinctive knowledge can be shared only with those who are "predisposed and predestined" for it—those who, in other words, possess instincts similar to Nietzsche's (BGE 30).

Once again, the language of embodiment is invoked to drive home this point. Alongside the references to taste and touch, auditory metaphors are also prominent. His teachings are only for the most sensitive ears (EH II, 7; Z I, 12). They are certainly inaccessible to those with donkeylike "long ears" for whom Zarathustra long ago "unlearned consideration" (Z IV, 3, 1). Moving from the auditory to the gastrointestinal, Nietzsche further delimits his readership by referring to Zarathustra's teaching variously as "man's fare" [*Meine Manns-Kost*], "warriors' food" [*Krieger-Kost*], and "conquerers' food" [*Eroberer-Kost*] (Z IV, 17, 1).

To be "predisposed and predestined" for his insights is not the same thing, however, as having a guaranteed grasp of them. Despite

16. I am speaking, of course, of the story of Zarathustra's repudiation and ridicule at the hands of the people in the marketplace (Z Prologue). By part IV Zarathustra considers his early attempt to share his wisdom with the many to have been a "great folly" (Z IV, 13, 1; cf. Z IV, 12).

their strong stomachs, sharp ears, and sensitive noses, those who share membership with him in the caste of stronger, higher human beings have fallen into grave difficulty in the modern era. In the next chapter I examine Nietzsche's account of how this could have happened as well as his various rhetorical strategies for "awakening" their dormant noble sensibilities. Before these strategies can be examined, however, Nietzsche's characterization of "strong" and "weak" human beings must be fleshed out.

One crucial element of this hierarchy has already been discussed. Nietzsche believes that the value of a human life is measured by "how much truth can a spirit *bear*; how much truth can a spirit *dare*" (EH Foreword 3; cf. BGE 39; WP 1041). One is stronger and thus of greater value than most if one is constitutionally equipped not simply to recognize the hard truths of reality but "to be happy and cheerful" in their presence (EH III, 3). This is what Nietzsche means by *Jasagen:* "Recognition, affirmation of reality" [*Die Erkenntnis, das Jasagen zur Realität*] is as much a necessity for the strong man as its opposite ("cowardice and *flight* in the face of reality") is for the weak (EH IV, 2). But this is not the only way in which the strength-weakness distinction is framed. Below we shall see how Nietzsche distinguishes the strong from the weak (a) in terms of "will to power" and, in a related way, (b) using a normative standard of nature.

Strength, Weakness, and the Will to Power Thesis

Many commentators from Heidegger and Jaspers to the present have assumed the will to power to be Nietzsche's cosmological theory of the innate workings of the universe, and admittedly there are textual passages that appear to vindicate this reading. Zarathustra's teaching "about life and about the nature of all living creatures" is encapsulated in the observation that "where I found a living creature, there I found will to power" (Z II, 12). Moreover, in Nietzsche's own voice we are told that "a living thing desires above all to *vent* its strength—life as such is will to power" and that "the really fundamental instinct of life . . . aims at *the expansion of power*" (BGE 13; GS 349; cf. GM II, 12; GM III, 7; WP 1067). Occasionally Nietzsche frames the will to power thesis as an ostensibly value-neutral, scientific observation rather than a form of approbation; that a "body . . . will want to grow, expand, draw to itself, gain ascendancy" is due not to "any morality or immorality" but simply to the fact that "it *lives* . . . [that] life *is* will to power" (BGE 259).

In light of the obvious weakness of any reductionist account of life that purportedly "explains" all sentient behavior in terms of "power," Kaufmann and several more recent commentators have argued against the cosmological interpretation in order to save Nietzsche's reputation as a serious philosopher. After noting that the bulk of Nietzsche's references to the will to power stem from his observations of human psychology, they conclude that the will to power speaks to the human world (rather than to "life" in general) and emerges from Nietzsche's own preference for power-seeking, aggrandizing individuals. Nietzsche, as Maudemarie Clark suggests, believes that "every enhancement of the human type depends on a strengthening of the will to power."[17] While I do not share these commentators' goal of "saving" Nietzsche from an indefensible cosmological thesis, I think they are right to highlight the primary relevance of the will to power thesis for Nietzsche's assessment of human relations.

Strong, ascendant forms of human life are said to embody a will to power in a joyous and unflinching manner. In *Beyond Good and Evil*, for example, Nietzsche speaks of an "unconditional will to power" that revels in the "art of experiment and devilry of every kind," a view also reflected in the notebooks unpublished in Nietzsche's time (the so-called *Nachlass*), where we learn that it is "the supreme will to power" to "impose upon becoming the character of being" (BGE 44; WP 617). Turning to those whom he identifies as weak, Nietzsche is of two minds. On the one hand, he claims that those "in decline" possess the will to power only in pitiably small quantities, as in this passage from *The AntiChrist*: "I consider life itself instinct for growth, for continuance, for accumulation of forces, for *power*: where the will to power is lacking [*wo der Wille zur Macht fehlt*] there is decline" (A 6; cf. A 17; WP 98, 855). If, in this vein, the will to

17. Clark, *Nietzsche on Truth and Philosophy*, p. 226.

power is associated with everything "that heightens the feeling of power" in man, then those who cannot feel their power in and through their own creative agency cannot "be" will to power (A 2). They might instead embody an urge to survive in relative comfort.

On the other hand—and, I would suggest, for the most part—Nietzsche also depicts the weak as capable of mustering a considerable amount of will to power—but in a form so misguided that it denies its own reality. Consider, for example, his derisive treatment of those political "leaders" of modern democracies who delude themselves into thinking that they are not really commanding but rather "obeying" or "serving" the people, God, or something else (Z III, 5, 2; cf. BGE 199; A 38). Such hypocrisy is the outcome of an essentially dishonest worldview that denies the fact that will to power drives everything. As Zarathustra observes in this spirit, "even in the will of the servant I found the will to be master" (Z II, 12).

Nature and Artifice: The Highest Human Type

Although Nietzsche describes both higher and lower human beings as "natural" in the sense described above (both human types are animals with instincts), he also insists that the higher, stronger type of human being is *much more* natural than the lower and weaker—natural in a specifically normative sense of that term that recalls a classical tradition in moral philosophy. As we examine Nietzsche's normative use of nature, the ethical vision that undergirds his ostensibly scientific view of reality should come out even more clearly.

"The virtues arise in us," declares Aristotle in the *Nicomachean Ethics*, "neither by nature nor against nature" (1103a25).[18] The meaning of the first part of this cryptic phrase seems straightforward: virtue is "unnatural" in that it does not develop spontaneously, without education or upbringing. In this sense hardly anything in human beings is "natural," including the use of language.[19] The second part, that virtue

18. Aristotle, *Nicomachean Ethics*, trans. Terence Irwin (Indianapolis: Hackett, 1985).
19. As Bernard Williams notes in his *Ethics and the Limits of Philosophy* (Cambridge: Harvard University Press, 1985), p. 47.

is not "against nature," suggests that an ethical disposition is part of the natural culmination of human development, where "natural" refers to the cultivation of certain essential human attributes in the context of an artificial (human-constructed) culture or community. Virtuous action that is part of the creative artifice of culture *is* natural in that it represents the *telos* of the correct development of a certain kind of animal: the human being. From this Aristotelian perspective, the standard nature-culture dichotomy popularized both by modern Romanticism and Kantian philosophy simply does not make sense.

Without ever acknowledging an intellectual debt to Aristotle, Nietzsche was drawn to this Aristotelian perspective on nature.[20] In his opening remarks to the early essay "Homer's Contest" (1872), Nietzsche stakes out a recognizably Aristotelian position from which, I would argue, he never departs:

> When one speaks of *humanity* [*Humanität*], the idea is fundamental that this is something which separates and distinguishes man from nature. In reality, however, there is no such separation: "natural" qualities and those called truly "human" are inseparably grown together. Man, in his highest and noblest capacities, is wholly nature [*ganz Natur*] and embodies its uncanny dual character [*unheimlichen Doppelcharakter*]. (HC)[21]

20. Scholars who have recognized Nietzsche's rejection of the nature-culture dichotomy include Bruce Detwiler, *Nietzsche and the Politics of Aristocratic Radicalism* (Chicago: University of Chicago Press, 1990), p. 80; Bernard Yack, *The Longing for Total Revolution: Philosophic Sources of Social Discontent from Rousseau to Marx and Nietzsche* (Berkeley: University of California Press, 1992), pp. 317–318; and Eric Blondel, *Nietzsche, The Body, and Culture: Philosophy as Philological Genealogy*, trans. Sean Hand (Stanford: Stanford University Press, 1991), p. 43. Blondel, however, fails to note any classical antecedent and appears to assume that Nietzsche was the first philosopher to have thought this way.

21. Kaufmann, whose rendition of "Homer's Contest" I use here, did not translate the entire piece for his *Portable Nietzsche* volume. Two new and complete English translations have recently appeared: one by Carole Diethe (with the title "Homer on Competition," as a supplement to *On the Genealogy of Morality*, ed. Keith Ansell-Pearson and trans. Carole Diethe [Cambridge: Cambridge University Press, 1994], pp. 187–194), and a second by Christa Davis Acampora in *Nietzscheana #5*, ed. Richard Schacht (Urbana, Ill.: North American Nietzsche Society, 1996).

Nietzsche maintains the view that fulfillment of the highest human being's true nature—that is, the attainment of human excellence—is to be found in "artificial" realms of creativity rather than through any rediscovery of a purportedly authentic, "natural" self unsullied by artifice (BGE 188). A fragment from 1887 succinctly states his position: "Man reaches nature only after a long struggle—he never 'returns'" (WP 120).

Nietzsche's critique of Romanticism can be understood in light of this insistence on "artificiality." His profound objection to the view that one could "return to nature" (and thus to virtue) by sloughing off the artifice of culture and recovering a pristine, "natural" self is well illustrated in part IV of *Zarathustra*, where Nietzsche burlesques the nostalgia for the noble savage by making one of his two kings—a so-called "higher man"—declare that the "finest and dearest man today is a healthy peasant, uncouth, cunning, obstinate, enduring" (Z IV, 3, 1). The fact that the lowly peasant is thoroughly "natural" is no reason to show him the respect due to higher orders of humanity.

Nietzsche despises the intellectual and artistic fashion of his time—associated both with Romanticism and with the literary Naturalism of Zola—that insists on the inherent worth of everything natural. He asserts that the fashionable Romantic idealization of rustic manners and the indiscriminate curiosity of the literary Naturalists toward everything "natural" embody an assault against that true nobility and decency he sees himself as championing: "Today we consider it a matter of decency not to wish to see everything naked, or to be present at everything, or to understand and 'know' everything" (GS Preface 4).[22]

Nietzsche's highest human type, to recapitulate, embodies a high degree of naturalness in virtue of being a man of cultural "artifice" and discrimination. He is the type described in the third essay of *The Genealogy* as a "great experimenter with himself, discontented and insatiable, wrestling with animals, nature, and gods for ultimate dominion," a being who "has dared more, done more new things, braved more and challenged fate more than all the other an-

22. For some examples of Nietzsche's distaste for literary Naturalism, see GS Preface 4; GS 347; TI IX, 7; and WP 821.

imals put together" (GM III, 13). Such a man does not attempt to listen to nature's "voice" à la Rousseau. As noted above, Nietzsche considers the amoral natural world to be an inappropriate model for superior human beings. In aspiring "to be other than this nature," the superior man becomes one of a very few "genuine artists of life" (BGE 9, 32).

Nature That Is Also against Nature

Although Nietzsche privileges the sort of will to power resulting in the creation of normative values, he insists that not all forms of value creation are equally praiseworthy. Debased forms originate with those who would prefer to think of themselves as not creating at all—those who, like the aforementioned democratic political "leader," consider themselves to be obeying something "higher" than themselves. This, he claims, is a monumental self-delusion, a flight from truth that diminishes the value of the creation.

Consider as well the character of the ascetic priest, whom Nietzsche treats as a higher, stronger type of human being gone bad (or "decadent"). Nietzsche often evinces a grudging admiration for those "ingenious" [Geistreich] individuals who have founded and perpetuated those religions with mass following and universalistic pretensions (GM I, 7). He recognizes their inherent ability, and insofar as he acknowledges his own extended flirtations with "decadence," he identifies himself as their kin (GM II, 24). Nietzsche's qualified respect for creativity in the service of religion is also illustrated in his warm treatment of the solitary hermit character in the Prologue of Zarathustra (Z Prologue 2). The ascetic project of service to God and truth, he concedes, evinces a kind of disciplined self-overcoming in its own way.[23]

Such qualified praise is crucially mitigated, however, by Nietzsche's identification of a paradox at the center of such a life. Although ascetic priests show great creativity in producing highly sophisti-

23. As Charles Taylor observes in his *Sources of the Self: The Making of Modern Identity* (Cambridge: Harvard University Press, 1989), p. 453.

cated human artifacts, their resulting products embody core values that calumniate and attempt to stamp out the human capacity to create. This bizarre spectacle of creativity-that-calumniates-creativity is so "new, profound, unheard of, enigmatic, contradictory" as to constitute a "sublime" spectacle worthy of "divine spectators" (GM II, 16). And while Nietzsche concedes that this turning of the human soul into a "torture chamber" may have made humankind more "interesting" (in the sense that the inner turmoil thereby generated has added depth to the human psyche), his praise of this spectacle—if one could call it that—is balanced by the claim that it has been responsible for "the most terrible sickness that has ever raged in man" (GM II, 16; GM II, 22).

The case of the ascetic priest is proof positive that man is the "sickliest" of animals (A 14). Out of all the species in the animal world, ours is the only one that produces decadent individuals, that is, those who marshal healthy species drives (for creativity, innovation, originality, etc.).in order to extirpate these same drives. The ascetic priest is a "gruesome hybrid of sickness and will to power" who continually "[denies] and condemn[s] the drive whose expression [he] is" (EH Foreword 4; WP 179). He is an example of "nature against something that is also nature" because he embodies a naturally creative will to power that denies its own creative nature and discourages this creativity in others (WP 228).

A truly noble and fully natural form of value creation, by contrast, refrains from seeking meaning in external sources and bases itself on the truths of science. Nietzsche's stress on the honesty and integrity of the sort of individual who can do this can scarcely be exaggerated. He who embodies this way of life openly and honestly[24]—who creates a table of values informed by a realistic grasp of the workings of the universe and who refuses to fudge or run away from "hard" truths—performs the task that Nietzsche claims he first set for him-

---

24. As Zarathustra declares, "I count nothing more valuable and rare today than honesty [*Redlichkeit*]" (Z IV, 13, 8; cf. D Preface 4; WP 404). Berkowitz perceptively highlights Nietzsche's identification of honesty as a cardinal virtue for the superior man. See his *Nietzsche: The Ethics of an Immoralist*, pp. 40, 102, 128, 250.

self in *The Birth of Tragedy:* "to see science under the lens of the artist, but art under the lens of life" (BT Preface 2).

But what of those unable to attain this summit? How do those who represent, in Nietzsche's eyes, the vast majority fit into this account of the dual character of human beings? In an echo of Aristotle's famous distinction in the first book of *The Politics* between mere life and the good life, Nietzsche refers disparagingly to the so-called virtue that is put into play merely "in order to live long and in a miserable ease [*erbärmlichen Behagen*]" (Z I, 6; cf. Z Prologue 3). Turning away from the noblest part of human life, the majority pursues what Nietzsche refers to as "the happiness of serfs" [*Glück der Knechte*] in its "will to existence," that is, its pursuit of the base ideal of mere self-preservation, physical health, and comfort (Z II, 8; Z II, 12; cf. WP 944). Having neither the capacity nor the desire for greatness, the majority is accused of "depriv[ing] existence of its *great* character" (EH XIV, 4). Again and again the many are revealingly described with animal imagery; they move together as a "herd" or "swarm," succumbing to the temptations of a merely animal-like existence focused on the fulfillment of immediate, basic needs. From the standpoint of the creative man, they are like the ape and treated as "a laughing-stock or a painful embarrassment"[25] (Z Prologue 3; cf. GS 351).

While this language is reminiscent of the more familiar nature-culture dualism and seems at times to suggest that superior human beings somehow transcend animality altogether,[26] Nietzsche subverts the standard dualist picture by insisting on the "unnaturalness" of the table of values that undergirds the majority's bovine existence (WP 204). Targeting "slave morality," as he terms the mode of ethical valuation predominant in Western civilization since the dawn of rabbinical Judaism and the early days of its Christian offspring, Nietzsche speaks of his "*attentat* on two millennia of anti-nature and the violation of man" (EH IV, 4). It is not, he confesses, just slave morality's epistemic errors

25. Bovine imagery takes over in the fourth part of *Zarathustra* when the majority is portrayed as cows whose cud-chewing masquerades as reflection (Z IV, 8).

26. Bernard Yack argues that Nietzsche falls into the familiar Kantian dualism of nature and culture in early works such as "Schopenhauer as Educator." Yack, *The Longing for Total Revolution*, pp. 318–319.

that horrify and offend him, not its lack "of discipline, of decency, of courage in spiritual affairs . . . —it is the lack of nature, it is the utterly ghastly fact that *anti-nature* itself has received the highest honors as morality, and has hung over mankind as law" (EH XIV, 7; cf. EH III, 5).

(Higher) Nature in Peril

Zarathustra suggests that the superior, "discerning man" at the height of his powers is confidently accurate in actions taken and judgments made; he considers all of his instincts "holy" (Z I, 22, 2). *Beyond Good and Evil* echoes this view in its suggestion that such a man evinces a "fundamental certainty which a noble soul possesses in regard to itself, something which may not be sought or found and perhaps may not be lost either" (BGE 287). Elsewhere Nietzsche speaks of a "complete automatism of instinct" as "the precondition for any kind of mastery, any kind of perfection in the art of living," and suggests that noble and maganimous types should "follow [their] own senses to the end" if they know what is good for them (A 57; GS 3).

For Nietzsche, however, the great calamity of the modern age is that higher human beings—with the exception of himself and a few other extraordinary modern figures such as Goethe and Napoleon—no longer know what is good for them. The picture of the superior man who listens to his bodily instincts is drawn as a normative ideal—perhaps as wishful thinking—rather than treated as a common occurrence. All too often, superior types have been led away from their instincts into beliefs and practices that are objectively bad for them. Having been raised in modern herd society and inculcated in its erroneous post-Christian democratic values, superior men no longer experience and revel in their authentic corporeal instincts. Their rational part—"spirit" [*Geist*]—claims Zarathustra, often "tells lies about the soul" [*Seele*] (Z III, 11, 2). It is to Nietzsche's diagnosis of the sorry state of higher human beings in the modern age, and to his projected rescue operation, that we must now turn.

t w o   **Nietzschean Consciousness-Raising**

I see them already *coming*, slowly, slowly; and perhaps I shall do
something to speed their coming if I describe in advance what
vicissitudes, upon what paths, I see them coming?
>   —*Human, All Too Human I Preface 2*

The *Ressentiment* of the Herd

As we have seen, Nietzsche traces "slave morality" back to the
cowardly inability of an essentially weak, declining type of
human being to joyfully embrace the fact that ethical valuation is "artifice," a construct of human agency. But this is not his only
genealogical account of "herd" values. In a second, complementary
genealogy, slave morality is explained as a defensive and vengeful

outgrowth of the majority's resentment of the superior individuals in its midst.

The root of slave morality, *ressentiment*, is attributed to the herd's essential lack of self-sufficiency, its inability to understand and promote itself in an autonomous, noncomparative way. Nietzsche's observations on vanity [*Eitelkeit*] as a servile trait are instructive in this regard.[1] The vain are "good actors" [*Schauspieler*] whose entire spirit is consumed with ensuring that others watch them because their sense of self-worth is wholly dependent upon the validation of others (Z II, 22). Zarathustra refers to them derisively as self-conscious singers "whose voices are softened, whose hands are eloquent, whose eyes are expressive, whose hearts are awakened, only when the house is full" (Z III, 11, 1; cf. Z II, 15). When Nietzsche ridicules those who ostentatiously display "the heaving bosom," who are quick to invoke "the big moral words . . . of justice, wisdom, holiness, virtue" and in whom moral seriousness [*Ernst*] becomes "imprinted on faces and gestures," he is criticizing a particularly tawdry and distasteful form of this dependency (TI I, 19; GS 359).

Nietzsche considers the need for applause to be a sure sign that real human excellence is absent. "Subtle fabricators and actors," claims Zarathustra, can evince only "pretended virtues" [*Aushänge-Tugenden*] and "glittering, false deeds" (Z IV, 13, 8). Only when a virtue is manifest away from an audience is a truly virtuous disposition present. Zarathustra challenges his "brothers" to move beyond such servile dependency and evince the courage of a hermit or an eagle, "which not even a god observes any more," rather than the so-called courage manifested only "in the presence of witnesses" (Z IV, 13, 4).

The vain man's attempt to develop a positive self-image by attracting attention and praise is destined to fail. In his heart of hearts

1. Ruth Abbey notes an important shift in Nietzsche's treatment of vanity: whereas in his middle period he was more inclined to identify vanity as part of the human condition in general—as "human, all too human"—in the late works it becomes a weakness of the "many, too many" and a central attribute of a servile table of values. See Abbey, "So Polyphonous a Being: Friedrich Nietzsche in His Middle Period" (manuscript, University of Western Australia, 1997). Some of the more important middle-period discussions of vanity include HAH 89, 137, 158, 170, 527, 545; AOM 234; WS 50; and D 385, 558.

he can never feel in confident possession of the virtues he so loudly praises and to which he lays claim because he simply lacks the natural equipment—the proper instincts—for human excellence. His public exertions are like those of a flat-footed dancer; all the effort in the world will not bring about what Zarathustra describes as his own "dancing virtue" [*Tänzers Tugend*] (Z III, 16, 6). In his awkward posturing the mere pretender remains one of those "beasts" whom Zarathustra describes as "clumsy-footed from birth," who can only "exert themselves strangely, like an elephant trying to stand on its head" (Z IV, 13, 19). In general, he observes, representatives of the "poor, sick type" of human being have "heavy feet" and "do not know how to dance" (Z IV, 13, 16).

Unaided by "*light* feet," that is, those healthy bodily instincts and elevated passions that are the *sine qua non* of human excellence, all studied effort goes for naught, and may even be taken as evidence of an inner deficiency. "Effort," as Nietzsche suggests in a late work, "is an objection," a view echoed in the *Nachlass:* "All perfect acts are unconscious and no longer subject to will; consciousness is the expression of an imperfect and often morbid state in a person" (TI VI, 2; WP 289; cf. WP 430; EH II, 9).[2]

Nietzsche claims that the futility of this search for validation through self-conscious, awkward performance is not lost on the pretenders to virtue themselves. Although they may flee from the hard truth about themselves and find temporary solace in each other's company, they remain tormented by inchoate, scarcely conscious feelings of inadequacy. Nietzsche speaks of the pervasiveness of "that inward-turned glance of the born failure which betrays how such a man speaks to himself—that glance which is a sigh! 'If only I were someone else,' sighs this glance: 'but there is no hope of that'" (GM III, 14). Sadness at the outcome of a natural lottery that has relegated them to inferiority gives way to outrage; Zarathustra notes that because the "despisers

2. The notion that fine action emerges out of visceral, inner compulsion rather than self-conscious effort also appears in the third essay of *The Genealogy*, when Nietzsche explains that the maxim "he who possesses is possessed" is held by his imagined, higher philosophers not because of a self-conscious "will to contentment and simplicity" aimed at attracting popular approval but rather because "their supreme lord demands this of them, prudently and inexorably" (GM III, 8).

of the body" are unable "to create beyond [them]selves" they become "angry with life and with the earth" (Z I, 4).

This frustration in the face of inadequacy is twinned with resentment and seething envy toward those who seem naturally graceful and sure-footed in their dealings. In the passage just cited Zarathustra speaks in this context of "unconscious envy" [*ungewußter Neid*], while elsewhere Nietzsche comments on the spectacle of those displaying "the heaving bosom" who "at the same time look with envy on the advantages enjoyed by those who live for the day" (TI I, 19). In such passages the herd appears to have an accurate—albeit scarcely articulate—understanding of its own inferiority. In the same vein Zarathustra warns one of his select, youthful interlocutors to be on guard against those who "still feel you are noble" (Z I, 8). "Everyone finds the noble man an obstruction," he observes, because the presence of innate grace in the midst of awkwardness serves to remind most people of their own inadequacy (ibid.). As Zarathustra cautions another of his interlocutors, "Before you they feel themselves small." Thus the higher type becomes "a bad conscience [*böse Gewissen*] to [his] neighbors" (Z I, 12).

Superior types unintentionally antagonize and exasperate the mediocre simply by being who (or what) they are. By refusing, for example, to resort to the pretentious moral phraseology that serves others as a crutch, they evince a "silent pride" that "offends [the] taste" of the mediocre (ibid.). Moreover, the crowd cannot abide the calm, polite way in which they refrain from flattery, envy, and other obvious signs of dependency on the opinion of others. Zarathustra notes, for example, that the people in the marketplace cannot forgive him for not being envious of their "virtues" (Z III, 5, 2).

Most unforgivable in the eyes of the majority, however, is the superior man's innate, instinctive contempt of those who do not share his lofty sensibility. Despite the higher type's magnanimous displays of polite, reserved gentleness, his disdain unquestionably shines through. "Even when you are gentle towards them," Zarathustra informs his youthful comrades, "they still feel you despise them; and they return your kindness with secret unkindness" (Z I, 12; cf. Z I, 17). In an apparent allusion to Nietzsche's own early experiences among his university colleagues, Zarathustra remarks that when he lived among scholars, he "lived above them. They grew angry with me for that. / They did not want to know that someone was walking over their heads" (Z II, 16). The idea that the herd's *ressentiment* is fueled by an inchoate perception of the condescension directed toward it is revisited in Nietzsche's late autobiographical reflections: "He whom I despise *divines* that I despise him: through my mere existence I enrage everything that has bad blood in its veins" (EH II, 10).

Nietzsche's use of the term "tarantulas" to refer to those experiencing "repressed envy" reveals the link between herd *ressentiment* and the vengeful desire to "sting" everyone who is not herdlike (Z II, 6). As suggested by Zarathustra's allusions to the herd's "secret unkindness" and "hidden vengeance," the sting is unleashed indirectly, in large part because of the majority's innate weakness and cowardly inability to evince its will to power openly and unapologetically (Z I, 12). In their "tyrant-madness of impotence," the many launch their project of revenge upon "everything that has power" (Z II, 6; cf. GM III, 14). Nietzsche identifies this project with a "slave revolt in morals" in which noble values are calumniated and herd values proclaimed the only true, respectable form of normative valuation.

The Moral Imperialism of the Herd

In his *Genealogy* Nietzsche distinguishes slave morality from nobler forms of valuation by highlighting what he sees as the former's essentially reactive nature (GM I, 10; GM II, 11).[3] Whereas the essence of nobility is to be self-regarding, to take oneself as good and praiseworthy and—almost as an afterthought—to dismiss what cannot attain one's level as bad [*schlecht*] and undesirable, those incapable of such psychological autarchy can only trumpet themselves as good by stigmatizing the dispositions of others—the noble sort—as evil [*böse*].

3. Although Nietzsche occasionally describes his alternative vision of human flourishing as a higher (master or noble) *morality* (e.g., BGE 202, 260; GM I, 10; A 24; EH II, 1; WP 268, 404), I prefer to speak of Nietzsche's "ethics" or "normative vision" and to associate the term "morality" with a large, extended family of religious and secular discourses that Nietzsche regards as questionable because of their emphasis on egalitarian and benevolent values (BGE 228).

The herd sees itself as "good" only in the wholly negative sense of being not-evil, of not evincing the capacities of stigmatized others.

That Nietzsche finds this a spiritually inferior form of valuation is no surprise. That he does not call for its utter eradication is less apparent, but nonetheless true. Nietzsche believes that the world will always be filled with unselfsufficient types needing some form of consolation and meaning. It is thus "understandable and forgivable" for people leading "empty and monotonous" lives to slide into religious belief (HAH 115). In this same middle-period passage, Nietzsche lauds Christianity's usefulness in this regard: "Within Christianity servility assumes the appearance of a virtue and is quite astonishingly beautiful" (ibid.; cf. WP 216). Hence his desire not to see the majority wrenched from its dogmatic convictions. As he proclaims in his notebooks, "the ideas of the herd should rule the herd" (WP 287). God may be dead, "murdered" by those in the know who have exposed him as an artifact of human ingenuity, but the fact that the majority continues to believe in his existence is by no means undesirable, so long as those capable of perceiving "the greatness of this deed" are allowed to do so and to live accordingly (GS 125).

This crucial proviso, however, is what "slave morality" rejects out of hand. The "secret desire" of its purveyors is "to be a truth for everyman," to insist that only their values are true and universal (BGE 43; cf. BGE 202, 221, 228; GS 345; A 11; WP 175, 185). What really enrages Nietzsche about a so-called "herd religion" such as Christianity is this "revolting" claim to unique conceivability (WP 186). It is one thing for the majority to live according to comforting illusions alongside and under the domination of other, higher forms of human life; future rulers might even "patronize and applaud" a herd religion because it "teaches obedience" and fosters in the mass "virtues that make [them] useful and submissive" (WP 216). It is quite another to attempt to banish competing modes of valuation and convert everyone to a herdish belief system.[4] Those with empty and monotonous lives, asserts Nietzsche, "have no right to demand

4. That Nietzsche has Christianity in mind when he speaks of this hegemonic ambition is apparent in his 1886 preface to *The Birth of Tragedy*, when he speaks of "Christian, unconditional morality" [*christlichen, das heißt unbedingten Moral*] (BT Preface 5; cf. BGE 203).

religiosity of those whose daily life is not empty and monotonous" (HAH 115). By asserting its own system of valuation as the one, true system, the majority overreaches itself by proclaiming its own visceral experiences of suffering, jealousy, resentment, and fear as the normative framework for all. Nietzsche takes this form of generalization "where generalization is impermissible" as a sign of baseness (BGE 198, 221, 272). "What is right for one," he insists, "*cannot* by any means therefore be right for another" (BGE 228).[5]

One form of herd imperiousness in the realm of values that particularly galls Nietzsche is the ascetic slander of worldly (especially bodily) pleasure. Although those with fine and unimpeded sensibilities tend to love life as they love themselves, seeing in life "a fountain of delight" and adopting a life-affirming stance, they tend to fall into the hands of "consumptives of the soul" who calumniate all of existence by projecting their self-loathing outwards (Z I, 9; Z II, 6; cf. Z III, 10, 2; Z III, 11, 16). The latter can see "only one aspect of existence," namely the misery, meanness, and ugliness of their own lives (Z I, 9). Their base instincts—referred to as "aching stomachs" in part III—filter out all of life's beauty and goodness, allowing only their own ugly projections to pass through (Z III, 11, 16).

Those who calumniate worldly pleasure and vitality are also predisposed to promote "moderation" as a universal virtue. In the hands of the hoi polloi and its priestly representatives, this notion is confused with mediocrity and associated with a contemptible aspiration for comfort and ease (WP 870; Z III, 5, 2; Z Prologue 3). The satirical portrait of the self-proclaimed preacher of "opium virtues" in part I of *Zarathustra* illustrates the same sentiment. This "wise man" counsels against sinning—indeed, against all innovative life experiments because they would be inconsistent "with good sleep." He claims that accruing a great deal of honor for oneself, in the manner of Aristotle's great-souled man, would "excite spleen" too much, while possessing no honor at all would make one sleep badly; the solution, he concludes, is to seek out a "moderate" (read: mediocre) form of honor: "a good name" in the eyes of the majority (Z I, 2).

5. Cf. Richard Schacht, *Nietzsche* (London: Routledge and Kegan Paul, 1983), p. 455.

Following the jaundiced view of the French moralist tradition typified by writers such as La Rochefoucauld, Nietzsche unmasks this risk-averse "virtue" as an inadequacy or deficiency. "In truth," confides Zarathustra, "I have often laughed at the weaklings who think themselves good because their claws are blunt!" (Z II, 13; cf. WP 355).[6] Herd "moderation" is truly a *verkleinernde Tugend*, a "virtue that makes small" (Z III, 5, 1). Nietzsche's grave concern is not that such a "virtue" exists—he thinks, after all, that "small virtues" are needed for "small people"—but that its universalization, along with the universalization of other "herd values," is stunting the spiritual growth of finer human beings and thus leading to a narrowing of the horizon of human achievement and potential (Z III, 5, 2).

The moral injunction that one ought not overreach oneself may be fine for those whose reach is short to begin with. When imposed upon those with the potential for reaching much farther, however, the consequences can be disastrous. Indeed, Nietzsche considers it a matter of principle that "the demand for *one* morality for all is detrimental to precisely the higher man" (BGE 228; cf. BGE 62, 82). The detriment lies precisely in the key role this hegemonic demand plays in the herd project of revenge. When herd values represent the only normative game in town, noble types who internalize them experience great spiritual torment because of the disjuncture between these alien values and their innate instincts. The spectacle of their torment, however, provides perverse satisfaction to the herd, compensating it for its own feelings of inadequacy.

6. Compare La Rochefoucauld, *Maximes* 308: "On a fait une vertu de la modération, pour borner l'ambition des grands hommes et pour consoler les gens médiocres de leur peu de fortune et de leur peu de mérite" [Moderation has been elevated into a virtue in order to curb the ambitions of the great and to console the second-rate for their lack of good fortune and the mediocrity of their talents] (*Maximes* [Paris: Éditions Garnier, 1961], p. 87; *The Maxims of the Duc de la Rochefoucauld*, trans. Constantine FitzGibbon [London: Millington, 1974], p. 92). On the influence of La Rochefoucauld on Nietzsche, see Ruth Abbey, "Dissent and Descent: Nietzsche's Reading of Two French Moralists" (Ph.D. diss., McGill University, 1994). The notion of "moderation" as a plot of the weak to diffuse the threat from the strong can be traced back to the ancient sophists. See especially Callicles' speeches in Plato's *Gorgias.* Brian Leiter notes the affinity between Nietzsche and at least some elements of Callicleanism in "Nietzsche and the Critique of Morality" (Ph.D. diss., University of Michigan, 1995), pp. 125–128.

Having been raised in modern herd society and steeped in Christian values (or in secular, Christian-influenced values), superior men no longer seem capable of experiencing and reveling in their corporeal instincts. Their "spirit" [*Geist*] often "tells lies about the soul [*Seele*]," and not simply because it has made some easily correctable miscalculations (Z III, 11, 2). When Nietzsche suggests that the deep internalization of otherworldly ideals has made "mankind itself . . . false down to its deepest instincts—to the point of worshipping the *inverse* values to those which alone could guarantee it prosperity," he does not presume that the instincts of the finest have been left untouched (EH Foreword 2). "Illusion" and "blundering" have "become body and will" in Nietzsche's imagined readers (Z I, 22, 2). Through the propagation of sophisticated but misanthropic transcendental notions of self-perfection, "everything has been distorted and twisted down to its very bottom" (Z III, 12, 28).

Nietzsche identifies two complementary weapons used in the herd's assault on noble bodily knowledge: the Christian view of free will and the dualistic form of philosophy introduced into Western civilization by Socrates. I discuss Nietzsche's assessment of Socrates' significance later in this chapter. First, however, we should examine his account of how the defenders of slave morality used "the superstition of free will" as a club with which to beat down healthy, superior men (GS 345). Duping these latter into an embrace of the free will doctrine represents a crucial victory over noble inclinations and sensibilities because it leads strong individuals to believe that they can (and should) "freely choose" not to manifest their strength against others. Their embrace of the belief "that *the strong man is free* to be weak and the bird of prey to be a lamb" is, of course, in the prudential interests of "lambs" who want to avoid being preyed upon (GM I, 13).[7] Once caught in the web of herd valuation, "mistrust of the instincts" becomes "second nature" in the strong; indeed, these

---

7. In *The Genealogy* Nietzsche also presents the free will doctrine as a psychological device that bolsters the herd's fragile self-esteem. In embracing free will the multitude is comforted by the illusion that it has "chosen" to be weak. To confront the hard truth—that their weakness is innate—would be unbearable (GM I, 13).

very instincts become "confused" (EH XIV, 8). Being true to one's aggressive instincts and exerting strength against weakness are henceforth stigmatized as "sin."[8]

Infused with a Christian notion of free will and sin and thus prevented from joyfully and spontaneously embracing its own lofty instincts, the noble psyche turns into a scene of self-torture as an alien "conscience" seeks to extirpate the body's intelligence. The guileless, open savagery evinced by the pre-Christian nobles of antiquity and praised in *The Genealogy* is turned inward in the strong but "self-lascerating" and "ill-constituted" human beings of modernity (A 22). Obliged to deny powerful instincts that refuse to ebb, the superior man in the grip of plebeian false consciousness seeks out "new . . . subterranean gratifications," developing a secretive, guilt-ridden personality that combines public self-abnegation with covert enjoyment of stigmatized and shameful inclinations (GM II, 16). Zarathustra recounts this psychological pathology: "And now your spirit is ashamed that it must do the will of your entrails and follows by-ways and lying-ways to avoid its own shame" (Z II, 15).

This sad spectacle comes to pass without any overt coercion on the part of the majority. "Morality," observes Nietzsche in one of his Prefaces of 1886,

> does not merely have at its command every kind of means of frightening off critical hands and torture-instruments: its security reposes far more in a certain art of enchantment [*Kunst der Bezauberung*] it has at its disposal—it knows how to 'inspire'. With this art it succeeds, often with no more than a single glance, in paralyzing the critical will against itself, so that, like the scorpion, it drives its sting into its own body. (D Preface 3; cf. Z I, 8)

The finest have been "enchanted" by the hegemonic slave morality to such an extent that herd sensibility becomes their "good con-

---

8. Interestingly, Nietzsche flirted briefly with a very different genealogy of free will in his middle period. In "The Wanderer and His Shadow" the origins of the free will doctrine are traced back to the strong rather than the weak; the latter, reasoned Nietzsche in 1880, could never have conjured up such an idea because they had no experience of strength or freedom (see WS 9). This alternative account disappears completely in the later works. I owe this point to Ruth Abbey.

science" and drives away any expression of independent, proud individuality: "As long as the good conscience [*gute Gewissen*] is called herd, only the bad conscience [*schlechte Gewissen*] says: I" (Z I, 15). To make matters worse, the "heavy words and values" of the herd are hammered into noble types at an impressionable age, taught and preached to them "almost in the cradle" (Z III, 11, 2). All nonconformity is stamped out early on by "old idol-priests" whose "palates" are "excited" by the prospect of taking on impressionable young people as charges (Z III, 12, 6).

Although a superior type raised in herd society may be tricked into thinking that the struggle for equal rights for all is synonymous with "justice," Nietzsche aims to show his readers that such ostensibly high-minded rights talk masks the herd effort at exacting revenge. "To hunt him [the free spirit] from his hiding place—the people always called that 'having a sense of right'" (Z II, 8; cf. Z II, 6). Nietzsche refuses to take the call for *equal* rights at face value, interpreting it as a vehicle for the herd's attempted domination of the talented few. In an invective launched at the "preachers of equality," Zarathustra claims that the demand for equality masks a "tyrant-appetite" (Z II, 6). The rhetoric of equal rights, like that of "free will," is deemed another form of herdish mystification, another crafty strategy for convincing the strong to refrain from exerting their will to power on the weak. "One speaks of '*equal rights*'," claims Nietzsche, when "one wants to prevent one's competitors from growing in power" (WP 86).

The strong, talented man who embraces such ideas and who mistakenly comes to think the multitude worthy of his guidance is, in Nietzsche's eyes, a tragic spectacle. In becoming a shepherd to the flock, he lets go of the discriminating sense of *Rangordnung* that protects finer sensibilities by keeping them apart from the common orders. He imitates what Nietzsche describes metaphorically in *Zarathustra* as that "weight-bearing spirit," the camel, in his willingness to kneel down before the herd and take its cares upon his back (Z I, 1). This camel wades into "dirty water," ignoring his innate, discriminating sense by refusing to disdain anyone: not even "cold frogs and hot toads." The camel-like creature, argues Zarathustra, "debases itself" by "making friends with the deaf," by loving "those who despise" those of noble sensibilities (ibid.). In part III Zarathustra returns to the image of the camel, bemoaning the lot of the higher man who "bears too many foreign things on his shoulders" (Z III, 11, 2).

Zarathustra denounces the type of person who takes advantage of this misguided weight-bearing, who drains the life-energy of the talented few, as "the most offensive beast of a man I ever found": the parasite (ibid.). Here again, Nietzsche's tendency to associate the many with lower forms of animal life comes to the fore. Parasitical human beings, unable to create but profiting from the creations of others, spend their lives "extract[ing] warmth from light-givers" (Z II, 9; cf. Z IV, 11). This shameless exploitation need not be part of a willed conspiracy; on the contrary, parasites may be quite unaware of their own parasitism, "want[ing] blood . . . in all innocence" (Z I, 8). Neither should it be imagined that their often obsequious flattery is innocent of this parasitism. "They buzz around you even with their praise," remarks Zarathustra to an interlocutor, "and their praise is importunity. They want to be near your skin and your blood" (ibid.). Although it may seem that "he who praises" the talented wishes thereby to "give back," the truth of the matter is that "he wants to be given more!" (Z III, 5, 2).

Given the routine association these days of Nietzsche with the debunking of all normative categories, it may seem surprising that Nietzsche speaks of injustice when denouncing this exploitation of the strong by the weak. Just as Aristotle argues in *The Politics* that it would be unjust to treat the better sort of man like everyone else, Nietzsche insists that "justice itself" supports his belief that deferential treatment and privilege, rather than expectations of service to the "common good," are the due of those like him (BGE 265).[9] "For men are *not* equal," intones Zarathustra, "thus speaks justice" (Z II, 16; cf. Z II, 7). Conversely, injustice "lies in the claim to '*equal*' rights," in a social order that has the temerity to "call into question

9. "Justice is thought by [men] to be, and is, equality—not, however, for all, but only for equals." Aristotle, *The Politics*, ed. Stephen Everson, trans. Benjamin Jowett with revisions by Jonathan Barnes (Cambridge: University of Cambridge Press, 1988), 1280a10–13. Leiter notes that "while Nietzsche might not dispute the general moral imperative that 'like cases should be treated alike' he clearly rejects the idea that we are, in fact, *all like cases*." Leiter, "Nietzsche and the Critique of Morality," p. 15.

the higher, greater, richer" (A 57; HAH I Preface 6).[10] Nietzsche claims that his approach to political and social life is premised on a different—and better—notion of justice. Nietzsche's "new philosophers" claim as their motto the words of Charlemagne's Anglo-Saxon advisor, Alcuin: "prava corrigere, et recta corroborare, et sancta sublimare" [Correct what is wrong, strengthen the right, and raise what is holy] (WP 977).

Stepping Out from the Domination of Chance and the Priesthood

While hopeful (most of the time) that a small number of individuals like himself do in fact exist,[11] Nietzsche is far from certain that his "slow search for those related to [him]" will be successful and that higher human beings will emerge to claim their rightful place in a revitalized political and cultural order (EH X, 1). In *Beyond Good and Evil* he anxiously contemplates "the terrible danger that they might not appear or might fail or might degenerate" (BGE 203).[12] Higher types have always been much rarer in human history than mediocre ones; they are described as "brief little pieces of good luck . . . that here and there come flashing up" and as "lucky hits" [*Glücksfälle*]" (BGE 224; GM III, 14; cf. BGE 276, WP 684). Indeed, "the higher the type of man a man represents, the greater the improbability he will *turn out well*" (BGE 62; cf. Z IV, 13, 15). The premature destruction of a higher man, he explains, is due not "to any special fatality or

10. Nietzsche's attack on the notion of equal rights is given further attention in Chapter 6.

11. We should note, however, Nietzsche's occasional suggestion that he is writing for a readership that has yet to come into being. See, for example, WP 958: "I write for a species of man that does not yet exist: for 'the masters of the earth.'" Cf. the comment in *Ecce Homo* that his Zarathustra, who "is still looking" for those "to whom one *ought* to communicate oneself . . . will have to look for a long time yet!" (EH III, 4).

12. Laurence Lampert understates this fear when he writes that "Nietzsche stood at the head of an army not yet mustered and outfitted, an army formed for public battles still a long way off and won in the mind of their instigator." *Nietzsche and Modern Times: A Study of Bacon, Descartes, and Nietzsche* (New Haven: Yale University Press, 1993), p. 389.

malevolence of nature, but simply to the concept 'higher type': the higher type represents an incomparably greater complexity—a greater sum of co-ordinated elements: so its disintegration is also incomparably more likely. The 'genius' is the sublimest machine there is—consequently the most fragile" (WP 684).

In the modern age, moreover, the danger faced by those with "the desires of an elevated, fastidious soul . . . has become extraordinary" (BGE 282). At a time when sickliness has taken on hegemonic ambition, "the corruption, the ruination of higher human beings, of more strangely constituted souls, is the rule; it is dreadful to have such a rule always before one's eyes" (BGE 269; cf. BGE 62, 268; EH II, 8). Alongside that traditional obstacle to the higher type's flourishing—capricious *Fortuna*—the petty vindictiveness of the herd and its priestly leadership have been added to the mix.

Nietzsche's dread at the prospect of the extinction of higher types like himself becomes even more understandable in light of his belief that the fate of the species as a whole depends on the condition of these talented few. If the exemplars of the species are abandoned to slave morality and left in their current spiritual torpor, the struggle to ensure "a *new* greatness of man, a new untrodden path to his enlargement" will be lost (BGE 212). Left unchecked, herd morality will succeed in securing itself as the only viable table of values, thus ensuring what Nietzsche considers "worst of all": an irreversible species-wide "degeneration" [*Entartung*] (Z I, 22, 1). Instead of securing the preservation and enhancement of the higher type of human being, we will witness "the physiological ruination of mankind" (EH VII, 2).[13] The somber pronouncement in his notebooks that "man as a species is not progressing" suggests that in his blacker moods Nietzsche believed that this feared degeneration was already

13. Nietzsche's talk of the need to preserve and protect a higher form of human life belies William Connolly's suggestion that Nietzsche rejected the notion of preservation in favor of self-overcoming. *Identity\Difference: Democratic Negotiations of Political Paradox* (Ithaca: Cornell University Press, 1991), p. 186. As Nietzsche argues in a fragment from 1884, although "rarer, subtler, and less average men" (himself, for example) are "enraged" by the instincts of self-preservation of that "profoundly average creature, the species man" [*das tiefe Durchschnittswesen, der Gattungsmensch*], superior men are themselves eager to declare, "'We are nobler [*Edleren*]! Our preservation [*unserer Erhaltung*] is more important than that of those cattle!'" (WP 873; cf. EH II, 8).

under way (WP 684). His picture of its terminus is evoked in the memorable Prologue to *Zarathustra*, where the mob becomes master and the comfortable nihilism of the "last man" emerges triumphant.

The danger besetting higher human beings and the imminent threat this poses to human excellence adds urgency to Nietzsche's proselytizing. Despite his occasional signs of despairing pessimism, Nietzsche refuses in the end to adopt a posture of resignation. Indeed, he takes to task those who continue to face the onslaught on noble instincts with a "fatality that lies concealed in the idiotic guilelessness and blind confidence of 'modern ideas'" (BGE 203). The time to act is now: whereas the "soil" of humanity may still be "rich enough" for the cultivation of a noble ethos, "one day" soon it will become too "poor and weak" for such a task (Z Prologue 5). Those who share his views are said to "have no other choice" but to direct their hopes "toward new philosophers . . . toward spirits strong and original enough to make a start on antithetical evaluations" (BGE 203). One must begin, he claims, by calling upon "tremendous counter-forces" to combat the contemporary "progress" toward uniformity (BGE 268).

Genealogy as Edification

Among the "tremendous counter-forces" posited by Nietzsche, his genealogical account of the battle between "slave" and "master" tables of value in antiquity plays a central role. As early as his 1874 essay "On the Uses and Disadvantages of History for Life," he urged those like him to take the examination of ancient societies ("classical studies") seriously, "for the benefit of a time to come," as part of a broader struggle against the dominant, servile ethos of the modern age (UD, Foreword). When he suggests that the noble type "goes backwards as everyone goes backwards who wants to take a big jump," Nietzsche's intention might be to entice his readers to cultivate themselves by learning from the mistakes made by fine men in the past (BGE 280).

The account in *The Genealogy* of the origins of injustice—the defeat of the original, pre-Christian nobility at the hands of the herd—is an example of an unhappy, cautionary tale that is meant to edify. Whereas the tormented, guilt-ridden noble type may well consider his own inner turmoil and struggles to be aberrant, Nietzsche aims at drawing him out of his isolation and convincing him that he is not alone in his anguish. The sad story of the infamous "blond beast" is meant to serve this purpose by eliciting a shock of recognition from a reader who is encouraged to see his own mistakes and suffering as part of a long, sad history that began with the blond beast's downfall. No longer an idiosyncratic, isolated case, the noble-spirited reader can thus take heart in viewing his struggle in terms of a millennial meta-struggle between master and slave forms of life.[14] By recounting the genesis of a form of valuation that has caused sensitive, creative individuals throughout the ages such grief, Nietzsche wants his readers to understand how dangerous it is to be an heir to this struggle.

How did the noble types of antiquity allow themselves to be tricked by the clever, vengeful machinations of the herd? Nietzsche points to three factors, the first being identified in both *The Genealogy* and *Zarathustra* as the superior man's "indifference to and contempt for security, body, life, comfort" (GM I, 11). The high-minded "imprudence" [*Unklugheit*] of the strong, their "bold recklessness whether in the face of danger or of the enemy," is contrasted favorably with the "timid mistrustfulness" of "cowardly souls" who evince a cautious self-concern in their every gesture (GM I, 10; Z III, 10, 2). Given their tendency to channel all resources into creative activity, the strong and resourceful have neither the time nor the energy for self-defensive prudence. Their resulting "helplessness" in the face of "everything small" is caused by the suspension of all "minor defensive capabilities" in the face of the "tremendous expenditure . . . presupposed by every *creative* deed" (EH IX, 5).

They tend, moreover, to shun the prospect of constant vigilance against the attacks of resentful inferiors. "I *must* be without caution," insists Zarathustra, "so my fate will have it" (Z IV, 5, 2). Refusing to

14. In "So Polyphonous a Being," Abbey notes that Nietzsche's tendency to subsume all of his psychological observations into a meta-narrative of masters versus slaves emerges only in his later period.

defend oneself against the thousand pinpricks or stings of the common folk is honorable, even though their gradual accumulation may prove fatal. "I will make light of you," Zarathustra says to the insect-like common folk surrounding him, "since I have *heavy things* to carry; and what do I care if beetles and dragonflies sit themselves on my bundle!" (Z II, 14). Better to be "without foresight" [*ohne Vorsicht*] than "to be prickly towards small things," which Zarathustra dismisses as "the wisdom of a hedgehog" (Z III, 5, 2; cf. EH II, 8).[15] Such freedom from suspicion, claims Nietzsche, is a double-edged sword; although he portrays it as a sign of nobility he also concedes that it renders the magnanimous soul highly vulnerable to the machinations of lower types.

A third vulnerable area of the premodern noble psyche, and one that Nietzsche treats as (at least in principle) excisable in his targeted contemporary audience, is its lack of critical self-understanding. Even the finest of ancient men, he concedes, held concepts that "were rather at first incredibly uncouth, coarse, external, narrow, straightforward, and altogether *unsymbolical* in meaning to a degree that we can scarcely conceive" (GM I, 6). Possessing what to our modern sensibilities must appear as an impoverished inner world— one stretched thinly "as it were . . . between two membranes" (GM II, 16)— and relying solely on their admirable "unconscious drives," noble types were highly vulnerable to a completely unprecedented development: the emergence of a morally charged and vengeful intellectual and spiritual revolt erupting from the masses and led by the standard-bearer of self-conscious reflection, Socrates.[16]

15. As Martha Nussbaum points out, the view that chronic suspicion and mistrustfulness are signs of a base character can be traced back to the ancient Greeks. "Euripides, Aristotle, and Thucydides concur in the view that . . . a mistrustful suspiciousness, which can come to an agent through no moral failing, but only through experience of the bad things in life, can be a poison that corrodes all of the excellences, turning them to forms of vindictive defensiveness." *The Fragility of Goodness: Luck and Ethics in Greek Tragedy and Philosophy* (Cambridge: Cambridge University Press, 1986), p. 418.

16. "Socrates belonged, in his origins, to the lowest orders: Socrates was rabble . . . [H]e contained within him every kind of foul vice and lust" (TI II, 3). Nietzsche claims that the essential morbidity of Socratic philosophy—and hence its affinity with the "sick" multitude—is proven by Socrates' apparent denigration of mortal life and willing embrace of death, as recounted by Plato in the *Phaedo* (TI II, 1, 12; GS 340).

Socrates' public dialogues were embraced by Athenian aristocrats, in Nietzsche's view, because they seemed to satisfy in a new and appealing way the Athenian desire for agonistic competition: "He introduced a variation into the wrestling-matches among the youths and young men" (TI II, 8; cf. TI IX, 23). In the end, however, Socratic dialectics proved to be the undoing of noble types with "small intellects and spacious souls" (Z II, 4). More at ease issuing commands than giving reasons, habituated to act spontaneously on instinct, these naïve aristocrats were reduced to shadows of their former selves, "to thinking, inferring, reckoning, co-ordinating cause and effect" (GM II, 16). Henceforth they were at their "weakest and most fallible," highly vulnerable to the noxious influence of morbid and vengeful types who were well schooled in logic and metaphysics (ibid.).

Critical self-consciousness thus became the Trojan horse allowing the weaker—though more "clever"—majority to capture the hearts and minds of the strong (TI IX, 14).[17] Nietzsche believes that philosophers since the time of Plato have been, with only a few exceptions, learned vulgarians who proselytize on behalf of the sort of Platonic and Christian metaphysics that teaches higher types to ignore or extirpate their bodily knowledge. Since the time of Socrates, "the weaker dominate the strong again and again," largely through the propagation of a conceptual and normative package that calumniates the body and the earth and instills self-misunderstanding, doubt, bad conscience, and self-loathing in the souls of the healthy (ibid.; cf. TI X, 2). Zarathustra illustrates this view of the unsavory normative role of philosophy since Socrates when he bemoans the fact that "hitherto all *knowledge* [*Wissen*] has grown up *beside* the bad conscience [*bösen Gewissen*]!" (Z III, 11, 7).

However, Nietzsche does not call upon his readers to emancipate themselves by repudiating rational self-consciousness altogether and returning to the blissful, naïvely confident state of the pre-Socratic noble. One simply cannot "take mankind back, *force* it back, to an *earlier* standard of virtue" (TI IX, 43; cf. GS 377). The Pandora's box of reflexive self-consciousness opened by Socrates and his followers

17. Nietzsche often associates cleverness [*Klugheit*] with a cowardly, calculating prudence. See, for example, Z I, 12; Z II, 16; Z III, 5, 2; GS 3.

can never be shut again.[18] Zarathustra expresses this sense of inevitability when he reminds his imagined comrades that "neither in the incomprehensible [*Unbegreifliche*] nor in the irrational [*Unvernünftige*] can you be at home" (Z II, 2; cf. Z I, 10; Z III, 15, 2).

Nostalgia is ruled out of court not only because of its futility—we can never recapture the prerational innocence of the "blond beast"—but also because of its ignominy. To pine for a long-lost antiquity would entail a servile conformity with received tradition that would be antithetical to Nietzsche's idea of a truly noble form of valuation.[19] In a manner reminiscent of Aristotle's *megalopsuchos*, Nietzsche's great man feels viscerally compelled to rebel against moral systems that equate fine action and motivation with obedience to something outside of the self. This refusal of all mimicry forms the background to Nietzsche's famous declaration that "we must overcome even the Greeks" (GS 340).

Yet we should be cautious about assuming that Nietzsche's rejection of romantic nostalgia entails a refusal on his part to take a stand between "master" and "slave" modes of valuation.[20] As Nehamas has

18. Bernard Williams rightly notes that the complexity of Nietzsche's attitude toward modernity stems, in part, "from his ever-present sense that his own consciousness would not be possible without the developments that he disliked. In particular his view of things . . . depended on a heightened reflectiveness, self-consciousness, and inwardness that, he thought, it was precisely one of the charms, and indeed the power, of the Greeks to have done without." Williams, *Shame and Necessity* (Berkeley: University of California Press, 1993), p. 9. Nietzsche's genealogy of heightened inwardness and self-consciousness can be profitably compared with Charles Taylor's discussion of the "radical reflexivity" of the modern identity in *Sources of the Self: The Making of Modern Identity* (Cambridge: Harvard University Press, 1989), pp. 130–131, 176–178.

19. Cf. Nietzsche's early assessment of the limitations of "antiquarian history" in UD 2 and 3. Peter Berkowitz's discussion of these passages in his *Nietzsche: The Ethics of an Immoralist* (Cambridge: Harvard University Press, 1995), pp. 32–36, is very useful. Nietzsche's criticism of nostalgic longing recalls Machiavelli's polemic against the fashionable cult of things ancient in his prefaces to *The Prince* and *The Discourses*.

20. Such caution is notably absent in many contemporary scholarly treatments of Nietzsche. Nietzsche's emphasis on creation is often assumed to entail a careful neutrality between the "masters" and the "slaves." See, for example, Walter Kaufmann, *Nietzsche: Philosopher, Psychologist, AntiChrist*, 4th ed. (Princeton: Princeton University Press, 1974), p. 297; Richard Schacht, *Nietzsche*, p. 412; and Tracy B. Strong, *Friedrich Nietzsche and the Politics of Transfiguration*, expanded ed. (Berkeley: University of California Press, 1988), pp. 148, 237.

suggested, although Nietzsche may believe it neither possible nor desirable to go back to the specific instance of pre-Socratic nobility, he may "still want us to go back to the *type* itself."[21] Certain aspects of premodern nobility were indeed admirable and worthy of emulation, but only a creative, mature form of appropriation—in the spirit of the Renaissance notion of *imitatio*—will do.[22] And an appropriation of this sort is possible only by opening oneself up to the possibility of a different form of cognition, one that complements the fine sensibilities of the strong, that exults rather than denigrates bodily knowledge. Whereas premodern noble types had only one path to self-consciousness open to them, a path that, *faute de mieux*, led them to paralyzing self-doubt and self-contempt, Nietzsche means to provide his readers with a "counter-ideal," a competitor to servile rationality symbolized by "the advent of Zarathustra" (EH XI).

The Personal and the Pedagogical

"In the final analysis," suggests Zarathustra, "one experiences only oneself," a sentiment Nietzsche embraces as a truth about all authentic acquisition of knowledge (Z III, 1). "In the case of every cardinal problem . . . a thinker cannot relearn but only learn fully—only discover all that is 'firm and settled' within him on this subject" (BGE 231). By extension, knowledge of one's character and of the presence of nobility therein can be unearthed only through the deepest, most personal form of self-examination: "If you have a virtue and it is your own virtue," insists Zarathustra, "you have it in common with no one" (Z I, 5). I noted in the previous chapter how this stress on the personal sometimes (but not always) leads Nietzsche and his literary

21. Alexander Nehamas, *Nietzsche: Life as Literature* (Cambridge: Harvard University Press, 1985), p. 254.
22. Given the unmistakably pejorative reputation of the modern notion of imitation (especially its use as a synonym for servile mimicry), the difficulties involved in grasping the Renaissance notion of *imitatio* are formidable. For a useful discussion of the older sense of this term and its eclipse in the modern era, see Wayne Booth, *The Company We Keep: An Ethics of Fiction* (Berkeley: University of California Press, 1988), pp. 227–260.

surrogate to reject impersonal modifiers: "not good taste, not bad taste, but *my* taste" (Z III, 11, 2).

This rejection would seem at first glance to imply a repudiation of any form of external ethical-spiritual guidance. *Zarathustra* continuously drives home the message that neither universal rules and methods nor mimicry of others are of any help in the highly personal matter of ethical and spiritual self-improvement. Experimentation with many paths is said to be an inevitable part of the precarious, extremely personal odyssey leading to ethical and spiritual development of the highest sort. When asked for "the way" to self-improvement, Zarathustra replies, "'This—is now *my* way: where is yours?' . . . For *the* way—does not exist!" (ibid.; cf. Z IV, 13, 10). The insistence on the solitary nature of personal development is further emphasized in Nietzsche's preface to *Daybreak*, in which he warns his readership not to think that he intends to "invite them to the same hazardous enterprise! . . . For he who proceeds on his own path in this fashion encounters no one: that is inherent in 'proceeding on one's own path'" (D Preface 2).

It seems to me, however, that Nietzsche's stress on the personal implies neither a lack of interest in the improvement of others nor a complete disregard for ways in which an experienced traveler could help kindred spirits get their own journeys under way. When Zarathustra observes that "he who is of my sort will also encounter experiences of my sort," he appears to be speaking not just of himself but of a broadly defined character type [*meiner Art*] of which he is an exemplar (Z III, 8, 1). As such, his *démarche* and experiences may be of some use to other representatives of this same type. Farther along in his own odyssey, Zarathustra clearly presents himself as a beacon for the "shipwrecked"— others of similarly lofty sensibility who are experiencing grave difficulties. As one who has "learned to climb . . . up high masts," he declares his readiness to "flicker" like a little flame so as to be "a great comfort to castaway sailors and the shipwrecked" (Z III, 11, 2).

Passages such as these suggest that Nietzsche sees no contradiction between writing in an intensely personal manner and expressing a keen desire to help others along in their ethical-spiritual development. "Shall my experience . . . have been my personal experience alone?" he asks in an 1886 preface to an earlier work (HAH II Preface 6). His negative answer is revealing: "Today I would like to believe the reverse; again and again I feel sure that my travel books were not written solely for myself, as sometimes seems to be the case" (ibid.). Nietzsche goes on to "commend" his books "to the hearts and ears" of those similar to himself, that is, those still struggling with and suffering from the "burden" of their past, the "most imperiled, most spiritual, most courageous men who have to be the *conscience* of the modern soul and as such have to possess its *knowledge* . . . whose comfort it is to know the way to a *new* health . . . a health of tomorrow and the day after" (ibid.).[23]

In appending an account of his own trials and tribulations to those of the long-vanished, fatally flawed "blond beast," Nietzsche strives to become the sort of philosopher evoked in his notebooks, a "great educator" who serves as an indispensable aid to those of similar makeup undergoing similar upheavals (WP 980). "Perhaps," muses Nietzsche in a preface to the first volume of *Human, All Too Human,* "I shall do something to speed [the] coming [of free spirits] if I describe in advance under what vicissitudes, upon what paths, I *see* them coming?—" (HAH I Preface 2). In a late work, Nietzsche returns once again to the therapeutic or pedagogical impact of his own writing: "He who is related to me through *loftiness* of will experiences when he reads me real extasies of learning" (EH III, 3).

In this approach to therapy or pedagogy, the "patient" or "pupil" actively participates in his own cure or lesson. As Zarathustra puts it, let the patient's "best healing-aid be to see with his own eyes," and let him look to his mentor as an inspiration, rather than a crutch (Z I, 22, 2; cf. Z I, 6). This is why Nietzsche takes pains to distinguish his preferred style of intervention from standard moral preaching. We make ourselves "ridiculous," he claims, when we turn to an individual and say, "'*You* ought to be thus and thus'" (TI V, 6; cf. WP 317; EH Foreword 4). His goal is rather "to *create conditions* that *require stronger men,*" to help them develop "a physical-spiritual discipline"

23. In another preface written in the same year, Nietzsche recalls how, at an earlier stage in his *démarche*, it was crucial for his "cure and self-restoration" to believe that he "was *not* thus isolated, not alone in *seeing* as [he] did" (HAH I Preface 1).

that "*makes them strong*!" (WP 981). This involves "breeding" a certain type of human being—a "gentleman" [*gentilhomme*], as he puts it in *Ecce Homo* (EH X, 2; cf. A 3).

Nietzsche begins his breeding enterprise by paradoxically urging his select readers to follow his example by not following anyone or anything but their own inclinations and instincts: "I need living companions who follow me because they want to follow themselves" (Z Prologue 9). The Nietzschean paradox of "follow me: command!" is succinctly encapsulated in the following aphorism: "I do not want to have people imitate my example; I wish that everybody would fashion his own example, as I do" (GS 255).

In describing his pedagogical role, Zarathustra refers to himself as a "drawer, trainer, and taskmaster" [*ein Zieher, Züchter und Zuchtmeister*] who can only urge his charges to "become what you are" (Z IV, 1). Ethical-spiritual development under the guidance of such a mentor becomes a highly personal journey allowing one to experience—perhaps for the first time—the innate, instinctive knowledge that defines what one truly is. It is a journey of liberation, for in this process of discovery one learns to free oneself from all manner of "foreign" accoutrements collected through early, misguided, and noxious indoctrination. The free spirit is one who has cast off that which is nonessential, thus "seiz[ing] possession of itself" (EH VI, 1).[24]

Master-types in the grip of a self-abnegating false consciousness have been raised to see virtue as an external, superior slave driver. Zarathustra illustrates this wrong-headed approach by rehearsing the plaintive cry: "'What I am *not*, that, that to me is God and virtue!'" (Z II, 5). Concerned that his readers have been seduced by "world-calumniators" and "world-slanderers" into believing that the way to transcendence is through renunciation of the body, Nietzsche tries to convince them to come down from "cloudland" and learn the nature of authentic, healthy transcendence. "Stay loyal to the earth," Zarathustra urges his "brothers." "Do not let [your bestowing love and your knowledge] fly away from the things of the earth and beat

24. The autobiographical origin of this view is made clear in Carl Pletsch's very useful account of Nietzsche's efforts to distance himself from the early influences of Wagner and Schopenhauer. See Pletsch, *Young Nietzsche: Becoming a Genius* (New York: Free Press, 1991).

with its wings against the eternal walls!" (Z I 22, 2; cf. Z III,12,15; Z III,16, 2; Z II, 4). Because "the best men have . . . often misunderstood themselves," Nietzsche focuses his enterprise on inciting them to recognize a profound truth that emerges from "the bottom of [their] souls": that "[their] virtue is [their Selves] and not something alien, a skin, a covering" (WP 870; Z II, 5).

Taking possession of oneself in this manner involves recovering or making initial contact with the corporeal "knowledge" of one's instincts and drives. Zarathustra expends much effort (a) berating his interlocutors for being out of touch with this knowledge, (b) urging them to think more deeply about their true selves, and (c) persuading them to embrace more authentic positions in line with their profoundest inclinations. He proposes to his "brothers" to "listen . . . to the voice of the healthy body [*die Stimme des gesunden Leibes*]: this is a purer voice and a more honest one" (Z I, 3). As Nietzsche informs us in his own voice, this proposal is meant to give back to men of lofty sensibilities "the courage to their natural drives" (WP 124).

Zarathustra describes the process of reacquainting oneself with innate, bodily knowledge in terms of a combination of transcendence and descent "into the depths" [*in die Tiefe steigen*] (Z Prologue 1). Ascent (in the sense of greater enlightenment) and descent are pictured as inextricably linked: "The soul which possesses the longest ladder," claims Zarathustra, "can descend the deepest" (Z III, 12, 19). Searching for an appropriate explanatory device, Zarathustra evokes a plethora of metaphors: for example, that of the tree, which rises to the heights and the light only by plunging its roots "into the depths—into evil" and that of the mountain rising from the sea: "The highest must arise to its height from the deepest" (Z I, 8; Z III, 1). That Nietzsche believes he has already attained an earthly transcendental view of this sort is clear from his declaration in *Ecce Homo* that "I come from heights no bird has ever soared to, I know abysses into which no foot has ever yet strayed" (EH III, 3).[25]

25. I discuss Nietzsche's conception of a transcendence that involves both ascent and descent in "The Objective Viewpoint: A Nietzschean Account," *History of Philosophy Quarterly* 13, 4 (October 1996): 483–502.

t h r e e   **Negation and Its Overcoming**

The Importance of Negation

In Zarathustra's portrayal of an essentially affirmative stance, the healthy, self-loving body/soul ostensibly places its own stamp on all things with a "bestowing" love: "You compel all things to come to you and into you, that they may flow back from your fountain as gifts of your love" (Z I, 22, 1). Everything is turned into a mirror around the virtuous man's "exalted body" and reflects his brilliance (ibid.; cf. Z III, 10, 2). A profound love of the earth is thus posited as an extension of the free spirit's self-regard. Free spirits strive for "the kingdom of earth" [*das Erdenreich*] and an "earthly virtue" [*Eine irdischen Tugend*] rather than for worlds beyond (Z IV, 18, 2; Z I, 5).

One could read into these passages an indiscriminate embrace of all forms of existence, both higher and lower, healthy and sick. But this is far from Nietzsche's intention. Although, as we shall see below, he thinks that the mature outlook of the higher sort involves an unflinching, unconditional affirmation of all that has been, Nietzsche does not believe that an easygoing, ecumenical endorsement or approval of all human practices and values is a proper starting point or goal for ethical-spiritual development. Indeed, he claims that the rejection of facile ecumenism in favor of extreme selectivity in the bestowing of love and respect is a precondition for proper development. He urges his readers to repudiate, for example, what he sees as the simple-minded, superficial optimism of the "all-contented" [*die Allgenügsamen*], those purveyors of panglossian views of a rational universe in which everything is as it should be in the best of all possible worlds (Z III, 11, 2).

Nobility requires a healthy, discriminating suspicion of all unfamiliar—and many all-too-familiar—things, persons, and ideas. Far from considering everything worthy of a fond embrace, Nietzsche's man of virtue "reacts slowly to every kind of stimulus, with that slowness which a protracted caution and a willed pride have bred in him—he tests an approaching stimulus, he is far from going out to meet it" (EH I, 2). As someone of discriminating tastes, he should shun and repudiate as well as embrace and affirm; his avoidance of ugliness is just as important as his pursuit of beauty. In a revealing autobiographical aside, Nietzsche notes that it is not in his "nature to love much or many kinds of things." His preferred stance, toward books as well as people, is one of "caution, even hostility," rather than of "neighborly love" (EH II, 3).

Nietzsche considers the Judeo-Christian precept of loving one's neighbor to be one more piece of false consciousness designed to dissuade the higher type from discounting that which should be discounted. Urging his readers to abandon their misguided concern for the fate of the majority, he claims that their true and best destiny lies in a much more "selfish" preoccupation with themselves and their own ethical-spiritual development. Zarathustra's interlocutors are urged to "stop [their] ears" to the notion of "love thy neighbor," which is derided as "the virtue only of petty people" who have neither the right to nor strength for a noble form of selfishness [*Eigennutz*] (Z IV, 13, 11).

A higher type shows more "prudence and providence," he claims, in his selfishness; his real "neighbor" is in fact his work and his will (ibid.). Here Nietzsche calls upon his readers to embrace what he claims is a noble form of self-regard, a "sound, healthy selfishness that issues from a mighty soul" (Z III, 10, 2; cf. Z II, 13). By negating the herd and perfecting himself, the noble type does far more than simply look after himself; his selfishness leads counterintuitively to "the greater perfection of all things" (Z III, 3).[1]

An acute sensitivity to rank and especially to one's superior position in the natural *Rangordnung* is said to be a precondition for healthy, life-affirming nobility. In his late autobiographical musings, Nietzsche reveals that he can form favorable first impressions only of those authentic "gentlemen" who demonstrate this sort of sensitivity, that is, those who have "a feeling of distance" [*ein Gefühl für Distanz im Leibe*] and "see everywhere rank, degree, order between man and man" (EH XIII, 4). Nobility is thus predicated upon an ability to negate as well as affirm. Only those with a "really swinish nature," claims Zarathustra, "chew and digest everything," that is, evince an indiscriminate fondness for and curiosity about everything (Z III, 11, 2). Zarathustra prefers to "honor the obstinate, fastidious tongues and stomachs" (ibid.). The point is underscored by his observation that while "he who wants to understand all things among men has to touch all things," Zarathustra's hands are "too clean for that" (Z III, 9).

In place of an indiscriminate ecumenism, Nietzsche wishes to draw out the visceral contempt for the rabble that he considers part of the higher type's instinctive knowledge. Contempt is treated as a form of wisdom, a sign that the higher type has resisted or overcome herdish false consciousness: "There is wisdom in the fact that much in the world smells ill," insists Zarathustra. "Disgust itself creates wings and water-divining powers" (Z III, 12, 14). The affirmative,

1. Nietzsche wishes to contrast this "glorious selfishness" with a "sick selfishness," that is, the small-minded form of self-preservation and self-indulgence characteristic of the "self-seeking cattle and mob" (Z III, 10, 2; Z I, 22, 1; WP 752). Whereas the latter involves nothing beyond the desire for a "pitiable comfort," the former allows higher types to achieve greatness.

loving stance of the healthy individual appears to require a healthy disdain for sickness and weakness. Zarathustra speaks in this sense of a "great, loving contempt [*das große, das liebende Verachten*] which loves most where it despises most," and claims "to love the great despisers, for they are the great venerators" (Z III, 14; Z Prologue 4; cf. Z IV, 13, 3). At the highest level of human existence, contempt for much of humankind is said to be inseparable from the love of creation, and its cultivation is treated as a crucial sign of progress toward a more refined form of love: "The lover wants to create, because he despises! What does he know of love who has not had to despise precisely what he loved?" (Z I, 17).

The Radical Retreat into Solitude

At times Nietzsche seems to suggest that the cultivation and maintenance of a healthy psychological distance from the herd is possible even in cases of close physical proximity. For those obliged to live among the crowd, an inscrutable aloofness and determined masking of one's true nature is recommended. "The higher the type, the more a man requires an incognito" (WP 943; cf. WP 985). Far from revealing a pervasive self-deflating irony, as some have suggested, this tactic is primarily invoked as a means of self-defense; it would be dangerous to bare one's soul in the midst of a populace that can only exploit greatness. As he suggests in *Ecce Homo*, the "self-defensive instinct" for disguise is merely another word for taste (EH II, 8). Zarathustra confides to his interlocutors that he shows the herd only his most austere, inscrutable side for this very reason: since "envious and injurious people" could not "endure [his] happiness," he reveals to them "only ice and winter on [his] peaks" (Z III, 6).[2]

In passages such as these Nietzsche appears to follow the Stoic view that an imperturbably virtuous character may be forged and

2. This same passage also suggests that Zarathustra's outward, inscrutable austerity conceals a warmth and lovingness that is being saved for a more select group of companions. Whereas the herd "hears only the whistling of [his] winter storms," Zarathustra also winds "girdles of sunlight" around his mountain in anticipation of a new form of comradeship (Z III, 6). See Chapter 4.

maintained even within a vice-ridden ambient culture. In this optimistic spirit Zarathustra suggests that "although there are swamps and thick affliction on earth, he who has light feet runs even across mud and dances as upon swept ice" (Z IV, 13, 17). The pitfalls of the surrounding servile culture may be skipped over, as it were, by the dancing virtuoso with nimble feet.

Elsewhere and for the most part, however, Nietzsche suggests that efforts at insulating oneself and one's virtue from ambient vulgarity are futile without some degree of physical distance from the crowd. That he leans in this direction is readily understandable in light of his recurring emphasis on embodiment and physicality. As I noted in Chapter 1, Nietzsche claims to detect and to find "utterly unendurable" the smell of "dissolution and decomposition" in the presence of the herd (TI IX, 20; GM I, 12). Any higher individual with an "instinct for cleanliness" would feel the need to escape such contamination (EH I, 8). In a similar vein Zarathustra warns that "all wells are poisoned" where the "rabble" drink, and speaks of how he was impelled to "fly to the height where the rabble no longer sit at the well" (Z II, 6; cf. Z II, 4).

The view that one's ethical-spiritual development is greatly influenced by the company one keeps, which seems more in line with Aristotelian than Stoic moral philosophy, can be gleaned from many passages in *Zarathustra*. The title character claims, for example, that traffic with those experiencing the unending, demoralizing pain and suffering of the multitude is undesirable. He hopes that his destiny leads him only across the path of those who "do not sorrow or suffer," of "those with whom I can have hope and repast and honey in common!" (Z II, 3). Later, in taking leave of the "ugliest man," he confesses how witnessing the morbid suffering of this pathetic character affected him in a viscerally debilitating way: "chilled and alone," he felt that he "had absorbed much coldness and loneliness, to such an extent that even his limbs had grown colder" (Z IV, 8). His confrontation with a Schopenhauerian figure, the gloomy prophet, appears to have a similar effect, for in the aftermath of this encounter Zarathustra claims to have become "wet with [the gloomy prophet's] affliction" (Z IV, 2). His self-prescribed cure for this contagious Schopenhauerian pessimism is to "shake [him]self and run away from [him], so that [Zarathustra] may become dry again"(ibid.).

Too long a delay in making a clean break with the herd community, warns Zarathustra, may have a deleterious effect on one's nobility. In particular, the aforementioned instinctive, defensive posture of aloofness and disguise, if retained in perpetuity, might stifle creative self-expression and frustrate the search for truth. Zarathustra confesses in this spirit that while he remained in close quarters with the many-too-many, his instinctive aloofness forced him to live "with truths held back" (Z III, 9). As an embattled, disguised figure, Zarathustra claims he was only too ready to "misunderstand *[him]self* so that [he] might endure *them*" (ibid.). Similarly, Nietzsche claims elsewhere that unless a "pathos of distance" is maintained between lower and higher human types, the latter will be less likely to fully explore their inner selves, less able to "long . . . for an ever-increasing widening of distance within the soul itself, the formation of ever higher, rarer, more remote, tenser, more comprehensive states" (BGE 257).[3]

Living in close proximity to the herd may lead, moreover, to the loss of the essentially optimistic, affirmative embrace of life that is a sine qua non of all healthy, higher types. One ought to surround oneself only with good things and good company if one is to preserve one's optimism (Z IV, 13, 15). Such optimism is absent in the "frothing fool" character encountered in part III, whom Zarathustra criticizes for having remained within shouting distance of a city that is likened to a swamp (Z III, 7). By remaining near the city, the fool has been overwhelmed by the vulgarity of its inhabitants and reduced to a caricatural prophet of doom, spewing overwrought damnations upon passers-by. He would have done better to have fled "into the forest" or to have explored "the sea" for some of its many "green islands" (ibid.).

The figure of the frothing fool is meant to warn those whose repeated exposure to plebeian vulgarity threatens to overwhelm their

3. Brian Leiter similarly discerns Nietzsche's link between the "overcoming" of vulgar elements within the self and the importance of maintaining distance from the herd in his "Morality in the Pejorative Sense: On the Logic of Nietzsche's Critique of Morality," *British Journal for the History of Philosophy* 3 (1995): 113–145.

optimism. Nietzsche claims that the best way to protect one's capacity to affirm life is to seek out environments where one is no longer in constant contact with that which should be negated. The idea is "to say *No as little as possible*. To separate oneself, to depart from that to which No would be required again and again" (EH II, 8). When one is forced repeatedly to negate, one's defensive posture becomes "a rule, a habit" that leads to "an extraordinary and perfectly superfluous impoverishment," a siphoning off of valuable energies (ibid.). In such a situation, the temptations of nihilism can become overwhelming: a noble contempt for vulgarity could easily be perverted into an indiscriminate "contempt for men" in general. When this happens, all hope of overcoming the vulgar and creating new values is abandoned.[4]

Zarathustra's treatment of the "frothing fool" reveals yet another reason for effecting what Nietzsche refers to as a "radical retreat into solitude" (GS Preface 1). As Zarathustra sees it, the fool's violent, denunciatory rhetoric is driven by a desire for the herd's flattery and praise. Because the herd did not flatter the fool to his satisfaction, he began "grunting" at them, "[sitting] down beside this filth . . . so that [he] might have cause for much *revenge*! For all [his] frothing . . . is revenge" (Z III, 7). The fool's great disappointment at not being recognized and valued by the many—and his desire to seek vengeance for their failure to acknowledge his "greatness"—reveal a misguided dependency on the opinion of those who ought to be despised.

In presenting the episode of the fool as one of his many cautionary tales, Nietzsche demonstrates his concern that his readers' close proximity to mainstream European culture and society might tempt them to take the same embittered, vengeful turn. Life in or near a big, modern city, he suggests in an almost Rousseauian spirit, is pervaded with the obsessive pursuit of honor, fame, and glory. Zarathustra speaks disparagingly in this context of the "lusting for eminence"

---

4. In the *Nachlass* Nietzsche asserts that the nihilist is guilty of a pathological "generalization": the assumption that all tables of value are empty and false simply because one (servile) set of values has been exposed as empty and false (WP 13). Unable to transcend the level of negation, the nihilist deems himself and the world as a whole to be "valueless" (WP 12a). Cf. Zarathustra's allusion to the nihilistic error of "hermits," whose wrong-headed rejection of life began with an initially sensible turning away from the "rabble" (Z II, 6).

characteristic of "the ambitious" (Z I, 17). As we have already seen, Nietzsche believes that high-minded and high-spirited people in full possession of themselves reject this sort of other-dependency. But in order to achieve and retain self-possession, a flight away from the crowd is advisable. Although solitude is not for everyone—"many should be dissuaded from [it]" because solitude is invariably a "poison" for unselfsufficient types—it seems the best medicine for those wishing to wean themselves from beliefs contrary to the highest form of human flourishing (Z IV, 13, 13; GS 359).[5]

The Discipline of Suffering

Nietzsche talks of solitude in terms of a therapeutic "recovery" [*Genesung*], a state in which one "returns" to oneself (EH II, 8). Something "voiceless" counsels Zarathustra to "go back into solitude," for only in this state will he "grow mellow" (Z II, 22). Solitude [*Einsamkeit*] is even personified as a woman who, in a memorable dialogue with Zarathustra, contrasts herself favorably with the loneliness [*Verlassenheit*] experienced in crowds and reminds him how much better she is for him than his previous life among the many (Z III, 9).

Nietzsche understands that such words may seem like cold comfort to those who, because of their upbringing in a herd community, can contemplate the prospect of abandoning their past loyalties and affections only with great reluctance. Given the deeply internalized nature of the false consciousness of his imagined readers, he readily concedes that a definitive break with the communities that breed slave morality will cause spiritual torment. Zarathustra forewarns his youthful interlocutors that "the voice of the herd will still ring within [them]" and that they will "lament" the day when they discover they no longer have "the same conscience" as their herdlike former companions (Z I, 17). He prophesies in particular the inner torment of one of his disciples, a young man who, upon breaking with his community of origin, still finds its "conscience" ringing in his ears. "No

5. Nietzsche insists on distinguishing between the solitude sought by the unhealthy type (e.g., the religious ascetic who flees to the desert) and that chosen by the strong and healthy (Z III, 6; cf. EH II, 10).

one speaks to me," the youthful rebel laments, "the frost of my solitude makes me tremble." His wish to "rise into the heights" has made him a pariah among his former comrades, and his resulting misery makes him doubt the wisdom of ostracizing himself: "What do I want in the heights?" (Z I, 8; cf. Z I, 12).

Someone in this position, concedes Nietzsche, may succumb once again to "the greatest of all mistresses of seduction," slave morality, and slink back into the familiar warmth and comfort of his former community (D Preface 3). A beleaguered, suffering noble type in the midst of a self-imposed desert exile may "blink thirstily at the islands filled with springs where living creatures rest beneath shady trees" (Z II, 8). While aware of the temptation, Nietzsche has only contempt for those who succumb to it. These are the backsliders who abandon their higher vocation, who succumb to the "common, comfortable" life and with hindsight slander "their morning boldness" (Z III, 8, 1). Whereas they once "lifted their legs like a dancer," now they return to the self-abnegating beliefs of their childhood, "creep[ing] to the Cross" (ibid.). In the end, speculates Zarathustra, they may not have had the stuff of true nobility after all, for they fail to demonstrate that which only the few, fine exemplars of humanity have in their hearts: "a long-enduring courage and wantonness" (ibid.).Their cowardice in retreating to the herd for comfort reveals their affinity with the many-too-many.

Hoping to bring aid and comfort to like-minded souls, Nietzsche exhorts his readers to take pride in their internal turmoil and anguish. The suffering that results from ostracism and loneliness is not only normal but also desirable as a sign of serious commitment to radical ethical and spiritual self-remaking.[6] One should not, he stresses, abandon it prematurely and seek relief in the "pitiable comfort" of herd existence. "The way to yourself," claims Zarathustra, is also "the way of your affliction" (Z I, 17). Throughout Nietzsche's account of Zarathustra's odyssey, suffering consistently appears as a reliable indicator of the authenticity of one's efforts at self-improvement: "Genuine [*Wahrhaftig*]—that is what I call him who goes into god-forsaken deserts and has broken his venerating heart" (Z II, 8). In the midst of Zarathustra's chastisement of the so-called higher men of part IV, we

6. That Nietzsche considers a pariah status among the majority to be a badge of honor is suggested in BGE 30, 43, and 220; Z II, 8; Z II, 6; and A 46.

learn that one of the clearest signs of their spiritual impoverishment is their not having "suffered enough" (Z IV, 13, 6).

In his own voice Nietzsche makes a clear distinction between the suffering of the many—the suffering that, as we noted in the last chapter, leads to *ressentiment* toward the talented few—and the pain experienced by those few who are of concern to him. For the latter, he considers "suffering, desolation, sickness, ill-treatment, indignities" to be formative. "I wish them the only thing that can prove today whether one is worth anything or not—that one endures" (WP 910). It is revealing that one of the features of slave morality identified by Nietzsche as most contemptible is its aspiration for an "*English* happiness," a life denuded of all suffering and dedicated solely to the pursuit of "comfort and fashion" (BGE 228).

A measure of the depth of our examination of life, claims Nietzsche, is the depth of our suffering [*das Leiden*] (Z III, 2, 1). The suggestion that suffering is a precondition for the cultivation of human excellence is also made powerfully in *Beyond Good and Evil:* "The discipline of suffering, of *great* suffering—do you not know that it is *this* discipline alone which has created every elevation of mankind hitherto?" (BGE 225; cf. BGE 270). There is "much bitter dying" in the life of the creative individual; one must be prepared to countenance repeated reexaminations—and even rejection—of one's most cherished beliefs and closest relationships in order to reemerge as a "child new-born" (Z II, 2). In drawing out this metaphor of childbirth, Zarathustra claims that one who aspires to be a "newborn" in knowledge and insight "must also be willing to be the mother and endure the mother's pain" (ibid.). This association of creative striving with maternal pain in childbearing is made once again in the preface to *The Gay Science*, when Nietzsche insists that "we have to give birth to our thoughts out of our pain. . . . Only great pain is the ultimate liberator of the spirit" (GS Preface 3).

Nietzsche exhorts his readers not to allow their thirst for companionship and their fear and anguish in its absence to tempt them into "becom[ing] like these comfortable creatures: for where there are oases there are also idols" (Z II, 8). Courageous are those who, while having an intimate knowledge of the fear and pain of social disapprobation, refuse to let these emotions dominate them (Z IV,

13, 4).[7] An important step in this self-mastery, this overcoming of the suffering associated with the overthrow of slave or herd morality, is successful passage through a particularly difficult—many would say dreadful—thought experiment.

The Eternal Return as Psychological Problem

Nietzschean higher types, as we have seen, must pass through periods of tremendous personal upheaval and anguish in order to fulfill their lofty potential. The crucial phase of their suffering arrives, however, only after they decide to confront a daunting hypothetical choice: if they had the opportunity to relive their lives in perpetuity, would they do so unhesitatingly and joyfully, knowing that everything in their past would recur unaltered? Would they have the fortitude, in other words, to relish the prospect of a continual repetition of the sorrows, humiliations, and defeats of the past along with past moments of joy and victory? If they can stomach this prospect, they become true lovers of fate—in Nietzsche's sense of *amor fati*—and attain "the highest formula of affirmation" (EH IX, 1). They thereby join the ranks of those few capable of what Zarathustra refers to as a "vast and boundless declaration of Yes and Amen" (Z III, 4).[8]

7. Cf. Aristotle's view that the man of virtue knows fear but masters it. *Nicomachean Ethics*, 1115a10–b20.

8. A well-known alternative interpretation of eternal return—eternal return as Nietzsche's cosmological theory of the actual workings of the universe—is effectively criticized by Maudemarie Clark, *Nietzsche on Truth and Philosophy* (Cambridge: Cambridge University Press, 1990), pp. 245–270, and Alexander Nehamas, *Nietzsche: Life as Literature* (Cambridge: Harvard University Press, 1985), pp. 141–169. As they indicate, the texts that Nietzsche himself published provide little support for this interpretation. One possible exception is a passage in *Zarathustra* where the title character's animals appear to formulate a cosmological doctrine of the literal recurrence of everything ad infinitum (Z III, 13, 2). Clark and Nehamas rightly observe, however, that Zarathustra himself treats his animals' cosmological musings with condescension and chastizes them for turning his idea into a tiresome "hurdy-gurdy song" (ibid.). Although my reading of Nietzsche's thought experiment differs from Clark's (see below), I think she is right to interpret it "as a practical doctrine, a directive concerning how to live, rather than a theory concerning the nature of the universe." Clark, *Nietzsche on Truth and Philosophy*, p. 247.

Nietzsche presents *amor fati* as an inescapable precondition for noble self-love. One must affirm everything that has directly or indirectly contributed to one's personal development, even the so-called errors: "The *blunders* of life, the temporary sidepaths and wrong turnings . . . have their own meaning and value. They are an expression of a great sagacity, even the supreme sagacity" (EH II, 9). Ultimately this austere and uncompromising formula for affirmation requires an embrace of everything. Since "in the actual world . . . everything is bound to and conditioned by everything else, . . . to think away anything means to condemn and think away everything" (WP 584). All things in the universe are causally interconnected—"chained and entwined together," as Zarathustra puts it—and should thus be affirmed as having contributed to what one is (Z IV, 19, 10).[9]

Not one shred of regret for the past can be tolerated; the pain and suffering caused by physical illness, the death of close friends or family members, public humiliation and ostracism at the hands of the herd, and even the most horrific of human-made or natural catastrophes—all have played a role in making one what one is. After inquiring of his interlocutors if they had ever said "Yes to one joy," Zarathustra insists that if they have done so, "then [they] said Yes to *all* woe as well" (ibid.). If, in other words, we love what we have become, we should be prepared to say yes to (*Jasagen*) the eternal return of all past things *unchanged*, in order to ensure the reappearance of our noble selves.

It is easy to understand why Nietzsche presents his initial reaction to such a prospect as one of horror, as the suggestion of a "demon" (GS 341). For his thought experiment requires higher types to posit and affirm "without reservation" the unending recurrence "even of suffering, even of guilt, even of all that is strange and questionable in existence" (EH IV, 2). One prescient interpreter of the eternal recurrence, Maudemarie Clark, shares Nietzsche's initial resistance to the uncompromising nature of this idea. "Why," she asks, "cannot I affirm life precisely by preferring a history stripped of its horrors to the exact recurrence of my life? Why isn't it a greater affirmation of life to want the repetition of the past without the bad things? That I cannot recur unless all of the horrors do too does not seem like a

9. For some other references to this notion of interconnectivity, see Z III, 2, 2; Z III, 16, 4; TI VI, 8; and WP 293, 331, 333, 634, and 1032.

very good or a very Nietzschean answer."[10] Writing near the end of the bloodiest century of human history, Clark takes a stance that is readily understandable; she, like most of us, would prefer to will the eternal return of "a world that is just like ours except for the absence of Hitler."[11] And since she maintains an unreservedly sunny view of Nietzsche, she is inclined to assume that he cannot maintain a position that seems so horrific.

But this benign view distorts. Nietzsche openly derides as "farcical" the expression "that should not have been" (WP 584). To will the eternal recurrence of only a selective version of the past—a prettified, idealized past denuded of its horrors, suffering, and ugliness—is, in his view, to remain in a brooding state of *ressentiment* where one pines away for "another" world that never has been and never will be. "Strong, full natures," by contrast, have "the power to form, to mold, to recuperate, and to forget" even the "misdeeds" of the past (GM I, 10). "So rich is joy," explains Zarathustra, "that it thirsts for woe, for Hell, for hatred, for shame, for the lame, for the *world*" (Z IV, 19, 11). This type of joy wants both the "honey" and the "dregs"; it demands not just the "gilded sunsets" but also the "graves" and "the consolation of graveside tears" (ibid.). As Nietzsche insists in *Ecce Homo*, "nothing that is can be subtracted, nothing is dispensable" (EH IV, 2).

Nietzsche's version of an affirmative *Jasagen*-ing stance toward life insists on an unconditional affirmation not only of all past evil and suffering but also of inferior forms of human life. "He who climbs upon the highest mountains," claims Zarathustra, "laughs at all tragedies, real or imaginary" (Z I, 7). Nietzsche understands, of course, that such a prospect cannot be faced lightly; he concedes that it is the "hardest test of character" and makes some of Zarathustra's initial reactions to it highly unfavorable (WP 934). When positing the notion of an "eternal recurrence even for the smallest" and most contemptible, Zarathustra, like Maudemarie Clark, initially recoils in "disgust" (Z III, 13, 2). The very idea of a ceaseless recurrence of baseness strikes him as an "abysmal thought," and he confesses how hard it is "to understand that small people are *necessary*" (Z III, 3; Z III, 5, 2). And in *Ecce Homo* Nietzsche gives voice to these sentiments

10. Clark, *Nietzsche on Truth and Philosophy*, p. 281.
11. Ibid.

in a strikingly personal way when he confides that "the deepest objection to the 'Eternal Recurrence', my idea from the abyss, is always my mother and my sister" (EH I, 3).[12]

But Nietzsche claims that those with intestinal fortitude can learn to *Jasagen* everything—even the existence of the weak and degenerate—without losing (a) healthy contempt for these latter and (b) faith in the possibility of a higher form of human life.[13] He points to his own Zarathustra as an example of a human type "who to an unheard-of degree says No, *does* No to everything to which one has hitherto said Yes," and yet remains "nonetheless . . . the opposite of a spirit of denial" (EH IX, 6). Nietzsche hopes that his readers will feel disdain toward the many while, like Zarathustra, affirming their existence as "bridges" or "steps" [*Stufen*] upon which higher men must tread in their journey to greatness[14] (Z IV, 11).

The Eternal Return and the Battle against "Lord Chance"

Once we are prepared to declare unreservedly and joyfully that we would will the ceaseless repetition of the past if we could, Nietzsche claims, the whole idea of "misfortune" as an independent, mendacious force loses its hold over our lives. Through sheer force of will,

12. See Chapter 5, note 16.

13. Thus I disagree with Robert Pippin's suggestion that the eternal recurrence image "suggests to Zarathustra a radical deflating of the *Übermensch* ideal." Pippin, "Irony and Affirmation in Nietzsche's Thus Spoke Zarathustra," in *Nietzsche's New Seas: Explorations in Philosophy, Aesthetics, and Politics*, ed. Michael Allen Gillespie and Tracy B. Strong (Chicago: University of Chicago Press, 1988), p. 54. Pippin's claim that the eternal recurrence is a "profoundly antiredemptive thought" appears to turn on the assumption that Nietzsche/Zarathustra believes all things do in fact recur eternally (ibid., pp. 55–57, 64). If Pippin were right, eternal recurrence would indeed disable any hope for cultural renewal and, as he suggests, engender a thoroughgoing ironic stance toward all redemptive ideals. But the literal interpretation is at odds with Nietzsche's declared opposition to "the now prevalent instinct and taste" in democratic countries for fatalistic theories that insist upon "the mechanistic senselessness of all events" (GM II, 12). Once eternal recurrence is seen as a thought experiment, its redemptive ambition becomes clearer.

14. In Chapter 6 I suggest that this need for lower human beings subverts Nietzsche's occasional claim that higher types can become (in principle) completely self-sufficient.

that which had once been seen as misfortune becomes a product of choice. One thereby graduates from "milk[ing]" the cow of "affliction" to "drink[ing] the sweet milk of her udder" (Z I, 5). This exercise of willpower over fate fills the superior man with a feeling of invulnerability.[15] Once the gauntlet of the eternal return has been run, tragic misfortune can never break one's spirit again.

At times Nietzsche seems to believe his thought experiment so empowering as to banish the very notion of accidental occurrence in the lives of superior men. Zarathustra gloats that "the time has passed when accidents [*Zufälle*] could befall me, and what *could* still come to me that was not already my own?" (Z III, 1). Zarathustra's struggle with "Chance" is predominantly featured, as is his boasting over his victory: "I am Zarathustra the Godless: I cook every chance in *my* pot. . . . And truly, many a chance came imperiously to me: but my *will* spoke to it even more imperiously, then it went down imploringly on its knees" (Z III, 5, 3).

Zarathustra's declaration in part III that he has freed chance from its "servitude under purpose" might seem to refute the view that Nietzsche wished higher men to subdue contingency to *their* purposes (Z III, 4). If we read this passage in context, however, it becomes clear that Zarathustra means to liberate contingency only from metaphysical notions of purpose—for example, the "eternal reason-spider"—rather than from all purposes (ibid.). Fortune cannot, must not, be honored as a god; it must serve the ends of the superior man, before whom there can be no rivals (Z IV, 6).[16] In this vein Zarathustra urges like-minded

15. Whether this talk of the higher man's will is consistent with Nietzsche's rejection of "free will" is an important question. One obvious answer, which would require an argument absent here, would be that there is no contradiction because Nietzsche's talk of willing—as opposed to the metaphysical notions of will he criticizes—refers to an embodied sense of agency emerging out of (rather than against) healthy, life-affirming instinct. Ruth Abbey argues that Nietzsche falls into serious inconsistency here in "So Polyphonous a Being: Friedrich Nietzsche in His Middle Period" (manuscript, University of Western Australia, 1997).

16. Peter Berkowitz rightly highlights the ethic of self-deification developed in works such as *Zarathustra* in his *Nietzsche: The Ethics of an Immoralist* (Cambridge: Harvard University Press, 1995), pp. 4, 15–20, 150, 207–210. I am not as convinced by his claim that part IV of *Zarathustra* and the post-*Zarathustra* writings exemplify a prudent retreat from this hubristic goal. TI I, 3 serves as one example of the continued importance of self-deification.

souls to consider themselves their own "fate": "And if you will not be fates [*Schicksale*], if you will not be inexorable: how can you—conquer with me?" (Z III, 12, 29). Like Machiavelli, who counsels prospective political leaders to forcibly subdue the female *Fortuna*, Nietzsche urges superior men to subordinate all of life to their dictates.

Zarathustra readily admits that becoming a "redeemer of chance" in this sense requires a breathtaking arrogance beyond the reach of those destined to remain Fortune's "prisoner" (Z II, 20; cf. Z III, 12, 3). The mob, claims Nietzsche, tends to think itself at the behest of forces beyond its control, whether these are understood as stemming from God or as completely independent and capricious. Unable to "will backwards" in the sense described above, the herd man "is only 'willed', he is the sport of every wave," a fact that fills him with regret and recrimination (Z III, 12, 16; cf. Z IV, 11). Bitterly resentful of the cards that "God" or "dreadful chance" [*grauser Zufall*] has dealt him, the weak man finds his predilection for revenge intensified (Z II, 20). Zarathustra observes how the weak, servile will turns ill-tempered and takes to "teeth-gnashing" in its awareness of its own impotence. Being unable "to go backwards," it takes revenge on others and makes them suffer for its own impotence (ibid.). "This alone," he explains, "is *revenge* itself: the will's antipathy towards time and time's 'It was'" (ibid.).

Invulnerable Men?

In positing invulnerability to fortune as a normative ideal, Nietzsche evinces an indebtedness to a long-standing tradition in Western moral and political philosophy associated primarily with Stoicism and ultimately traceable back to Socrates. In its many guises, this tradition gives expression to the pervasive desire to believe that acting and living well, as Martha Nussbaum writes, "are things that depend only on human effort, things that human beings can always control, no matter what happens in the world around them."[17] Nussbaum

17. Martha Nussbaum, "Tragedy and Self-Sufficiency: Plato and Arisotle on Fear and Pity," *Essays on Aristotle's Poetics*, ed. Amélie Oksenberg Rorty (Princeton: Princeton University Press, 1992), p. 263.

identifies the first philosophical expression of this desire in Plato's *Apology*, where Socrates claims that a good man cannot be harmed. The Stoics later radicalized this thought, insisting that the good man ought to disengage himself psychologically from that which fortune controls or influences: the "external goods" of wealth, political freedom, friendship, and community. In the Stoic view, one could be bereft of all these goods and still lead an upstanding, admirable life.[18]

With his doctrine of the eternal return Nietzsche aims at radicalizing the Socratic-Stoic ideal of invulnerability. For the Stoics, as well as for later thinkers such as Machiavelli, fortune remains a formidable force in the lives of even the most admirable men. What separates the virtuous from the majority is the former's ability to erect barricades of a psychological and/or political nature to stem fortune's tide. The adoption of compensatory strategies, such as the psychological disengagement from all external goods and Machiavellian political *virtù*, implicitly acknowledges fortune's great power. Nietzsche, by contrast, urges upon his ideal readers a mindset that ostensibly would *banish* the role of contingency in their lives. Although pure contingency always plays a determinant role in the lives of the weak, the same, he insists, cannot be said for those few who can cry out "once more!" when faced with the prospect of the eternal recurrence of all that has been.

In light of this sometimes delusional stress on self-sufficiency and invulnerability, it might seem incongruous to suggest that Nietzsche also argues for the importance of "external goods" such as friendship in the lives of superior men. How could he hold that the superior man can master contingency while at the same time insist that certain inherently contingent goods are necessary for his full flourishing? I intend to argue that he tries to retain both views—unsuccessfully. While drawn to the Stoic-Socratic ideal of personal invulnerability, Nietzsche is also pulled in another direction, toward an alternative view of the human condition whose roots in the Western tradition are just as deep. Associated with the great tragedians of ancient Greece and given its first philosophical expression in Aristo-

18. See Julia Annas, *The Morality of Happiness* (New York: Oxford University Press, 1993), pp. 262–290, 385–411.

tle, this tradition recognizes, as Nussbaum says, that luck is "seriously powerful," that "it is possible for a good person to suffer serious and undeserved harm."[19]

The next chapter shows that Nietzsche feels the force of this discourse even as he clings tenaciously to Stoic ideals of personal autarchy. The result is a seriously problematized body of thought. Perhaps the most significant problems emerge in Nietzsche's treatment of friendship and community.

19. Martha Nussbaum, *The Fragility of Goodness: Luck and Ethics in Greek Tragedy and Philosophy* (Cambridge: Cambridge University Press, 1986), pp. 384–385. Bernard Williams also gives voice to this perspective when he speaks of the possibility of "social reality [acting] to crush a worthwhile, significant, character or project without displaying either the lively individual purposes of a pagan god or the world-historical significance of a Judaic, a Christian, or a Marxist teleology." Williams, *Shame and Necessity* (Berkeley: University of California Press, 1993), p. 165.

f o u r   **Overcoming Solitude**

> All company is bad company except the company of one's equals.
> —*Beyond Good and Evil* 26

The Limitations of Solitude

G iven Nietzsche's repeated praise of the therapeutic effects of solitude and his insistence on intensely personal, inimitable paths to ethical-spiritual development, it is tempting to read into his work an unremitting hostility toward any and every form of sociability and community.[1] His radical individualism seems

1. The consensus view of Nietzsche as a radical individualist extends over a very broad field, encompassing scholars who disagree in many other respects. Some of the

apparent when he teaches that the exceptionally creative individual "stand[s] out" [*sich abzuheben*] and should value himself as one to whom *préférences*, in Montesquieu's sense, are owed (TI IX, 37). "A great man," observes Nietzsche, "finds it tasteless to be familiar" (WP 962).

Nietzsche, moreover, finds that noble self-sufficiency is woefully absent in the "gregarious" [*heerdenhaft*] lower orders, where an ethic of "love thy neighbor" reigns out of necessity rather than virtue (WP 886). He detects a spiritual void and even self-loathing in the sort of sociability that feeds upon the glances of others and eats praise out of the hands of flatterers. In *Beyond Good and Evil* he speaks of a "subservient, unauthoritative and un-self-sufficient species of man" who is a "lover of his neighbor" out of weakness rather than strength. Such a man performs his "good works" (including scientific research) with an eye for "honor and recognition" because a "constant affirmation of his value and his utility" is needed to shore up his shaky sense of self-worth (BGE 206). The dependent type of person cannot bear the thought of existence without the warmth generated by close proximity to other herd animals (ibid.; Z Prologue 5). As Zarathustra observes, such a person can hardly endure to be alone with himself and flees to the company of his neighbor (Z I, 16).

---

better-known studies making this assumption include Walter Kaufmann, *Nietzsche: Philosopher, Psychologist, AntiChrist,* 4th ed. (Princeton: Princeton University Press, 1974), p. 162; Richard Schacht, *Nietzsche* (London: Routledge and Kegan Paul, 1983), p. 407; Tracy Strong, *Friedrich Nietzsche and the Politics of Transfiguration,* expanded ed. (Berkeley: University of California Press, 1988), p. 112; and Mark Warren, *Nietzsche and Political Thought* (Cambridge: MIT Press, 1988), p. 61. Philosophers and political theorists not known as Nietzsche scholars who also view Nietzsche as a strictly "nomadic" thinker include William Connolly, *Identity\Difference: Democratic Negotiations of Political Paradox* (Ithaca: Cornell University Press, 1991), p. 187; Bonnie Honig, *Political Theory and the Displacement of Politics* (Ithaca: Cornell University Press, 1993), p. 230; Alasdair MacIntyre, *After Virtue: A Study in Moral Theory* (Notre Dame: University of Notre Dame Press, 1984), p. 258; and Martha Nussbaum, "Pity and Mercy: Nietzsche's Stoicism," in *Nietzsche, Genealogy, Morality: Essays on Nietzsche's "On the Genealogy of Morals,"* ed. Richard Schacht (Berkeley: University of California Press, 1994), p. 158.

Yet it would be hasty to infer that passages such as these reflect an uncompromising repudiation of all forms of sociability. Although the radical individualist reading is vindicated in textual passages that seem to posit an austere vision of personal autarchy, much of Nietzsche's praise of solitude and self-sufficiency emphasizes a selective distaste for the company of the mass of ordinary human beings and leaves open the prospect of "a refined conception of friendship" in the lives of stronger, healthier individuals (BGE 260).

Repudiating the "pitiable comforts" of herd life and successfully passing through a psychologically trying thought experiment may be necessary as preconditions for full human flourishing, but they do not suffice. Beyond the imperative of breaking with mediocre communities and joyfully willing the infinite repetition of one's past life, Nietzsche gestures (at least most of the time) toward another, higher type of sociability required for self-overcoming. The suggestion that great men consider it tasteless to be familiar is balanced by another notebook entry suggesting that these same great ones "want to embed themselves in great communities" (WP 964). Even at his most isolated and friendless, Nietzsche felt that his "cure and self-restoration" required him at the very least to dream of a "relatedness and identity in eye and desires, a reposing in a trust of friendship, a blindness in concert with another without suspicion or question-marks" (HAH I Preface 1). In *The Genealogy*, moreover, unending solitude appears as a fall-back plan rather than the most desired state: "Let us have good company, *our* company! Or solitude, if it must be [*wenn es sein muss*]!" (GM III, 14).

In his later writings, the perceived need for a higher form of solidarity pervades *Zarathustra* in particular, where the title character's relief at having escaped the stifling atmosphere of herd society soon gives way to a deep yearning, often couched in metaphor, for new, meaningful connections with like-minded others.[2] The pursuit of

2. Ruth Abbey argues that Nietzsche's treatment of sociability in his later work pales in comparison with the rich evocations of friendship and solidarity in the middle period and speculates that this change can be traced back to the aggravation of Nietzsche's personal isolation in the mid- to late 1880s. Abbey, "Nietzsche and the Excluded Middle," presented to the Annual Meeting of the Midwest Political Science Association, Chicago, April 1997.

wisdom, as we have seen, requires a period of "voluntary living in ice and high mountains" (EH Foreword 3). But once solitude has been attained, Zarathustra cannot help but cry out, "My hand is burned with ice! . . . [N]ow my longing breaks from me like a well-spring—I long for speech [*Rede*]" (Z II, 9). It seems that the "speech" of companions is needed to counteract the "threatening, suffocating, heart-tightening" effects of a solitude that encircles and embraces the now-isolated, ostracized seeker of truth. This view of the spiritual emptiness of unending solitude is reiterated in one of the prefaces from 1886, when "this morbid isolation" [*dieser krankhaften Verein-samung*] on the icy peaks is described as but "a long road to that tremendous overflowing certainty and health . . . to that *mature* freedom of spirit" (HAH I Preface 4).

Zarathustra clearly does not wish to end up like the hermit he meets in the Prologue. While he does feel a kinship of sorts with this ascetic loner (suggested by their warm parting from each other), his later comments suggest that the radical retreat into solitude, however laudable as a self-protective measure, may lead to certain pathologies if unchecked by a more mature, selective search for suitable companions. In the first place, the absence of the right sort of company might lead an initially sound and healthy desire to repudiate the many-too-many into a nihilistic repudiation of humankind *in toto*. In this vein Zarathustra notes sadly that "many a one who turned away from life" initially had "turned away only from the rabble" (Z II, 6).

Second, too long a period of self-imposed isolation may render the ostracized superior type so "needy," so starved for human contact, that he may ignore the warning of his discriminating taste and fall back into the mediocre companionship from which he escaped in the first place. "The solitary," observes Zarathustra, "extends his hand too quickly to anyone he meets" (Z I, 17). This message is re-iterated in his declaration that the greatest danger for the solitary man is an indiscriminate love, a "love of any thing *if only it is alive!*" (Z III, 1). Farther along in the text this lapse of the instinct for *Rangordnung* is criticized as "the folly of hermits" [*die Einsiedler-Torheit*], a folly to which Zarathustra himself succumbs in the Prologue, when, after a long period of solitude, he sets out to speak to everyone in the marketplace. In retrospect, Zarathustra claims to understand that by attempting to speak to everyone, he "spoke to no one" (Z IV, 13, 1).[3]

Alternatively, a life bereft of all friendship may lead to another hermit's folly: excessively morose introspection. Zarathustra offers a parallel between his own, solitary self and the hermit, for whom "there are too many depths" (Z I, 14). Without a friend to engage him in a conversation that would draw him out of himself, Zarathustra is in danger of falling into the same humorless moral pedantry that, as we saw in Chapter 2, Nietzsche ruthlessly mocks as a sign of self-loathing and *ressentiment*. In prolonged, unending solitude even the most optimistic of spirits may repeatedly go over past slights and personal failures, turning bitterly resentful and lusting secretly after revenge (Z I, 19; cf. Z II, 13). A sociable world where conversation among kindred spirits remains possible is more likely to preserve an affirmative stance toward life: "Where there is talking, the world is like a garden to me. How sweet it is, that words and sounds of music exist" (Z III, 13, 2).[4]

3. Zarathustra's own acceptance of some highly suspect company in part IV of his odyssey seems to cast doubt on the depth of his own understanding of this lesson. Robert Pippin notes that the quality of Zarathustra's interlocutors scarcely improves from the Prologue to part IV and interprets this clear lack of progress as evidence of Nietzsche's ironic undercutting of Zarathustra's redemptive project. "Irony and Affirmation in Nietzsche's *Thus Spoke Zarathustra*," in *Nietzsche's New Seas: Explorations in Philosophy, Aesthetics, and Politics,* ed. Michael Allen Gillespie and Tracy B. Strong (Chicago: University of Chicago Press, 1988), p. 62. Peter Berkowitz similarly sees part IV of *Zarathustra* as a "retreat from the extremes." *Nietzsche: The Ethics of an Immoralist* (Cambridge: Harvard University Press, 1995), pp. 211–227. There is, however, another way of interpreting the presence of the so-called higher men of part IV. Averse to facile, pollyannaish happy endings, Nietzsche may have placed these ridiculous characters near the end of the book to underline the great difficulty facing anyone of his sort who attempts to find (or create) suitable companions. As noted above, Zarathustra declares at the beginning of part IV that he and his destiny "do not speak to Today, neither do we speak to the Never" (Z IV, 1). I take the last part of this phrase as an indication that the redemptive hope is retained, however chastened. (The ironically named "higher men," moreover, serve as important vehicles for Nietzsche's pedagogy, as further negative examples to his imagined readers.)

4. The image of a dialogical community of superior men is also evoked in the following *Nachlass* passage: "What dawns on philosophers last of all [is that] they must no longer accept concepts as a gift, nor merely purify and polish them, but first *make* and *create* them, present them and make them convincing" (WP 409).

Yet Nietzsche's preferred life of rarefied sociability would not be one of constant *bavardage*. Paradoxically, just as one needs to flee from the herd in order to overcome loneliness, so one requires the company of kindred spirits to attain a healthy, peaceful silence. This insight comes to Zarathustra after years of self-imposed isolation: "I have belonged to solitude too long: thus I have forgotten how to be silent" (Z II, 1). This same idea of a healthy, mature silence that paradoxically requires the presence of worthy companions reappears in part III, when Zarathustra speaks of having attained a "silence [that] has learned not to betray itself by silence" (Z III, 6). He has learned, in other words, not to destroy the satisfying silence among friends by retreating once again into the forced introspection of solitude. Elsewhere in part III Zarathustra similarly observes that the "lonely height" of isolation may not always be "sufficient to itself" [*selbst begnüge*] (Z III, 10, 2).

That solitude is meant to be a temporary, transitional state is suggested by the test Zarathustra springs upon his admirers in part III. Comparing his "childen and companions" to trees, he insists that it is his duty to "uproot" them and "set each one up by itself, that it may learn solitude and defiance and foresight" (Z III, 3). This enforced isolation, he explains, is meant to determine whether each tree "is of my kind and my race" [*meiner Art und Abkunft*] (ibid.). At this point in the narrative, Zarathustra's devotees have not yet proved their mettle to his satisfaction. Although they have taken the important first step of negating their communities of origin, he believes them to be still in danger of forming a new, servile cult of devotion and worship, with Zarathustra as its godhead. Unless they are pushed onto solitary paths, they may come to resemble the pathetic "higher men" burlesqued in part IV, who hang onto Zarathustra's every word and find meaning and value only in his person (Z IV, 11). To those who pass the test, Zarathustra crucially extends an invitation to rejoin him on an equal footing, to become his "companion [*Gefährte*] and a fellow-creator and fellow-rejoicer [*Mitschaffender und Mitfeiernder*]" (Z III, 3).

With terms such as "fellow-creator" Nietzsche evokes a rarefied notion of companionship that recalls the Aristotelian model of a friendship of magnanimous men grounded in virtue. Like Aristotle, he makes a hierarchical distinction between lower-order solidarities and the comradeship of kindred, noble spirits bound together in equality and virtue.⁵ Lower-order human beings cannot become friends in the highest sense; they simply do not possess what Zarathustra claims the virtuous man loves most about his friend: "the undimmed eye and the glance of eternity" (Z I, 14).

Because true friends are equally endowed with fine instincts, they recognize themselves in the reflection of each other's undimmed eye. A friend's face, claims Zarathustra, "is your own face, in a rough and imperfect mirror" (ibid.). Recognizing in the friend another self, Nietzsche's noble soul bestows upon his equal "the same . . . tender reference as it applies to itself" (BGE 265). Thus love for one's friend is an expression of self-love. And this is not all; in a letter to one of his own friends Nietzsche also suggests that healthy self-love is dependent upon maintaining a love for friends. "One ceases to love oneself *aright* when one *ceases* to give oneself exercise in loving others."⁶

Like Aristotle, moreover, Nietzsche sees in the highest form of friendship an essential vehicle for self-discovery. In light of the difficulty we experience in seeing our own lives clearly and without bias, it is particularly useful to study ourselves secondhand, as it were, embodied in another good life. Blinded as we are by our partiality, we may in fact end up being a greater source of insight for our friends than for ourselves. As Zarathustra puts it, "many a one cannot deliver himself from his own chains and yet he is his friend's deliverer" (Z I, 14).⁷

The Bestowing Virtue

"I want to go to man once more," announces Zarathustra. "I want to go under *among* them [*unter ihnen will ich untergehen*], I want to give them,

5. Of the three grounds for friendship identified by Aristotle in the *Nicomachean Ethics*—pleasure, advantage or utility, and good character—the third is said to be the best by far (1157a30–b22). Friendship rooted in virtue is considered superior because it involves a "sharing of conversation and thought" among virtuous men, rather than a herdlike "sharing [of] the same pasture" (1170b12–14). In *The Politics* he notes that the highest type of friendship presupposes "likeness and equality" (1287b32).

6. Letter to Peter Gast, 18 July 1880, in *Selected Letters of Friedrich Nietzsche*, ed. and trans. Christopher Middleton (Indianapolis: Hackett, 1996), p. 173.

7. Cf. Aristotle, *Nicomachean Ethics*, 1169b28–1170a4.

dying, my richest gift!" (Z III, 12, 3). That Zarathustra should express the desire to "go under"—that is, to undergo a figurative "death" in the process of radical self-transformation—in the midst of others reveals the great importance of companionship to Nietzsche's whole project. It also reveals the importance of the act of *giving* to fellow higher humans.

Just as the brilliance of the sun and every other star depends on a shining on objects external to themselves, so is the happiness and virtue of Nietzsche's superior man dependent on his "shining on" others. At the very beginning of his adventures and again near their end, Zarathustra gives voice to his feelings of kinship with the sun when he cries, "Great star! What would your happiness be, if you had not those for whom you shine!" (Z Prologue 1; Z IV, 20). Just as Zarathustra and his animals bless the sun for its "superfluity" [*Über-fluß*] and draw strength from it, so do lofty men draw sustenance from each other's overflow. Both Zarathustra and the sun are "super-abundant" [*überreiches*], requiring others to take in their energy.

Switching metaphors but in a similar spirit, Zarathustra compares himself at the start of his journey to a bee gathering too much honey that needs "hands outstretched to take it" (Z Prologue 1). Until others have experienced his overflow, he cannot claim to be a human being in the highest sense of the word: "This cup wants to be empty again, and Zarathustra wants to be man again [*wieder Mensch werden*]" (ibid.). After the debacle in the marketplace, of course, Zarathustra comes to see his earlier generosity toward the mass of ordinary people as misguided and begins to search for more worthy recipients of his beneficent overflow. The idea of the necessity of giving, however, of the "bestowing virtue" [*der schenkenden Tugend*], remains the same. Hence the highest man's sense of thankfulness for the presence of others to give to: "Does not the giver owe thanks to the receiver for receiving? Is giving not a ne-cessity?" (Z III, 14). The idea that the full expression of virtue requires a bestowal upon others is given metaphorical expression when Zarathustra compares his compulsion to share with that of a stream that flows inexorably into the sea. Further on in the same section he speaks of needing to release a storm of cloudlike "tension" (Z II, 1).[8]

8. Invoking yet another metaphor from nature, Nietzsche has Zarathustra com-pare the exceptional man's need to share his "superabundance" with others with the mother's physical need to nurse her child (Z III, 14).

As suggested earlier, however, these evocations of mutual dependency coexist uneasily with Nietzsche's occasional insistence that any such arrangement is tantamount to servility. The star and sun metaphors are also pressed into service to evoke this opposing vision of the creative individual as a completely self-contained source of light. When Zarathustra insists, for example, that "I live in my own light, I drink back into myself the flames that break from me. / I do not know the joy of the receiver," he seems to repudiate the dimension of reciprocity so crucial to the sustenance of any long-term, satisfying human relationship (Z II, 9). Creative beings, in this section, appear doomed to remain isolated from other sources of meaning and value: "Many suns circle in empty space: to all that is dark they speak with their light—to me they are silent" (ibid.). This passage also suggests that the human contact experienced by the emitters of light tends to be asymmetrical and exploitative, as uncreative, "obscure, dark ones" scramble to "extract warmth" and "comfort" from them while giving nothing of worth in return (ibid.). The same Nietzsche who insists on the necessity of giving as a precondition for virtue here faces a Nietzsche who belies these insights and refuses to acknowledge that even the most talented and self-sufficient needs to receive as well as to give.

Agonistic Friendship

Early on in his personal journey Zarathustra becomes aware of the temptations of a facile, lazy type of happiness that must be rejected in favor of more difficult paths that precipitate ethical-spiritual growth. He has this sort of "desire for love" in mind when he declares: "To desire [*Begehren*]—that now means to me: to have lost myself" (Z III, 3). Nietzsche exhorts his readers to cultivate a "hatred of love" of this sort because of its potential for steering higher human beings away from the difficult task of perpetual self-improvement (HAH I Preface 3). He sets out to convince those predisposed to understand that the best form of love—the love of noble types for themselves and for each other—shuns this ersatz variety.

The finest sort of love should actually precipitate suffering—both in oneself and in others—in order to facilitate constant self-betterment. As Zarathustra claims, "there is a bitterness in the cup of even the best love: thus it arouses longing for the Superman, thus it arouses thirst in you, the creator!" (Z I, 20). "What can be loved in man," after all, is not his ability to serve as a source of commiseration and sympathetic ear for our complaints but rather his being "a *going-across* [*Übergang*] and a *down-going* [*Untergang*]" (Z Prologue 4; cf. Z IV, 13, 3). The self-loving noble type rejects self-indulgence, cultivates "harshness" [*Härte*] as one of his habits and never "spares" himself because he knows that he who takes the easy path "sickens at last through his own indulgence" (EH III, 3; Z III, 1).

Nietzsche's suspicion of complacency and comfort explains his insistence that his "refined conception of friendship" has no room for the "soft" sort of love that excuses and even encourages expressions of weakness and vulnerability. Echoing Goethe's fear that "the world will become a large hospital and each will become the other's humane nurse," Nietzsche counsels a stoic "hardness" as an antidote to overindulgent commiseration.[9] Only when life becomes "harder and harder," claims Zarathustra, will "man grow to the height where the lightning can strike and shatter him" (Z IV, 13, 6). "Creators," we learn elsewhere, "are hard" (Z III, 12, 29; cf. Z III, 1). Their virtue has "its origin and beginning" in a rejection of the easy life, of "the soft bed and what is pleasant [*das Angenehme*]" (Z I, 22, 1).

The hardness with which we treat our loved ones, he argues, is first and foremost a reflection of the stringent standards to which we hold ourselves accountable. If our refusal to spare ourselves is a manifestation of self-concern and self-love, why, then, should we spare our loved ones, those who are a mirror image of ourselves? Zarathustra proposes that the finest sort of love is that which spurs our friends

9. The citation from Goethe is from his letter to Frau von Stein, 8 June 1787, quoted in Kaufmann, *Nietzsche: Philosopher, Psychologist, AntiChrist*, p. 369. Nietzsche evokes the hated hospital model of society in GM III, 14. Martha Nussbaum notes Nietzsche's debt to the ancient Stoics in this regard; the Stoics were also fond of using images of softness and hardness "to contrast vulnerability to external conditions with dignified absence of such vulnerability." Nussbaum, "Pity and Mercy: Nietzsche's Stoicism," p. 146.

to achieve their highest potential (Z I, 10). Representing "an arrow and a longing for the Superman," we ought to provide them not an oasis of easy respite but rather "a resting-place like a hard bed, a camp-bed: thus you will serve him best" (Z II, 3). A hard stance toward our friends, in other words, is in their best interests, however difficult it may be to maintain in practice.

Zarathustra acknowledges that resisting the temptations to mollycoddle is no easy feat. In the act of "being hard" toward friends one might initially think oneself insensitive and cry out plaintively, "Where have the tears of my eye and the bloom of my heart gone?" (Z II, 9). But our hearts' tendency to melt at the sight of a loved one's suffering can be resisted if we remind ourselves of the probable consequences of soft-heartedness. The indulgence of the soft-hearted [*Weichlichen*] toward their comrades is more likely to contribute to the dissipation of their creative potential. Through our harsh treatment we cultivate in our friends the same qualities of harshness so necessary for ethical-spiritual *épanouissement:* "In order to grow *big*, a tree wants to strike hard roots into hard rocks!" (Z III, 5, 3).

Nietzsche is particularly derisive toward the notion that higher-order companions ought to pity one another and counts the overcoming of pity [*die Überwindung des Mitleids*] among the "*noble virtues*" (EH I, 4; cf. Z II, 3). Why is this so? Why does he think that "the hands of pity can under certain circumstances intrude downright destructively into a great destiny"? (EH I, 4). Expressions of pity, in his view, disempower the pitied by reinforcing their own sense of powerlessness and victimhood. To pity someone is to presuppose his or her vulnerability to the vagaries of fortune. We pity the person who has fallen victim to bad luck and has thus sustained a serious loss of some sort.[10] As noted in the previous chapter, however, Nietzsche is convinced that a mature noble type is capable of taking charge of his destiny and mastering fortune through

10. I have profited from Martha Nussbaum's reflections on the psychological and ethical dynamic underlying pity. See "The Stoics on the Extirpation of the Passions," *Apeiron* 20, 2 (1987): 129–158, and "Therapeutic Arguments and Structures of Desire," *Differences* 2, 1 (1990): 46–66.

an imaginative form of "willing backwards." Thus to treat such a man as requiring pity is to condescend to him, to consider him as an inferior because of his apparent inability to take charge of his life.[11]

This, I would argue, is why Nietzsche claims in a work from his middle period that "to offer pity is as good as to offer contempt" (D 135).[12] He considers it especially insidious because its ostensibly benign, nurturing face masks a noxious leveling effect, whereby noble types are gently but assuredly discouraged from continuing their upward trek—and (what is worse) even rewarded for abandoning it. Pity is thus numbered alongside patience, humility, and insipid "friendliness" [*Freundlichkeit*] as one of the slavish virtues and is decried as "the most sinister symptom of our sinister European civilization" (BGE 260; GM Preface 5). Instead of indulging oneself and one's friends in commiseration, one should "keep a nice tight reign on one's sympathy" and "*persist* in one's *own* ideal of *man;* one should impose one's ideal on one's fellow beings and on oneself overpoweringly, and thus exert a creative influence!"[13]

Nietzsche introduces an explicitly martial dimension to his austere, edifying notion of friendship, suggesting that among free spirits the hardness of friendship becomes almost indistinguishable from pure enmity. In the late works in particular, a conflict-ridden socia-

11. One might suppose that Nietzsche would be prepared to countenance pity toward weaker individuals who (in his view) must invariably remain the playthings of chance. This, however, is not the case. Alongside his disapproval of expressions of pity toward higher men, Nietzsche also considers "active sympathy [*das Mitleiden*] for the ill-constituted and weak" to be "more harmful than any vice" (A 2). Chapter 7 examines why.

12. Abbey argues that middle-period works such as *Human, All Too Human* and *Daybreak* also evoke a more benign notion of pity, a discreet, sensitive and respectful form worthy of higher, free-spirited individuals. Abbey, "So Polyphonous a Being: Friedrich Nietzsche in His Middle Period" (manuscript, University of Western Australia, 1997). As the citation from D 135 suggests, however, even in the middle period this alternative view coexisted uneasily with Nietzsche's more common view of pity. The idea of a form of pity suitable for higher human beings completely drops out of his work by the early 1880s.

13. Letter to Malwida von Meysenbug, August 1883, *Selected Letters of Friedrich Nietzsche*, p. 216. For some other examples of Nietzsche's disparagement of pity, see GS 345; BGE 199, 202, 222, 225; TI IX, 37; and A 7.

bility is contrasted repeatedly and favorably with a contemptible desire for peace and tranquility. Given his self-characterization in *Ecce Homo* as "warlike" by nature, it is unsurprising that he imagines his ideal friends as "brothers in war," at war with each other as much as against a common adversary (EH I, 7; Z I, 10). Zarathustra reminds his youthful admirers that they should consider their friend "[their] best enemy" and that their hearts should feel closest to a friend "when you oppose him" (Z I, 14). The friend/enemy is valued for his role in providing the free spirit with the "resistances" needed to maintain the sharpness of his heightened instincts (EH I, 7). Moreover, as Zarathustra parts from his admirers into another long period of therapeutic, self-imposed isolation, he suggests that the heartfelt intimacy experienced by his type of friend can quite appropriately encompass feelings of hatred: the "man of knowledge [*Der Mensch der Erkenntnis*] must be able not only to love his enemies but also to hate his friends" (Z I, 22, 3).[14]

Friendship across Gender Lines?

Is this "refined conception of friendship" applicable to male-female relationships?[15] To a limited extent it is, for the theme of agonistic struggle and its salutary effect remains prominent in Nietzsche's depiction of the ideal sort of relationship between a free spirit and his female consort. Even in his relations with the opposite sex the Nietzschean warrior male is expected to shun the safe, pitiable comforts sought by the herd male. Because "the true man" [*der ächte Mann*] wants "danger and play" out of life, he consorts with "woman, as the most dangerous plaything [*das gefährlichste Spielzeug*]" (Z I, 18). As a means of testing his mettle even in his amorous relations, he seeks

14. Hatred—as opposed to contempt—is treated by Nietzsche as a sign of respect for one's equals, be they friend or foe. See, for example, GM I, 10: "How much reverence [*Ehrfurcht*] has a noble man for his enemies!—and such reverence is a bridge to love.— For he desires his enemy for himself, as his mark of distinction."

15. In this section I draw freely upon my article "The *Übermensch*'s Consort: Nietzsche and the 'Eternal Feminine,'" first published in *History of Political Thought* 18, 3 (1997): 512–530, copyright © Imprint Academic, Exeter, U.K.

out not the submissive shrinking violet of a lesser man's fantasies but rather a "strangely wild" creature, a "dangerous, creeping, subterranean little beast of prey" whose attractiveness lies in the challenge she poses (BGE 239; EH III, 5).

It is neither possible nor desirable for the free-spirited higher man to subdue this "wild" creature completely. Nietzsche imagines that such a woman, possessing an "inner savagery" that inspires "respect" and "fear" [*Furcht*], would remain a forceful presence in the life of her man and indeed of her society, just as many strong-willed women in the past have exercised considerable power behind the scenes (BGE 239; cf. BGE 131). Nietzsche speaks approvingly in this context of "the world's most powerful and influential women (most recently the mother of Napoleon)," who "owed their power and ascendancy over men precisely to the force of their will" (BGE 239).

Nevertheless, he balks at the idea of such women attaining agonistic *equality* with their warrior mates.[16] While believing that "healthy" women can attain certain specifically female forms of excellence—to which he attributes greater value than "herd virtues"[17]—he maintains that the ultimate form of human flourishing is reserved only for a few male exemplars of the species. As we have already seen, Zarathustra's teachings are characterized as "man's fare" or "warriors' food" that would be indigestible to children and "fond little women, old or young." Thus he concludes: "I am not their teacher and physician" (Z

16. Here, once again, I am speaking primarily of Nietzsche's better-known later writings. Ruth Abbey suggests that the works of Nietzsche's middle period countenance the prospect of a truly equal relationship between the sexes. But even in the middle period, it is easy to find evidence of the masculinist views that later became dominant. See Abbey, "Beyond Misogyny and Metaphor: Women in Nietzsche's Middle Period," *Journal of the History of Philosophy* 34, 2 (April 1996): 244–256.

17. Sarah Kofman recognizes Nietzsche's view that "some women are more affirmative than . . . some men." Kofman, "Baubô: Theological Perversions and Fetishism," in *Nietzsche's New Seas: Explorations in Philosophy, Aesthetics, and Politics*, ed. Michael Allen Gillespie and Tracy B. Strong (Chicago: University of Chicago Press, 1988), p. 193. Berkowitz makes a similar observation in his *Nietzsche: The Ethics of an Immoralist*, p. 170. Thus my disagreement with Bruce Detwiler's labeling of Nietzsche as a misogynist. See his *Nietzsche and the Politics of Aristocratic Radicalism* (Chicago: University of Chicago Press, 1990), pp. 15, 193. It is possible to be against the idea and practice of gender equality without being a hater of women (although such a position is both unfamiliar and objectionable in a feminist era).

IV, 17, 1). It is also of note that *Ecce Homo* compares the healthy sort of woman with the Maenads of ancient Greek mythology, who were the female followers—rather than equals—of Dionysus (EH III, 5).

However much of a challenge they may pose to their male partners, healthy women are said to find their deepest fulfillment in service to deserving men. As Zarathustra puts it: "The man's happiness [*Glück*] is: I will. The woman's happiness is: He will" (Z I, 18). At some deep level, claims Nietzsche, the finest women admire only strong and audacious men and crave to be dominated by them. This point is made in a passage that identifies wisdom metaphorically as a woman, when Zarathustra claims that she "never loves anyone but a warrior" (Z I, 7).[18] It reappears in the preface to *Beyond Good and Evil* when Nietzsche, who this time supposes truth to be a woman, suggests that she reveals herself only to a certain type of virtuoso, one without the "gruesome earnestness" and "clumsy importunity" that have characterized dogmatic philosophers heretofore (BGE Preface; cf. GS 345). Only those men who have resisted the emasculating efforts of centuries of servile moral teaching are deemed worthy of a fine woman's attentions. To those whose constitutions predispose them to servility, respect is neither owed nor given. "In the long run," as Nietzsche suggests, "the little women [*die Weiblein*] . . . play the deuce with selfless, with merely objective men [*aus selbstlosen, aus bloß objektiven Männern*]" (EH III, 5). This same idea is apparent in part I of *Zarathustra* when the title character asks, "Whom does woman hate most?" and immediately provides his own answer: "Thus spoke the iron to the magnet: 'I hate you most, because you attract me, but are not strong enough to draw me towards you'" (Z I, 18).

The idea that a superior man and his consort could form a friendship of equals is further belied by Nietzsche's view that even the most ideal woman is inherently "shallow" and thus unable to comprehend the depths of the superior man's nature (ibid.).[19] As evidence of

18. Compare Machiavelli's infamous suggestion at the end of chapter 25 in *The Prince* that "since fortune is a woman," she will be "well disposed" to young men "because they are less cautious and more aggressive, and treat her more boldly." *The Prince*, ed. Quentin Skinner and Russell Price (Cambridge: Cambridge University Press, 1988), p. 87.

19. See also Nietzsche's comparison of woman's shallowness with that of the German in *Ecce Homo*: "With the German, almost as with the woman, one never gets to the bottom, *he has none*: that is all" (EH XIII, 3).

woman's superficiality Nietzsche points to her ostensibly inferior manner of loving: whereas the woman's love for a man typically is characterized by "total devotion . . . with soul and body, without any consideration or reserve," presupposing an "unconditional renunciation of rights" and a "will to renunciation," for a healthy man such a desire for total devotion would be "alien" (GS 363). "A man who loves like a woman," he concludes, "becomes a slave; while a woman who loves like a woman becomes *a more perfect woman*" (ibid.). Passages such as these highlight the resemblance of Nietzsche's picture of male-female friendship to Aristotle's. Aristotle also posits a hierarchy of *philoi* in the *polis*, with the friendship between virtuous males deemed the most perfect and that between the man of virtue and his wife and children an inferior—although hardly insignificant—variety.[20]

The paragraph from *The Gay Science* quoted above highlights an important aspect of Nietzsche's view of women and gender relations that has been either studiously avoided or dismissed outright by commentators who invoke Nietzsche in the name of a feminist antiessentialism.[21] As I have argued at greater length elsewhere, Nietzsche's attack on nineteenth-century feminists for their attempt "to enlighten men about 'woman as such' [*das Weib an sich*]" and for their hubristic "elevation of *themselves* as 'woman in herself'" should be seen not as an illustration of a broader combat against an essentialist view of the feminine but rather as an attempt to cast aspersions on one particular—liberal feminist—interpretation of women's essence in the name of another (ostensibly more accurate) version (EH III, 5; BGE 232).[22] That Nietzsche considers himself a *connoisseur* of woman's nature is suggested in the obvious pride with which

20. Cf. *Nicomachean Ethics*, bk. 8, chaps. 7–12; *The Politics*, bk. 1, chaps. 2, 5, 12, 13.

21. See, for example, the collection *Nietzsche and the Feminine*, ed. Peter J. Burgard (Charlottesville: University Press of Virginia, 1994), and especially Burgard's introduction, pp. 1–32. See also the contributions to *Nietzsche, Feminism, and Political Theory*, ed. Paul Patton (London: Routledge, 1993).

22. Fredrick Appel, "The *Übermensch*'s Consort: Nietzsche and the 'Eternal Feminine.'" Nietzsche does not take a consistent line with the women's movement, however. While at times criticizing its proponents for putting forward a faulty conception of feminine essence, he accuses them in other passages of commiting a great error—a "stupidity"—by attempting to talk men out of the idea "that there is something eternally, necessarily feminine [*Ewig- und Notwendig-Weibliches*]" (BGE 239). Notwith-

he reports to his friend Peter Gast that August Strindberg regards him "as the greatest psychologist of women."[23]

The "dangerous plaything" role discussed above is not the only form of service to men that Nietzsche assigns to his superior women. The second is directly related to procreation. His view of the complementarity of these two roles is encapsulated by Zarathustra: "There are many things so well devised that they are like women's breasts: at the same time useful and pleasant [*nützlich zugleich und angenehm*]" (Z III, 12, 17). Another remark relating more directly to the division of labor between the sexes makes the same point: "This is how I would have man and woman: the one fit for war [*kriegstüchtig*], the other fit for bearing children [*gebärttüchtig*], but both fit for dancing with head and heels" (Z III, 12, 23; cf. Z I, 18; BGE 239).

Greatly respectful of women's procreative capacity, Nietzsche believes that woman's virtue—her "highest hope" in Zarathustra's parlance—consists in part in bearing the next *Übermenschlich* generation (Z I, 18). Earlier in this section, Zarathustra includes the following homily: "Everything about woman is a riddle, and everything about woman has one solution: it is called pregnancy. / For the woman, the man is a means: the end is always the child" (ibid.).[24] The great importance he attributes to this role is further demonstrated in his criticism of Christianity's "abysmal vulgarity" with respect to "procre-

---

standing this inconsistency, the commitment to gender essentialism remains constant throughout his mature period. In an attempt to recuperate Nietzsche for an antiessentialist feminism, Maudemarie Clark suggests that Nietzsche's decision to place quotation marks around the phrase "woman as such" (*das Weib an sich*) in paragraph 231 of *Beyond Good and Evil* reveals an ironic stance toward essentialist categories as such. See Clark, "Nietzsche's Misogyny," *International Studies in Philosophy* 26, 3 (1994): 7. While she is surely right that Nietzsche wishes to dissociate himself from the Kantian flavor of a phrase such as *Weib an sich*, I argue in "The *Übermensch*'s Consort" that this does not entail a break with all manner of talking about woman's essence.

23. Letter to Peter Gast, 9 December 1888, in *Selected Letters of Friedrich Nietzsche*, p. 331.

24. Cf. *Ecce Homo:* "Has my answer been heard to the question how one cures— 'redeems'—a woman? One makes a child for her. The woman has need of children, the man is always only the means: thus spoke Zarathustra" (EH III, 5). Also of note is *Beyond Good and Evil*'s declaration that a woman's "first and last profession is to bear strong children" (BGE 239).

ation [*die Zeugung*] . . . women, [and] marriage" (A 56). The tendency of Christianity's ascetic strain to "slander" the body is said to involve an unwarranted and disrespectful vilification of female procreative functions. By contrast, he contends, the Indian Law of Manu treats these matters "seriously, with reverence [*Ehrfurcht*], with love and trust." The "old greybeards and saints" who composed the laws of Indian caste society, he believes, "have a way of being polite [*artig*] to women which has perhaps never been surpassed" (ibid.).

The Feminist Woman as Source of Corruption

The elitism pervading all aspects of Nietzsche's thought does not leave his treatment of women unaffected. Far from believing all women to embody certain "essential" characteristics simply in virtue of their gender, he presents certain "feminine" roles and dispositions as paradigmatic virtues that only superior ("healthy") women exemplify. Those who reject gender stereotypes and fight for equality of the sexes, such as the suffragettes and salon women of Nietzsche's day, are relegated to the bottom run of the *Rangordnung* of femininity.

Given Nietzsche's predilection for tracing all normative claims and psychological orientations back to physiology and instinct, it is not surprising that he attributes feminist demands for the vote and other legal rights to physiological pathology. "The struggle for *equal* rights," he diagnoses, "is even a symptom of sickness: every physician knows that" (EH III, 5). A woman who tries to talk men out of the idea of woman's inferiority clearly evinces "a crumbling of the feminine instinct [*weiblichen Instinkte*]" (BGE 239). Specifically, she is alleged to be physiologically deficient in an area where, as we have just seen, healthy women are said to perform one of their greatest services: biological reproduction. Feminists are "*abortive* women, the 'emancipated' who lack the stuff for children" (EH III, 5).

In this portrait the feminist's alleged infertility is inextricably linked to a morbid set of instincts that produces a woman secretly envious of and bitterly resentful toward the healthy, fertile woman of

Nietzsche's imagination. His account of a feminist activism driven by envy and *ressentiment* mirrors his more familiar account of the motivations of the feminist's degenerative male counterpart, who is also preoccupied with the secret plotting of revenge upon superior types: "'Emancipation of woman'—is the instinctive hatred of the woman who has *turned out ill*, that is to say is incapable of bearing, for her who has turned out well. . . . At bottom the emancipated are the *anarchists* in the world of the 'eternal-womanly', the underprivileged whose deepest instinct is revenge" (ibid.).[25] Nietzsche's sterile, resentful woman thus shares with the herd male the mantle of the plebeian or lower sort of human being.

Although the feminist woman remains convinced that she is working for the true interests of her sex, Nietzsche claims that she ensures a contrary result. A "real woman" [*ein wohlgeratenes Weib*] in touch with her "most womanly instincts" understands this: "The more a woman is a woman [*Das Weib, je mehr Weib es ist*] the more she defends herself tooth and nail against rights in general" (BGE 239; EH III, 5). It would be in women's best interests to submit to the natural order of unequal gender relations, for they would thereby retain the advantages of their abilities in one crucial area where, as we noted above, he thinks they can exert great power: that of personal relations with men. "The state of nature, the eternal *war* between the sexes puts her in a superior position by far" (EH III, 5). In this private realm of gender relations, men of honor provide a "tribute of respect" [*Achtungszoll*] to their consorts, something that modern, degenerate women have perversely come to see as "almost offensive," preferring as they do the "competition for rights" (BGE 239).

But when they insist on "equal rights," that is, equal access to "grammar school education, trousers and the political rights of voting cattle [*Stimmvieh-Rechte*]," women actually abandon their great natural advantages in exchange for the opportunity to compete with men in a man's game, thereby "lower[ing] the general rank of woman" [*das allgemeine Rang-Niveau des Weibes "herunter" bringen*]

25. Nietzsche considers anarchism to be no less an exemplification of modern herd morality than socialism, liberalism, democracy, or feminism. For a sampling of his castigation of anarchists and anarchism, see D Preface 3; GS 370; GM I, 5; and A 58.

(EH III, 5).[26] "Since the French Revolution," he concludes, "the influence of woman in Europe has grown *less* in the same proportion as her rights and claims have grown greater" (BGE 239).

We have already seen (in Chapter 2) how Nietzsche treats the doctrine of equal rights as a rhetorical weapon used by the mediocre against their natural superiors. This, he argues, is exactly how unhealthy women use rights talk: to dominate men in both the public and domestic spheres. Zarathustra raises the specter of the ambitious female who, as a "dressed-up lie," conceals her domineering streak behind a veil of submissiveness during courtship, only to unleash it upon an unsuspecting, gullible groom after marriage (Z I, 20). Having sought after a bride and believing himself to have found "a handmaiden with the virtues of an angel," the naïve husband suddenly finds himself "the handmaiden of a woman" (ibid.).

The unhealthy woman's success in dominating her man in this manner is attributed to the basic servility—unmanliness—of the modern herd male. "If one tests your virility," Zarathustra declares mockingly to the "men of the present," "one finds only sterility!" (Z II, 14). Echoing the civic humanist discourse of Aristotle, Machiavelli, and Rousseau, Nietzsche points out instances of what he sees as female domination in his age and interprets them as unmistakable signs of widespread cultural degradation and decline.[27] In a corrupt

26. The parallel with Rousseau is striking. Compare, for example, the following passage from *Emile:* "Woman is worth more as woman and less as man. Wherever she makes use of her rights, she has the advantage. Wherever she wants to usurp ours, she remains beneath us." *Emile, or On Education*, trans. Allan Bloom (New York: Basic Books, 1979), pp. 363–364. Cf. Penelope Deutscher, "'Is it not remarkable that Nietzsche . . . should have hated Rousseau?' Woman, Femininity: Distancing Nietzsche from Rousseau," in *Nietzsche, Feminism, and Political Theory*, ed. Paul Patton (London: Routledge, 1993), pp. 162–188.

27. Nietzsche also adopts the classical civic humanist association of public virtue with tight male control over women: the ancient Greeks "from Homer to the age of Pericles," he believes, understood "how necessary [*notwendig*]" it was to become "more strict with women" [*strenger gegen das Weib*] "with the *increase* of their culture and the amplitude of their powers" (BGE 238; cf. HAH 259).

society, where men's will to power is weak or channeled into either religious-ascetic self-renunciation or lazy self-indulgence, many women seize the opportunity to step outside the domestic sphere and assert themselves publicly. Decadent European culture, bereft of the "manliest drives and virtues" [*männlichsten Tugenden und Trieben*], has allowed unhealthy, resentful women to begin aping the male virtues (A 17; TI I, 28). "There is little manliness here" [*Des Mannes ist hier wenig*], observes Zarathustra of the ambient, "herd" society. "Therefore their women make themselves manly. For only he who is sufficiently a man will—*redeem the woman* in woman" (Z III, 5, 2).[28]

Nietzsche's concern for the cultivation of a disposition of "hardness" should be understood in light of this fear of the "castrating" influence of a degenerate, emasculated culture that prefers a tranquilizing, self-indulgent benevolence over robust acts of creative will.[29] Zarathustra issues an ominous warning that "what is womanish [*Weibsart*], what stems from slavishness [*Knechtsart*] . . . now wants to become master of mankind's entire destiny" (Z IV, 13, 3). It is no accident that Nietzsche refers disparagingly to "the whole of European *feminism*" in the course of a polemical harangue on everything that annoys him about modern European civilization (D Preface 4). "Woman," he opines in the *Nachlass*, "has always conspired with the

28. See also Nietzsche's disparaging comments about the "literary woman" [*das Litteratur-Weib*] of eighteenth- and nineteenth-century Europe in *Twilight of the Idols* and *Beyond Good and Evil* (TI IX, 27; BGE 233). Madame de Staël, for one, is described as a "masculinized woman" of "unbridled presumption," apparently because she engaged in scholarship, an inherently masculine pursuit (BGE 209; cf. BGE 144). Only ten years earlier Nietzsche was corresponding with the writer Malwida von Meysenbug and complimenting her on her books, another indication that his views on women underwent a marked shift by the early 1880s. See, for example, the letter of 14 April 1876 in *Selected Letters of Friedrich Nietzsche*, p. 142.

29. "To demand that everything should become 'good man', herd animal, blue-eyed, benevolent, 'beautiful soul', . . . would mean to deprive existence of its *great* character, would mean to castrate mankind and to reduce it to a paltry Chinadom" (EH XIV, 4). Nietzsche's critique of the "emasculation of social life" in the Europe of his day is noted by Keith Ansell-Pearson in *An Introduction to Nietzsche as Political Thinker* (Cambridge: Cambridge University Press, 1994), pp. 180–199.

types of decadence, the priests, against the 'powerful,' the 'strong,' the men—. Woman brings the children to the cult of piety, pity, love" (WP 864).[30]

In calling for the cultural regeneration of Europe, Nietzsche hopes to see the reappearance of warrior figures like Napoleon, who emerged out of a plebeian political culture to make Europe "virile" [*Vermännlich*] again. Napoleon's virile example gave modern Europeans a *soupçon* of what it would be like for man to regain control "over the businessman and the philistine—and perhaps even over 'woman' who has been pampered by Christianity and the enthusiastic spirit of the eighteenth century, and even more by 'modern ideas'" (GS 362).

---

30. Sarah Kofman notes that for Nietzsche, "the weak act like *women:* they try to seduce, they charm, by misrepresenting and disguising nihilistic values under gilded trim." Kofman, "Baubô: Theological Perversions and Fetishism," p. 179. The view that slave morality evinces seductive feminine qualities is also expounded in *Beyond Good and Evil*, where Nietzsche speaks of "every unegoistic morality" as both "a seduction [*Verführung*] and injury [*Schädigung*] for precisely the higher, rarer, privileged" (BGE 221; cf. D Preface 3).

five   **The Higher Breeding of Humanity**

> You shall *make amends* to your children for being the children of
> your fathers: *thus* you shall redeem all that is past!
> —*Thus Spoke Zarathustra III, 12, 12*

Breeding Companions

When the prospect of finding those worthy of his company seems remote, Nietzsche feels "haunted by a feeling blacker than the blackest melancholy" and is sorely
tempted to throw off all hope and embrace a nihilistic "contempt of
man" (A 38). To combat such pessimism he resorts to numerous
stratagems. The eternal return thought experiment, for one, permits

him to believe—at least some of the time—in his own immunity to misfortune. By "willing backwards" Nietzsche convinces himself that his "lack of adequate company" is both necessary and salutary, hence his insistence that friendlessness has never prevented him "from being brave and cheerful" (EH II, 2).[1]

Another strategy to fulfill the psychic need for comradeship involves the creation of a fantasy world populated by idealized friends. At an early stage of the *Zarathustra* narrative the title character counsels his interlocutors to follow this route, deeming it preferable to "create your friend and his overflowing heart out of yourselves" than to "endure . . . any kind of neighbor" (Z I, 16). In an 1887 preface to an earlier work, Nietzsche admits to having recourse to "companions" of this sort:

> Thus when I needed to I once also *invented* for myself the 'free spirits' to whom this melancholy-valiant book . . . is dedicated: 'free spirits' of this kind do not exist, did not exist—but . . . I had need of them at that time if I was to keep in good spirits while surrounded by ills (sickness, solitude, unfamiliar places, *acedia*, inactivity): as brave companions and familiars with whom one can laugh and chatter when one feels like laughing and chattering, and whom one can send to the Devil when they become tedious—as compensation for the friends I lacked. (HAH I Preface 2)[2]

1. See Chapter 3. It is difficult, however, to detect any cheerfulness in the following *cri de coeur:* "Where may I look with any kind of hope for my kind of philosopher himself, at the least for my need [*meinem Bedürfniß*] of new philosophers?" (WP 464). That a lack of companionship clearly disturbed Nietzsche in his last years of sanity is even more evident in his personal correspondence. In a letter from 1888, after having "given humanity its profoundest book" (presumably *Zarathustra*), he confesses to "constantly being wounded" by "not hearing any answer, [by] having to bear, most terribly, on one's own shoulders, alone, the burden which one would have liked to share, to shed (why else should one write?)." Letter to Malwida von Meysenbug, end of July 1888, in *Selected Letters of Friedrich Nietzsche*, ed. and trans. Christopher Middleton (Indianapolis: Hackett, 1996), p. 302.

2. In 1885 Nietzsche confessed to his mother and sister that "there is nobody living about whom I care *much*; the people I like have been dead for a long long time—for example, the Abbé Galiani, or Henri Beyle, or Montaigne." Letter to Franziska and Elisabeth Nietzsche, 31 March 1885, in *Selected Letters of Friedrich Nietzsche*, p. 238.

Given Nietzsche's avowed commitments to worldliness and embodiment, however, it would be odd if these purely imaginative devices for creating "companions and children of his hope" exhausted his arsenal (Z III, 3). There is clear evidence that Nietzsche envisions other ways of seeking out suitable companions that involve action in the real world. As we noted in Chapter 2, he never abandoned hope of finding the "raw material" for worthy friends and companions. Real, flesh-and-blood companions, as distinct from imaginary friends, are still in the offing:

> That free spirits of this kind *could* one day exist, that our Europe *will* have such active and audacious fellows among its sons of tomorrow and the next day, physically present and palpable and not, as in my case, merely phantoms and hermit's phantasmagoria: *I* should wish to be the last to doubt it. I see them already *coming*, slowly, slowly . . . (HAH I Preface 2)

This reference to the slowness of their appearance—and to the patience required by those wishing to hasten their arrival—appears elsewhere in Nietzsche's later writings. As a "fisher of men," he knows that patience is a cardinal virtue for those with his vocation (Z III, 8, 2; cf. EH X, 1). Zarathustra informs us that he and his "destiny . . . do not speak to Today, neither do we speak to the Never: we have patience and time and more than time" (Z IV, 1). He reassures his interlocutors that although they may be unable to produce a "beautiful new race" [*neuen schönen Art*] overnight, they "could transform [themselves] into forefathers and ancestors [*Vätern und Vorfahren*] of the Superman" (Z II, 2; cf. Z III, 12, 12).

I argue below that Nietzsche's "slow search for those related to [him]" includes a serious consideration of questions of lineage and inheritance and even a desire to instigate forms of selective breeding that would ensure the continued propagation of higher human types (EH X, 1). I argue further that the notion of breeding is invoked to service not only his need for companionship but also his politics—as one of the "tremendous counter-forces" required to stem the tide of mediocrity that, in Nietzsche's view, threatens to engulf Europe (BGE 268).

Literal and Figurative Breeding

Recent studies have tended to follow Kaufmann in either dismissing outright or underplaying the idea that Nietzsche seriously countenanced the notion of breeding in the literal sense of eugenics.[3] Although the pervasiveness of procreative imagery in his work is readily acknowledged, it is often given a strictly metaphorical interpretation. The apparent strength of this reading lies in Nietzsche's undeniably frequent use of procreative imagery to metaphoric effect. When he refers to the "continually creative person" as "a 'mother' type in the grand sense" [*eine "Mutter" von Mensch*] or as "the motherly human type" [*die mütterliche Art Mensch*] the association of creativity with fertility is clear (GS 369; GS 376).[4] As early as *Daybreak*, Nietzsche declares that the creative type is no more in conscious control of the ideas or deeds gestating within him than the mother is in control of her offspring's rate of growth or time of birth (D 552). The "birthing" of ideas and deeds is equated with that of infants when he exhorts his readers to "give birth to our thoughts out of our pain and, like mothers, endow them with all we have of blood, heart, fire, pleasure, passion, agony, conscience, fate, and catastrophe" (GS Preface 3; cf. Z II, 2). In *The Genealogy*, moreover, we learn that the "fruitfulness" of the new (male) philosopher is to be found not in the sphere of biological reproduction but rather in his work [*Werk*], which is to its creator as the child is to its mother (GM III, 8; cf. BGE 206).

3. "Nietzsche looked to art, religion and philosophy—and not to race—to elevate man above the beasts." Walter Kaufmann, *Nietzsche: Philosopher, Psychologist, Anti-Christ*, 4th ed. (Princeton: Princeton University Press, 1974), p. 285; cf. p. 303. Tracy Strong briefly takes up the possibility of a literal dimension to Nietzsche's talk of breeding in his book, noting that Nietzsche "repeatedly uses the word *züchten*, which means to breed, raise, rear, grow or cultivate, a word normally used in connection with animals or plants." But despite his claim to have taken the call for breeding "at face value," Strong shies away from seriously examining its role in Nietzsche's vision of a "new transfigured world." This vision, he claims, is "so complex as to defy . . . all attempts" at description. Strong, *Friedrich Nietzsche and the Politics of Transfiguration*, expanded ed. (Berkeley: University of California Press, 1988), pp. 274, viii, 292.

4. And as we noted in the previous chapter's discussion of "infertile" (feminist) women, mediocrity is analogously described as a type of barrenness. Zarathustra considers uncreative, herd men to be "unfruitful" [*Unfruchtbare*] and "sterile" (Z II, 14; cf. Z IV, 13, 9).

These rhetorical tropes have, of course, a long history in moral and political philosophy,[5] and the importance of that tradition in Nietzsche's writings is beyond dispute. I maintain, however, that his rhetoric of procreation is most profitably seen on a continuum, with the metaphorical treatment at one end, the evocation of "breeding" as a form of education and/or upbringing in the middle range, and a frank consideration of experimentation in eugenics at the other extreme. The task of placing various textual passages along the continuum is a delicate one, complicated by the fact that the German term for breeding, *Züchtung*, has (like its English counterpart) both cultural and biological connotations. In English as in German the term "well-bred" is used typically as a synonym for "well-trained."[6] Nietzsche's use of the German term for discipline, *Zucht*, alongside its etymological cousin *Züchtung*[7] further highlights the importance of the cultural dimension in Nietzsche's treatment of breeding and reminds us of what was discussed in Chapter 2, namely his desire to cultivate a "new nobility" [*neuen Adel*] whose members are not literally his own children (Z III, 12, 12).

When Nietzsche speaks of breeding in this nonliteral, pedagogical-therapeutic sense, his preference for the term *Züchtung* is reinforced by his suspicion of the standard German terms for education and culture. In his eyes *Bildung* is irretrievably tainted by its association with slave morality,[8] and in *Ecce Homo* the other common term for education, *Erziehung*, is treated with equal suspicion: "All questions of politics, the ordering of society, education [*der Erziehung*] have been falsified down to their foundations because the most injurious men have been taken for great men" (EH II, 10). Nietzsche is also inclined, however, to invoke *Erziehung* for his own purposes. His description in his notebooks of the new, higher sort of philosopher as a

5. Aristotle, for example, claims in the *Nicomachean Ethics* that "a human being originates and fathers his own actions as he fathers his children" (1113b18).

6. As Bruce Detwiler reminds us in his *Nietzsche and the Politics of Aristocratic Radicalism* (Chicago: University of Chicago Press, 1990), p. 111.

7. Nietzsche envisages "great enterprises and collective experiments in discipline and breeding [*Zucht und Züchtung*]" in BGE 203.

8. For a sampling of some caustic remarks on European *Bildung*, see GS 86; Z II, 14; and TI VIII, 5. Mark Warren notes Nietzsche's preference for *Züchtung* over *Bildung* in his *Nietzsche and Political Thought* (Cambridge: MIT Press, 1988), p. 262.

"great educator" [*Erzieher*] comes to mind, as does a middle-period passage which evokes an expansive notion of breeding that has both biological and cultural components: "Education [*Die Erziehung*] is a continuation of procreation [*der Zeugung*], and often a kind of supplementary beautification of it" (WP 980; D 397).

As this latter passage suggests, a serious concern for breeding as education need not imply a lack of interest in questions of propagation. Indeed, in Nietzsche's view the former ultimately becomes ineffectual without serious attention to the latter. Sound pedagogical practices and institutions ultimately are ineffectual in the absence of a means of ensuring the appearance of future generations of free-thinking, high-spirited individuals predisposed by instinct to live and learn in a healthy manner. His aim is to help fulfill the need for "institutions . . . in which people live and teach as I understand living and teaching" (EH III, 1).[9] Such institutions—including, notably, that of marriage[10]—are of course discussed with his imagined companions in mind. More important, however, Nietzsche wants his institutions to flourish over the *longue durée*, in what Zarathustra grandiosely envisages as a "thousand-year empire" (Z IV, 1). Hence the need for measures to ensure the breeding of a "new ruling caste [*regierenden Kaste*] for Europe," a truly "master race" [*Herren-Rasse*] that could avail itself of these institutions over the long haul (BGE 251; WP 960; cf. BGE 208).

It is Nietzsche's view that the children born of superior men and women and raised in an environment that encourages self-expression and self-esteem (rather than conformity and self-abnegation) would stand a better chance at becoming exemplars of excellence than those whose birth and upbringing are left to the vagaries of chance. Believing, as we noted in Chapter 2, that the appearance of higher human beings has always been irregular and infrequent heretofore, he announces a grandiose aim of bringing about a society in which these "brief little pieces of good luck" are "willed" into being (BGE 224; A

9. Chapter 6 provides a more extensive discussion of Nietzsche's interest in institution building.

10. Nietzsche is especially desirous of fostering marriage because of its status as "the most enduring form of organization" that provides "security" for society "to the most distant generations" (TI IX, 39).

3; cf. WP 979). The key question, he declares, is "what type of human being one ought to *breed*, ought to *will*, as more valuable, more worthy of life" (A 3; cf. EH IV, 4; WP 957).

One of the best-kept secrets of recent scholarly commentary on Nietzsche is his positive stance toward childbearing and child rearing. In the course of his critique of ascetic "preachers of death," for example, Nietzsche identifies as particularly noxious their deprecation of a life of child raising. These ascetic "consumptives of the soul," observes Zarathustra, renounce the begetting of children because of their view that "lust is sin," that "giving birth is laborious," and that "one gives birth only to unhappy children" (Z I, 9).

In light of the aforementioned comment in *The Genealogy* that the "fruitfulness" of the new philosophers will manifest itself in something other than children, we might be disinclined to interpret Zarathustra's repeated talk of children literally. When, however, one considers his repeated suggestion that the "garden of marriage" can assist one in propagating oneself "not only forward but upward," and that marriage can best be described as "the will of two to create the one who is more than those who created it," it seems plausible that Nietzsche countenances the propagation of future generations as an important way in which higher human beings can manifest their fruitfulness (Z I, 20; cf. Z III, 12, 24). The propagation and nurture of children as potential creators is one way—although of course not the only way—for the healthy body to "create beyond itself" (Z I, 4).

Breeding and Inheritance

Nietzsche's enthusiasm for marriage and reproduction is hardly extended to all marital and reproductive arrangements. In *Zarathustra* propagation is recommended only to those prospective parents who have gone through an intense period of self-examination and self-development: "You should build beyond yourself [*Über dich . . . hinausbauen*]. But first you must be built yourself [*selber gebaut sein*], square-built in body and soul" (Z I, 20). One should take steps, in other words, to "become what one is" and throw off all false consciousness before taking on the responsibility of raising the next generation.

However, no amount of preparation for parenthood will guarantee the appearance of children "more worthy of life" if the prospective parents are "decadent." Nietzsche looks askance upon the offspring of those whose desire to reproduce has been driven by "the animal and necessity," or "isolation," or "disharmony with yourself" (ibid.). When Zarathustra asks rhetorically, "Are you a man who *ought* to desire a child?" (ibid.), the implication seems to be that only certain reproductive arrangements are especially praiseworthy. A child born from spiritually weak parents can hardly be considered a potential creator of values. As we learn in *Beyond Good and Evil*, "it is quite impossible that a man should not have in his body the qualities and preferences of his parents and forefathers: whatever appearances may say to the contrary" (BGE 264). Thus the sterile, conformist propensities of modern scholars are traced back to deficiencies in their lineage,[11] while creative, free-spirited types are more likely to issue from creative, free-spirited parents desirous of producing "living memorials" to their "victory and . . . liberation" (GS 348, 349; Z I, 20).

The link between superiority/inferiority of instinct and birth is made explicitly in *Beyond Good and Evil:*

> For every elevated world one has to be born [*geboren*] or, expressed more clearly, *bred* [*gezüchtet*] for it: one has a right to philosophy—taking the word in the grand sense—only by virtue of one's origin [*Abkunft*]; one's ancestors [*Vorfahren*], one's 'blood' [*Geblüt*] are the decisive thing here too. Many generations must have worked to prepare for the philosopher; each of his virtues must have been individually acquired, tended, inherited, incorporated. (BGE 213)

A similar conclusion is found in the *Nachlass*, where we discover that "there is only nobility of birth [*Geburtsadel*], only nobility of blood

11. The tendency to attribute normative-spiritual inferiority to low birth is also evident in Nietzsche's criticism of Socrates. Socrates' valorization of reason over instinct is explained by pointing to his plebeian origins, which supposedly made it impossible to grasp the lofty notion of trust in one's instincts (TI II, 3; cf. TI X, 3). Similarly, the plebeian nature of the Protestant Reformation is attributed to Luther's peasant origins and allegedly consequent vindictiveness (A 61; cf. GS 358; BGE 50; GM III, 22).

[*Geblütsadel*]. . . . When one speaks of 'aristocrats of the spirit,' reasons are usually not lacking for concealing something. . . . For spirit alone does not make noble [*Geist allein nämlich adelt nicht*]; rather, there must be something to ennoble the spirit. —What then is required? Blood [*Des Geblüts*]" (WP 942).

Although the emphasis on inheritance and blood is conventionally aristocratic, Nietzsche's understanding of who should be considered an aristocrat is far from conventional in its rejection of the more typical nineteenth- and twentieth-century obsession with the "purity" of blood.[12] Declaring that he has taken the concept of "gentlemen" more "radically" than it has ever been taken heretofore, Nietzsche finds the blood of Europe's nineteenth-century aristocracy wanting (EH X, 2). The so-called aristocrats of the modern world, claims Zarathustra, far from being well-bred in his sense, demonstrate their decadence by serving plebeian, mercantile values.[13] He accuses them of selling their supposedly high birth to "shopkeepers with shopkeepers' gold" (Z III, 12, 12). Moreover, they have "become a bulwark to that which stands," knee-jerk defenders of a woeful political status quo in which real political power has fallen into the hands of herd politicians (ibid.). Having abdicated all real power and reponsibility, they are accused of debasing the very notion of nobility by subsuming it into servile *Höflichkeit*, that is, courtly manners and gestures. These aristocrats in name only, having "grown courtly at courts," have "learned to stand for long hours in shallow pools, motley-coloured like a flamingo: / for *being able* to stand is a merit with courtiers; and all courtiers believe that part of the bliss after

12. Benedict Anderson argues that modern racist doctrine, developed by the Comte de Gobineau, flowed easily from earlier aristocratic preoccupations with blood. In the age of nationalism, the notion of superior races characterized by pure blood was "democratized" to include whole nations or peoples in the privileged elite. See Anderson, *Imagined Communities: Reflections on the Origin and Spread of Nationalism*, rev. ed. (London: Verso, 1991), pp. 149–150.

13. Strong rightly notes that in Nietzsche's view "there is no reason why someone who occupies the status of a president or king might not be slavely moral. One does not have slave morality in the same manner as one has social-economic status." *Friedrich Nietzsche and the Politics of Transfiguration*, p. 239. Peter Berkowitz makes a similar point in his *Nietzsche: The Ethics of an Immoralist* (Cambridge: Harvard University Press, 1995), p. 119.

death is—*being allowed* to sit!" (ibid.). Zarathustra decries the mindless servility that associates the whole of virtue with being able to wait endlessly in courts (Z IV, 3, 2).

Thus even as he attributes the possession of fine instincts to the right sort of blood, Nietzsche associates the latter neither with any conventional European aristocracy nor with a particular race or ethnic group, Aryan or otherwise.[14] In *Zarathustra* the suggestion is made that the raw material for a noble order of the future will come from the margins of contemporary herd societies, from individuals who have broken with the mainstream. Zarathustra issues his call to them: "You solitaries of today, you who have seceded from society [*ihr Ausscheidenden*], you shall one day be a people [*ein Volk*]: from you, who have chosen out yourselves, shall a chosen people spring— and from this chosen people, the Superman" (Z I, 22, 2). Nietzsche imagines these marginals and deviants coming together to form a new "master race" that is multiracial (rather than "pure-blooded") in character (GS 377).

In *The Genealogy* he claims that noble types have arisen in many areas of the world and spring from many peoples—Scandinavian, Japanese, and Arabic, for example—and never suggests that the origins of the future ruling caste will be anything other than cosmopolitan (GM I, 11). Hence his view that the new ruling caste would emerge out of—and be continually replenished by—"international racial unions" [*internationalen Geschlechts-Verbänden*] (WP 960). His comments on how the "slave revolt" led to an unfortunate, promiscuous mingling of the races might appear to suggest something quite different—a concern for the purity of the ruling caste's blood (GM I,

---

14. Cf. Detwiler, *Nietzsche and the Politics of Aristocratic Radicalism*, p. 111. An exception must be made for the Germanocentrism of an early work such as *The Birth of Tragedy*. After throwing off the early influence of Wagner, Nietzsche invariably imagines his readership as "good Europeans" rather than members of a particular nationality or ethnic group. Carl Pletsch notes that the shift toward cosmopolitanism began with the appearance of *Human, All Too Human* in 1879. Pletsch, *Young Nietzsche: Becoming a Genius* (New York: Free Press, 1991), p. 202. For some examples of Nietzsche's understanding of higher human beings as good Europeans, see HAH II Preface 6; GS 377; BGE Preface; BGE 241, 256; and WP 132.

9; cf. BGE 200).[15] In the offending passages, however, Nietzsche's difficulty is not with interracial breeding in principle; he is well disposed toward an interbreeding of disparate individuals deemed (by him) superior. What he frowns upon is the genetic mixture of "bad blood" [*schlechtes Blut*]—belonging to those he deems of "the lower orders"—with the blood of essentially noble types (EH I, 3; EH I, 8; EH II, 10). Nowhere in Nietzsche's work are "lower human beings" associated with a particular racial or ethnic group.

Ascription vs. Achievement

Notwithstanding this unusual insistence on the multiracial character of nobility, the emphasis on inheritance remains a central (although not exclusive) concern of Nietzsche's later works. In scoffing at the expression "aristocracy of the spirit" in the *Nachlass* passage quoted above, he aims to expose what he sees as the wishful thinking implied in the Enlightenment call for an overthrow of inheritance and birth in favor of merit. Ascension to the real aristocracy simply is not open to just any educated individual. The idea that genealogy essentially prescribes one's potential and determines one's fate is strongly suggested in Zarathustra's advice to his interlocutors: "Follow in the footsteps of your fathers' virtue," he counsels, for "it would be a piece of folly" to "pretend to be saints in those matters in which your fathers were vicious" (Z IV, 13, 13; cf. Z II, 7). Moreover, *The Gay Science* speaks of how character is governed by certain "capacities" [*Vermögen*] transmitted through the bloodline and "accumulated from generation to generation, becom[ing] domineering, unreasonable, and intractable" (GS 361).

This stress on lineage is rather awkward for Nietzsche personally because it forces him to reconcile his own self-understanding as a strong, higher type "*summa summarum*" with his view of his immedi-

15. This is the conclusion of Hubert Cancik in his "'Mongols, Semites, and the Pure-Bred Greeks': Nietzsche's Handling of the Racial Doctrines of His Time," in *Nietzsche and Jewish Culture*, ed. Jacob Golomb (London: Routledge, 1997), p. 61.

ate family as common and vulgar [*canaille*]. That he held this latter view is borne out by an examination of his comments on his immediate family in *Ecce Homo*. The Protestant minister's son reveals that his father, although "lovable," was "delicate" [*zart*] and "morbid" and derides his mother and sister for their "incalculably petty" instincts (EH I, 1; EH I, 3). Nietzsche is well aware of the problem: "To be related to such *canaille* [as his mother and sister]," he declares, "would be a blasphemy against my divinity" (EH I, 3).

Two separate strategies are invoked to redeem his "divinity." The first, which involves clinging steadfastly to the aristocracy of birth model, involves a scarcely lucid and rather pathetic vaunting of a wholly reinvented personal lineage: "I am a pure-blooded Polish nobleman," he insists, "in whom there is no drop of bad blood, least of all German" (ibid.).[16] On a charitable reading of this move, Nietzsche thereby stakes a claim to a hybrid genealogy, a "two-fold origin . . . from the highest and the lowest rung of the ladder of life," with the dominant "Polish" side of his constitution allowing him to overcome decadence (EH I, 1).

A second, less fanciful track has Nietzsche returning to a more strictly meritocratic view of nobility characteristic of his middle period.[17] In a work such as *Human, All Too Human* the notion of an aristocracy "of the spirit" that is independent of birth is embraced rather than ridiculed (HAH 210, 261). The criteria of free spiritedness include the ability to break not only with established customs and beliefs but also with one's "origin, environment . . . [and] class" (HAH 225). In this work Nietzsche gestures toward the possibility of acquiring abilities—rather than simply inheriting them—when he balances a discussion of "inborn talent" with an emphasis on "acquired toughness, endurance and energy" (HAH 263). The thrust of this approach, summed up admirably by the declaration that free

16. This passage, which also includes the reference to Nietzsche's mother and sister as *canaille*, was suppressed by Nietzsche's sister, Elisabeth Förster-Nietzsche, in her posthumous edition of his works. The suppressed passage was later reinserted into the edition used by Hollingdale for his translation, which I make use of here. Another effort at trumpeting a fictitious Polish aristocratic background is made in a letter to Georg Brandes, 10 April 1888, in *Selected Letters of Friedrich Nietzsche*, p. 293.

17. See Ruth Abbey, "Descent and Dissent: Nietzsche's Reading of Two French Moralists" (Ph.D. diss., McGill University, 1994), pp. 213–224.

spiritedness represents a "victory of education over the arrogance of ancestry," jostles uneasily with an aristocracy of birth model and captures a side to Nietzsche that embraced the ideals of the Enlightenment (HAH 237).[18]

Although the aristocracy of birth model becomes more prominent in the late works, its meritocratic rival still makes forceful appearances and competes for attention, notably in Zarathustra's exhortation to his interlocutors to "let where you are going, not where you come from, henceforth be your honor" (Z III, 12, 12). Although one may stem "from the race of the hot-tempered or of the lustful or of the fanatical or of the vindictive," with the proper encouragement one might find the resources within oneself to turn all of one's "devils [into] angels" (Z I, 5).

The meritocratic view also seems to fit well with the sort of unconditional affirmation of the past and present implied in the eternal return thought experiment. Nietzsche speaks in this context of how, after a long period of shame and despair—"What child has not had reason to weep over its parents?"—he learned to affirm even his father's priestly asceticism (Z I, 20). Although it tilted him early on toward an ethereal transcendentalism, Nietzsche came to appreciate how its project of service to God and truth instilled in him a "heroic" discipline and suspicion of *laissez-aller* that became important in his own, worldly project of self-overcoming (Z II, 4). Thus he learned to embrace the title of "heir" [*Eben*] to this self-discipline and to accede to its (hypothetical) eternal recurrence even as he pledges to redirect it in ostensibly healthier directions (D Preface 4).

After acknowledging and even affirming his tainted ancestry in this manner, Nietzsche finds himself in a position to transcend his immediate parentage and embrace a loftier, fanciful (that is, willed) genealogy: "One is least related to one's parents. . . . Higher natures have their origins infinitely farther back, and with them much had to be assembled, saved and hoarded" (EH I, 3). It is in this context that we should understand Nietzsche's claims to be "related" to political

18. Middle-period passages that perpetuate the aristocracy of birth model include HAH 442 and D 205, 272. Nietzsche's use of the perplexing phrase "born aristocrats of the spirit" [*die geborenen Aristokraten des Geistes*] in HAH 210 highlights his frequent tendency in these works to slide between the two models.

figures such as the thirteenth-century antipapist emperor Friedrich the Second (EH IX, 4). Having made his peace with his past, the noble type can find a new sort of kinship "through *loftiness* of will" (EH III, 3).

This reference to a kinship resting on the will rather than physiology should caution us against hastily interpreting all of Nietzsche's remarks on breeding as a call for controlled eugenic experimentation. As I have argued above, however, the instances where "breeding" is discussed as a nurturing form of pedagogy are not inconsistent with calls for procreation in the literal sense. Indeed, Nietzsche's literary surrogate evokes their compatibility when he suggests to his interlocutors that talents developed in overcoming the unfortunate aspects of one's lineage can be used to become a better parent: "You shall *make amends* to your children for being the children of your fathers: *thus* you shall redeem all that is past!" (Z III, 12, 12).

Although the exact nature of his breeding project (as procreation, pedagogy, or both) is often left ambiguous, Nietzsche is clear about its eminently political nature—about the need for a political-institutional framework to ensure its establishment and sustenance. Now we must turn to the matter of Nietzsche's politics.

s i x   **The Art of Politics**

> *The first part of this chapter, up to "Plato's Perfect State," is coau-*
> *thored by Ruth Abbey and Fredrick Appel and has been revised by*
> *Fredrick Appel.*

Beyond Petty Politics?

Given Nietzsche's many deprecatory remarks about the political realm and his self-description as a thinker above politics, it is understandable that many have characterized him
as a thinker unconcerned with or despairing of politics in general.[1]

1. See the Introduction, note 26 for some examples of influential antipolitical in-
terpretations of Nietzsche.

He undeniably derides the "long-drawn-out comedy of [Europe's] petty states and the divided will of its dynasties and democracies" and condemns Germany's imperialist pretensions (BGE 208). He scorns German nationalism and nationalist movements in general as examples of a "névrose nationale with which Europe is sick, [an] eternalizing of the petty-state situation of Europe, of petty politics [*kleinen Politik*]" (EH XIII, 2; cf. GS 377; WP Preface 2; WP 748). Such pettiness clearly has a great deal to do with democratic catering to the interests and needs of the majority. Zarathustra "turned [his] back upon the rulers" after finding their political activity to be nothing more than "bartering and haggling for power—with the rabble!" (Z II, 6) Only small-minded people, in his view, entertain ambitions for power in herd society: only the "superfluous [*Überflüssigen*] . . . strive towards the throne" (Z I, 11).

Does this mean, however, that Nietzsche reduces all politics to petty, herdlike behavior, beneath the dignity of his higher human beings? I argue that equating his criticisms of the modern state and his condescending treatment of democratic politics with an opposition to politics in general is premature.[2] Indeed, the aforementioned passage from *Ecce Homo* castigating petty politics gestures toward a different and higher type of politics by asking, "Does anyone except me know a way out of this blind alley? . . . A task great enough once again to *unite* the peoples?" (EH XIII, 2). Some alternative is evoked again in Nietzsche's prediction that "the *compulsion* to grand politics" will supersede "petty politics" (BGE 208). In *Daybreak*, moreover, the declaration that "political and economic affairs are not worthy of being the enforced concern of society's most gifted spirits" is immediately followed by a critique of contemporary economic and political arrangements and attitudes, in particular the idea that the state should provide universal security (D 179). Even in the earlier *Human, All Too Human*, the requirement that "a few must first of all be allowed, now more than ever, to refrain from politics and to step a little aside" is followed by the anticipation of a time when these few

2. Gerald Mara and Suzanne Dovi similarly caution against the antipolitical reading in their "Mill, Nietzsche, and the Identity of Postmodern Liberalism," *Journal of Politics* 57 (February 1995): 5. See also Bruce Detwiler, *Nietzsche and the Politics of Aristocratic Radicalism* (Chicago: University of Chicago Press, 1990), p. 59.

will take "permission to speak" (HAH 438). Thus while those who read Nietzsche as nonpolitical or antipolitical are correct in claiming that he denounces "petty politics," they fail to consider the possibility that this might be in the name of a higher, grander conception of the political, one that includes cultural-cum-ethical concerns.

The reading of Nietzsche as a thinker uninterested in or ultimately scornful of politics can be buttressed by a narrow interpretation of his aestheticism.[3] His accent on cultivating the individual as an artist of the self is often taken to be incompatible with a concern for social and political projects.[4] For Nietzsche, however, such rivalry between the aesthetic and the ethical or the political does not always exist. Even art in the conventional, limited sense is not isolated from questions of power and ethical judgment. Artists, he claims, are engaged in the eminently ethical endeavor of ranking types of human existence. That art inspires discriminating, practical judgments about human flourishing is suggested in *Twilight of the Idols:* "What does all art do? does it not praise? does it not glorify? does it not select? does it not highlight? . . . [this is] the prerequisite for the artist's being an artist at all" (TI IX, 24; cf. TI III, 6; WP 821).

Yet the relationship among aesthetics, ethics, and will to power runs deeper, for the aesthetic in Nietzsche's work is often taken to encompass any form of bold, original creativity. He repeatedly invokes the image of the artist to convey an action-oriented, produc-

3. As Martha Nussbaum observes, Nietzsche's remarks about existence being justified only as an aesthetic phenomenon (e.g., BT Preface 5; GS 107) are often "taken to imply some sort of moral aestheticizing of existence, a playful overturning of all moral and political categories in the name of detached aesthetic values." Nussbaum, "Transfigurations of Intoxication: Nietzsche, Schopenhauer, and Dionysus," *Arion* 1, 2 (Spring 1991): 101.

4. See, for example, Walter Kaufmann's claim that Nietzsche "was concerned with the artist, the philosopher, and those who achieve self-perfection. . . . [Those who] affirm their own being and all eternity, backward and forward, have no thought of tomorrow." *Nietzsche: Philosopher, Psychologist, AntiChrist,* 4th ed. (Princeton: Princeton University Press, 1974), p. 322. Echoes of this reading can be found in Alexander Nehamas, *Nietzsche: Life as Literature* (Cambridge: Harvard University Press, 1985), pp. 136–137; Leslie Paul Thiele, "The Agony of Politics: The Nietzschean Roots of Foucault's Thought," *American Political Science Review* 84, 3 (September 1990): 913; and Bonnie Honig, *Political Theory and the Displacement of Politics* (Ithaca: Cornell University Press, 1993), p. 231.

tive life. Artists are a "productive" species-type "to the extent that they actually alter and transform" (WP 585a). This broad aesthetic impulse is characteristic of higher human beings, for "the strong, the mighty want to form" (WP 941). To Zarathustra, "man is formlessness, material, an ugly stone which requires the sculptor" (EH IX, 8). His "ardent, creative will" drives him "again and again . . . to mankind . . . [I]t drives the hammer to the stone" (ibid.; cf. Z II, 2).

As the capacity to create and transform includes the ability to work on, shape, order, and organize human beings, it is unsurprising that Nietzsche construes politics as aesthetic activity. Barbarians "who come from the heights: [are] a species of conquering and ruling natures in search of material to mould" (WP 900). We are told that the violent beginnings of the polity were forged by men "who can command, . . . who [are] by nature 'master,' . . . who [are] violent in act and bearing. . . . Their work is an instinctive creation and imposition of forms; they are the most involuntary, unconscious artists there are. . . . [T]hey exemplify that terrible artists' egoism" (GM II, 17). Nietzsche refers to their "artists' violence" and to "those artists of violence and organizers [*Gewalt-Kunstlern und Organisatoren*] who build states" (ibid.; GM II, 18).[5] Discussing the power the great man feels over a people, he speaks of the desire "to give a single form to the multifarious and distorted" (WP 964).

Nietzsche's general claim that the great man is "always intent on *making* something out of" the people he comes into contact with is illustrated by Caesar and Napoleon, who work "on their marble, whatever the cost in men" (WP 962; WP 975). Confucius, Napoleon, and the *Imperium Romanum* are numbered as the "great artists of government so far" (WP 129). Christians, by contrast, are castigated as "not high or hard enough for the artistic refashioning of *mankind*" (BGE 62). Nietzsche envisages one "with . . . some divine

---

5. As Julian Young writes, "art, in short, is . . . *action*. Nietzsche's activist vocabulary for talking about artists—he refers to them as *creators, makers, doers, violators* and as *rapists* (TI IX, 8)—continually emphasizes this. And it is this perspective on the artist that provides the basis for inclusion of conquerors and builders of states and empires among the ranks of 'artists.'" *Nietzsche's Philosophy of Art* (New York: Cambridge University Press, 1993), p. 121. Cf. Peter Berkowitz, *Nietzsche: The Ethics of an Immoralist* (Cambridge: Harvard University Press, 1995), p. 88.

hammer in his hand" reacting to the sight of the distorted humanity wrought by Christianity by wailing, "Was this work for your hands! How you bungled and botched my beautiful stone!" (ibid.).

These remarks abundantly illustrate Nietzsche's broad notion of the aesthetic and his thinking about grand politics as aesthetic activity. Indeed, he imagines the goal of redeeming the human species from its current decline as the ultimate artistic project. His "higher concept of art" encompasses the "artist-philosopher," and he wonders how such a man "can place himself so far distant from other men that he can form them" (WP 795). The time is coming "when politics will have a different meaning" [*wo man über Politik unlernen wird*], and Nietzsche sees a master race of the future working "as artists upon 'man' himself" (WP 960).

Politics as Architecture

In light of passages such as paragraph 287 of *Beyond Good and Evil*, which underline the importance of the quality of motivation in the determination of nobility, many recent commentators follow Kaufmann's conclusion that Nietzsche "does not write to endorse a course of action" and that his "primary concern is not with particular actions."[6] However, the stress on the importance of motive need not entail a neutral stance toward the content and outcome of actions. Many passages illustrate Nietzsche's view that an individual's worth depends on the quality of his life's work and that his identity derives partly from his deeds. Simply thinking about oneself in a certain way cannot create self-transformation; this can occur only when actual behavior is attended to and life projects altered. Nietzsche dismisses the belief that "mere evaluation should produce

6. Kaufmann, *Nietzsche: Philosopher, Psychologist, AntiChrist*, p. 248. Cf. Tracy Strong's assertion that Nietzsche does not concern himself with "actual behavior" in his *Friedrich Nietzsche and the Politics of Transfiguration*, expanded ed. (Berkeley: University of California Press, 1988), p. 13; cf. p. 91. Similar claims are made by Nehamas in *Nietzsche: Life as Literature*, p. 203. Berkowitz's Nietzsche locates nobility not in actions but in "the self-knowledge of the noble soul." *Nietzsche: The Ethics of an Immoralist*, p. 252; cf. p. 255.

'works'" as "unnatural." Instead, "one must practice deeds, not strengthening of one's value-feelings" (WP 192; cf. WP 210). Part of the definition of nobility is "that one constantly contradicts the great majority not through words but through deeds" (WP 944). Becoming what one is requires the discharge of talents and toughness "in works and actions" (HAH 263). The power of actions to define identity also appears in Nietzsche's condemnation of Christians, for they do not engage "the *works* which Jesus demanded" (WP 191; cf. A 38).

Nietzsche thus parallels his *Rangordnung* of higher and lower humans with a hierarchy of deeds: superior individuals perform praiseworthy actions, the mediocre and contemptible engage in base activity. This explains why his complaints about the decrepit condition of the human species are accompanied by claims such as the following: "How few 'works' for the sake of which life on earth is worth while! And alas no more 'deeds' whatever!" (WP 395).

What, for Nietzsche, characterizes a great deed? This same passage from the *Nachlass* refers to "*great* works that have remained and not been washed away by the waters of time," which illustrates his focus on formal properties of fine action such as its ambition and long-term scope (ibid.). The doer of great deeds possesses the will to create things of lasting value. "It must seem bliss to you," remarks Zarathustra to an imagined comrade, "to press your hand upon the millennia as upon wax, / bliss to write upon the will of millennia as upon metal"(Z III, 12, 29). When it comes to politics, Nietzsche endorses Machiavelli's claim that "the great goal of statecraft should be *duration*, which outweighs everything else" (HAH 224).

Nietzsche's model for those farsighted artists who strive to create works that endure is the architect: "The most powerful men have always inspired architects; the architect has always been influenced by power. Pride, victory over weight and gravity, the will to power, seek to render themselves visible in a building; architecture is a kind of rhetoric of power, now persuasive, even cajoling in form, now bluntly imperious" (TI IX, 11). In the modern world, however, the human type based on the architect [*der Baumeister*] has been superseded by that based on the actor [*der Schauspeiler*], with baneful consequences:

The strength to build becomes paralyzed; the courage to make plans that encompass the distant future is discouraged; those with a genius for organization become scarce: who would still dare to undertake projects that would require thousands of years for their completion? For what is dying out is the fundamental faith that would enable us to calculate, to promise, to anticipate the future in plans of such scope, and to sacrifice the future to them—namely, the faith that man has value and meaning only insofar as he is *a stone in a great edifice*. (GS 356)

Nietzsche follows Machiavelli and Aristotle by likening the work of the master legislator to that of the architect. The task of the greatest architects resembles that of founders of constitutions who aim at "[eternalizing] a grand organization of society, the supreme condition for the prosperity of life" (A 58). This approach is most evident in his immense admiration for the political and constitutional achievements of ancient Rome. "Nobody stronger and nobler has yet existed on earth" in large part because of the Romans' audacity to enact plans for social and political engineering that were millennial in scope (GM I, 16; cf. A 38). They established institutions so sturdy as to survive "the accident of persons" (A 58). Nietzsche marvels at the development of a "most grandiose form of organization . . . in comparison with which everything before and everything since is patchwork, bungling, dilettantism" (ibid.). The *Imperium Romanum*, "this most admirable of all works of art in the grand style, was a beginning, its structure was calculated to *prove* itself by millennia—to this day there has never been such building, to build in such a manner *sub specie aeterni* has never been so much as dreamed of!" (ibid.; cf. D 71).

Nietzsche bemoans the subversion of the impressive Roman structure by the Christian table of values and its hostility toward the political. Faced with the Roman edifice of institutions and practices, Christians could only ask, "What is the point of public spirit, what is the point of gratitude for one's descent and one's forefathers, what is the point of co-operation, trust, of furthering and keeping in view the general welfare? . . . So many 'temptations,' so many diversions from the 'right road'" (A 43). The political quietism of Paul is also condemned: "There is nothing more false or deceitful in the world," declares Zarathustra, than to say, "'Let him who wants to slaughter and kill and harass and swindle the people; do not raise a finger against it! Thus they will yet learn to renounce the world'" (Z III, 12, 15).[7] Paul, we are informed, drew his followers from an "absolutely unpolitical and withdrawn species of *little people*" (WP 175). Once it gained popularity, the Christian ideal proved destructive of the political and social because it

> detaches the individual from people, state, cultural community, jurisdiction; it rejects education, knowledge, cultivation of good manners, gain, commerce—it lets everything go that comprises the usefulness and value of man. . . . Unpolitical, anti-national, neither aggressive nor defensive—possible only within the most firmly ordered political and social life, which allows these holy parasites to proliferate at public expense. (WP 221; cf. WP 204, 211)

Christians are "parasites" who focus on otherworldly goals while living off the political-architectural achievements of lofty-minded, worldly others, even as they denigrate the achievements of the latter as "vainglory." A modern political movement like the French Revolution is "the daughter and continuation of Christianity," for one of the things it inherits is the Christian devaluation of politics, which "destroy[s] the instinct for a grand organization of society" (WP 184, 90). The pervasive influence of Christianity on political thought and action helps to explain why Nietzsche finds so much to condemn in the politics of modernity: "No one any longer possesses today the courage to claim special privileges or the right to rule, . . . the courage for a *pathos of distance*. . . . Our politics is *morbid* from this lack of courage!" (A 43; cf. WP 212).

In what he sees as a vital first step in the establishment of the "thousand year empire" envisioned by Zarathustra, Nietzsche exhorts his imagined readers to overthrow this antipolitical Christian

---

7. Nietzsche echoes the criticism of Christian quietism advanced by Machiavelli in *The Discourses* II.2 and Rousseau in *The Social Contract*, IV. 8. As we shall see below, however, Nietzsche follows Machiavelli (but not Rousseau) in deeming Christian quietism wholly appropriate for the mass of ordinary people.

and post-Christian mindset and to recapture the sort of political will that gripped the ancient Romans. The latter owed their achievement to the fact that their political vision and ambition were matched by their will, and Nietzsche hopes that this same quality of will could one day manifest itself again in Europe. "Europe would have to . . . acquire a single will by means of a new caste dominating all Europe, a protracted terrible will of its own which could set its objectives thousands of years ahead" (BGE 208; cf. BGE 212, 213). Thus Nietzsche's insistence that "strength of the will" be listed as part of the "preparation for becoming the legislators of the future, the masters of the earth" (WP 132).

The Most Comprehensive Responsibility

Nietzsche's occasional talk of a healthy form of "selfishness" would seem at first glance to suggest that his nobles have obligations only to themselves and their self-perfection. However, obligation toward the self and obligation to others need not be mutually exclusive; rather, his preferred index of value and rank concerns "how *far* one could extend one's responsibility" (BGE 212). Nietzschean nobles instinctively seek heavy responsibilities, and it is considered a sign of nobility not to want to "relinquish or share our own responsibilities" (WP 944; BGE 272; cf. BGE 213).[8] The majority of human beings are, by contrast, "weak and growing weaker in . . . responsibility" (WP 898).

Nietzsche's political vision cannot be understood apart from this notion of the highest types' responsibility. Among the proper cares and concerns of free spirits is whether leaders who can sustain the weight of responsibility for transvaluing modern democratic political

---

8. Bernard Williams notes that "it has been in every society a recognizable ethical thought . . . that one can be under a (moral) requirement . . . simply because of who one is and of one's social situation." *Ethics and the Limits of Philosophy* (Cambridge: Harvard University Press, 1985), p. 7. Nietzsche resurrects the spirit of ancient moral philosophy in this regard. (This is no way means that Nietzsche thinks higher human beings ought to be responsible for the security and well-being of their ostensible inferiors. Chapter 7 explains why.)

values will emerge and endure (BGE 203). Nietzsche compares the highest men of the future to Caesar or Napoleon, for they too must "bear the *greatest responsibility* and *not* collapse under it" (WP 975).[9] As we noted in Chapter 2, this "most comprehensive responsibility" entails a concern not simply with the spiritual self-perfection of superior individuals but with the fate of the species as a whole (BGE 61). Nietzsche's politics is therefore driven by the conscience his new philosophers will share for a particular kind of creative activity: "the collective evolution of mankind" (ibid.).

Nietzsche's new dispensation reverses the way in which the welfare of the great is currently interwoven with that of the many. Whereas under the democratic status quo those with the potential for greatness are beholden to and bound up with (and held down by) the many, Nietzsche's new politics would require that the majority of ordinary human beings be restored to their proper place in the social order. It must be realized that society is justified "only as a foundation and scaffolding upon which a select species of being is able to raise itself to its highest task and in general higher existence" (BGE 258; cf. BGE 126; WP 679, 681, 898, 997). As *The Genealogy* decrees, "mankind in the mass sacrificed to the prosperity of a single *stronger* species of man—that *would* be an advance" (GM II, 12).

It is, therefore, the responsibility of the few to restore this proper balance to social and political organization and to appreciate that the mass is there to serve them in their quest for heightened nobility. They must grasp and act upon the fact that "this homogenizing species requires a justification: it lies in serving a higher sovereign species that stands upon the former and can raise itself to its task only by doing this" (WP 898).

9. Robert Solomon, by contrast, suggests that Nietzsche's philosophy "does not talk about 'responsibility' or 'authenticity.'" Introduction to *Reading Nietzsche*, ed. Robert C. Solomon and Kathleen M. Higgins (New York: Oxford University Press, 1988), p. 10. Laurence Lampert is closer to the mark when he argues that *Beyond Good and Evil* "is a book that assigns the greatest responsibility to the philosopher as one who knows what religions are good for, who knows how to order the politics of fatherlands, who commands and legislates how the world ought to be, and who has the whole future of mankind on his conscience." *Nietzsche's Teaching: An Interpretation of "Thus Spoke Zarathustra"* (New Haven: Yale University Press, 1987), p. 247.

Commanding and Obeying

Nietzsche's catalogue of complaints about contemporary politics includes the almost complete ignorance of "the art of commanding" [*des Kunst des Befehlens*] (BGE 213; cf. BGE 203). Worse still is the way this art is discredited and disavowed, even by those who exercise power:

> The herd instinct of obedience has been inherited best and at the expense of the art of commanding. If we think of this instinct taken to its ultimate extravagance there would be no commanders or independent men at all; or, if they existed, they would suffer from a bad conscience and in order to be able to command would have to practise a deceit upon themselves: the deceit, that is, that they too were only obeying. This state of things actually exists in Europe today. (BGE 199)

Nietzsche thus imputes to the noble personality a traditionally political capacity—the ability to rule. Sometimes this is coupled with the ability to be ruled, echoing Aristotle's belief that citizens of the polis should be able to command and obey.[10] At other times, however, only the capacity to command is seen as vital to higher types and the art of obeying is relegated to inferiors. In a fragment from 1887, for example, Nietzsche lists the "will and capacity to command" along with the will to power and to enjoyment as features of "the relatively strong and well-turned-out type of man (those in whom the grand effects were still unbroken . . .)" (WP 98).[11]

Following the classical view, Nietzsche requires the capacity to rule others to be coupled with that for self-rule: the new aristocracy is "based on the severest self-legislation" (WP 960). The truly sover-

10. Aristotle, *The Politics*, II, 2, 1261a22; III, 4. Nietzschean echoes of the Aristotelian dictum "to rule and be ruled in turn" are found in GS 283; BGE 251; WP 912 and 918.

11. Nehamas characteristically depoliticizes the Nietzschean capacity to command by rendering it self-reflexive and confining it to the personal realm. For him, "the question whether one is or is not a genuine philosopher is just the question whether one can indeed command and legislate, whether one can fashion a life of one's own." "Who Are 'The Philosophers of the Future'?: A Reading of *Beyond Good and Evil*," in Robert C. Solomon and Kathleen M. Higgins, eds., *Reading Nietzsche* (New York: Oxford University Press, 1988), p. 65.

eign individual is acutely aware of how his "mastery over himself also necessarily gives him mastery over . . . all weaker-willed and less reliable creatures" (GM II, 2; cf. Z II, 12). And just as the great individual is capable of command, so the inability to command is characteristic of the herd: "Small spirits must *obey*—hence cannot possess *greatness*" (WP 984). Such types can only evince a "herd instinct of obedience" and show a crude appetite for direction that "accepts whatever any commander—parent, teacher, law, class, prejudice, public opinion—shouts in its ears" (BGE 199; cf. WP 279).

Nietzsche is even audacious enough to contend that lower-order human beings would be better off submitting to the domination of their betters. Once again echoing Aristotle, Nietzsche claims that the natural slave-type "needs someone who will use him" (A 54). In a liberal-democratic society this need is frustrated and regrettably leads to the majority's perversion. Encouraged by an ambient democratic culture to forswear a natural, healthy instinct of deference to one's betters, the herd develops distasteful character traits, notably "untoward intemperance," "narrow enviousness," and "a clumsy obstinate self-assertiveness" (BGE 264; cf. A 57). Democratic ideology has become so much a part of mainstream common sense that all implicit knowledge of rank order and of the "need" of the weak-willed for "a master, a commander," is lost (BGE 242). "The mob," observes Zarathustra, "does not know what is great or small, what is straight and honest" (Z IV, 13, 8).[12] Encouraged to think of themselves as no worse than anyone else and as capable of anything, the lower orders succumb to what he refers to as the "evil falsity" of willing beyond one's powers (ibid.). Democratic reformers think they are working in the best interests of the majority, but in fact they accomplish the opposite: "He who makes the lame man walk," intones Zarathustra, "does him the greatest harm: for no sooner can he walk than his vices run away with him" (Z II, 20).[13]

12. Nietzsche sees his own compatriots as particularly damaged in this regard: "In the end the Germans have no idea whatever how common [*gemein*] they are; but that is the superlative of commonness [*der Gemeinheit*]—they are not even *ashamed* of being mere Germans" (EH XIII, 4).

13. Mark Warren rightly observes that Nietzsche "registers occasional sympathy for the working classes." *Nietzsche and Political Thought* (Cambridge: MIT Press,

Nietzsche's proposed hierarchical political order redeems the plebeian in the plebeian, allowing the mass to evince the "herd virtues" [*Heerdentugenden*] of which they are capable:

> That which is available only to the strongest and most fruitful natures and makes their existence possible—leisure, adventure, disbelief, even dissipation—would, if it were available to mediocre natures, necessarily destroy them—and actually does. This is where industriousness [*Arbeitsamkeit*], rule [*die Regel*], moderation [*die Mäßigkeit*], firm "conviction" [*die fest "Überzeugung"*] have their place—in short, the "herd virtues." (WP 901; cf. WP 356)

The inferior, untalented individual would be liberated of all unrealistic hopes (along with their attendant disappointments and resentments) and would at last follow the path that Zarathustra associates with (lower-order) virtue: "Thus speaks virtue: 'If you must be a servant, then seek him whom you can serve best'" (Z II, 8).

Thus the natural slave would flourish—in his own limited manner—in and through service to his master: "'Thus you yourself will thrive with your lord's spirit and virtue!'" (ibid.). In a properly ordered society the natural slave finds an intrinsic satisfaction in the fulfillment of his or her limited capacities: "To be a public utility, a cog, a function," claims Nietzsche, is a "natural vocation" or a "kind of *happiness* of which the great majority are alone capable, which makes intelligent machines of them. For the mediocre, it is happiness to be mediocre" (A 57).

Modernity's Self-Overcoming

Despite his very real concern that higher human beings will not heed his call and will remain in the grips of a servile false consciousness,

---

1988), p. 224. I would argue, however, that his sympathy stems not from any feeling of solidarity with them but rather from his reading of how egalitarian ideas and political movements have perverted their originally docile psyches.

Nietzsche believes that the seeds for their ascendancy are being sown within the liberal-democratic order itself. One of democracy's unintended consequences is a general weakening of the people's will, which increases the opportunities for strong-willed individuals to command. The majority's descent into nihilism "brings to light the weaker and less secure among them and thus produces an order of rank according to strength, from the point of view of health: those who command are recognized as those who command, those who obey as those who obey" (WP 55).

What is required for realizing the potential inherent in this situation is that the new elite hearken to Nietzsche's urgings and "employ democratic Europe as their most pliant and supple instrument for getting hold of the destinies of the earth" (WP 960; cf. WP 898). Without subscribing to any doctrine of historical inevitability, he remains hopeful that they will do so:

> I have as yet found *no* reason for discouragement. Whoever has preserved, and bred in himself, a strong will, together with an ample spirit, has more favorable opportunities than ever. For the trainability of men has become very great in this democratic Europe; men who learn easily and adapt themselves easily are the rule: the herd animal, even highly intelligent, has been prepared. Whoever can command finds those who *must* obey; I am thinking, e.g., of Napoleon and Bismarck. The rivalry with strong and unintelligent wills, which is the greatest obstacle, is small. (WP 128; cf. WP 898, 956)

Thus Nietzsche discerns a double movement in democratization: while weakening the majority, it creates circumstances propitious for "the breeding of *tyrants*—in every sense of that word, including the most spiritual" (BGE 242).

Along with democratization, Nietzsche identifies the burgeoning industrial and commercial culture as creating enabling conditions for a new elitist order.[14] Far from oblivious to economic change and its

14. This issue is more thoroughly discussed in the middle period than in the later works, although as we shall see it does not vanish altogether. Pertinent middle-period passages include HAH 585; WS 218, 220, 278–280, 283, 288; D 175, 186, 308; GS 21, 31, 42, 188.

salience for politics, as some contend,[15] Nietzsche applauds industrialization for its transformation of "mankind into a machine" (WP 866). His endorsement stems not from an enthusiastic embrace of the ethos of capitalism—Nietzsche never lost his aristocratic disdain for the rampant materialism and "indecent and perspiring haste" of his era[16]—but rather from a belief that industrialism generates the large caste of "weak-willed and highly employable" types required to facilitate the leisure of a higher-order elite (BGE 242; cf. HAH 439).

Modern industrialism, in other words, provides the "new slavery" required for Nietzsche's "new order" (GS 377). "Every strengthening and enhancement of the human type," he insists, "also involves a new kind of enslavement" (ibid.; cf. BGE 257). Nietzsche speaks not simply of enslaving manual laborers, but also of exploiting the expertise of the specialized technician and scientist. "The *ideal* scholar" possessing "the scientific instinct" is deemed "one of the most precious instruments there are" who "belongs in the hand of one more powerful" (BGE 207).

The problem with capitalist industrialism, for Nietzsche, has been the "lack of noble manners" of the employers, whose sudden accumulation and ostentatious, vulgar display of wealth seem to call into question the very idea of a natural rank order, thereby lending credence to egalitarian ideologies. The spectacle of the vulgar industrialist leads the factory worker to think "that it is only accident and luck that have elevated one person above another. Well then, he reasons: let *us* try accident and luck! let us throw the dice! And thus socialism is born" (GS 40). But while casting a disapproving glance at "the notorious vulgarity of manufacturers with their ruddy, fat hands" (ibid.), Nietzsche applauds their relegation of the majority to

15. Keith Ansell-Pearson claims that Nietzsche "ignored the changed conditions of work through modern industrialized production." *An Introduction to Nietzsche as Political Thinker* (Cambridge: Cambridge University Press, 1994), p. 214. Karl Löwith writes similarly of Nietzsche's "lack of concern for social and economic questions." *From Hegel to Nietzsche*, trans. David E. Green (London: Constable, 1965), p. 176.

16. D Preface 5. Cf. HAH 285; D 203, 204; GS 21, 40; BGE 189; WP 943. Nietzsche's criticisms of the worship of money cast doubt on Nancy Love's claim that his ideal of a leisured elite is bourgeois and thus an ideological support for capitalism. Love, *Marx, Nietzsche, and Modernity* (New York: Columbia University Press, 1986), pp. 18, 189, 200. It is more likely that his model is the ancient slave economy.

"intelligent machines" who "exist for service and general utility and . . . *may* exist only for that purpose" (A 57; BGE 61).[17]

However, this evocation of the need for a new, industrial form of slavery subverts Nietzsche's own occasional endorsement of a stoic notion of noble self-sufficiency. The autarchic ideal, already problematized by Nietzsche's stress on the importance of friendship, recedes even further when he speaks of how a mastery over "all more short-willed and unreliable creatures" is part and parcel of the noble type's self-mastery (GM II, 2). Nietzschean self-sufficiency ultimately succumbs to the superior type's need for lower individuals as "steps" to tread upon in the ascent toward the summit of human development (Z II, 7; cf. BGE 259). In the words of Zarathustra, "must there not exist that which is danced *upon*, danced across? Must there not be moles and heavy dwarfs—for the sake of the nimble . . .?" (Z III, 12, 2).[18]

Mastering Christianity

When Nietzsche declares that "it is the intrinsic right of *masters* to create values," a nonpolitical reader such as Nehamas interprets this to mean that Nietzschean philosophers of the future could only be concerned with themselves "and perhaps a few others like them" (BGE 261).[19] To subdue the herd politically, he reasons, would entail subsuming both the herd and the elite under the same set of values. Nietzsche, given his concern for maintaining a "pathos of distance" between castes, could look upon such a prospect only with distaste. Hence, concludes Nehamas, those preoccupied with value creation must remain completely uninterested in politics.

17. Apart from its infrastructural role of making leisure possible for the elite, manual labor also has the salutary effect of dulling the pain that necessarily attends the inferiority of the majority (GM III, 18). Of course, any kind of specialized (and especially manual) labor is totally unsuited for those with noble sensibilities (A 57, WP 943).

18. Keeping this in mind helps us interpret comments such as the following: "We must think of the masses as unsentimentally as we think of nature: they preserve the species" (WP 760). Such passages call into question Tracy Strong's insistence that Nietzsche's masters and slaves do not depend on each other in any way. *Friedrich Nietzsche and the Politics of Transfiguration*, p. 353.

19. Nehamas, "Who Are 'The Philosophers of the Future'?" p. 57.

We need not follow Nehamas and other Nietzsche scholars in adhering to this familiar "either-or" scenario—either the *Übermenschen* as value creators are completely disengaged from the herd or they must mix higher and lower together by creating one overarching set of values for all. It would be more fruitful to pursue another possibility: that a key aspect of the Nietzschean elite's hegemony is the power to prescribe different values for different sections of society. Even as he calls upon those like him to move "beyond good and evil," Nietzsche "demand[s] that herd morality . . . be held sacred unconditionally" (WP 132). His elite would not only create new values but would also respect Zarathustra's observation that "small people" need "small virtues" (Z III, 5, 2). Nietzsche's new rulers would endorse some existing values—including Christian ones—insofar as they serve to legitimate the new elite's rule in the eyes of the many. Thus in a Nietzschean polity, Christianity would not become completely obsolescent.[20]

There is no shortage of passages in the Nietzschean opus where Christianity joins nihilism, democracy, and industrialization as a force inadvertently preparing the way for the rise of a new elite. Consider, for example, the admission in Nietzsche's notebooks that although "we good Europeans . . . are atheists and immoralists, for the present we support the religions and moralities of the herd instinct: for these prepare a type of man that must one day fall into our hands" (WP 132). Anticipating the future tasks of the philosopher-ruler, *Beyond Good and Evil* acknowledges the need to "make use of the religions for his work of education and breeding, just as he will make use of existing political and economic conditions" (BGE 61). The strategic value of religion is further underlined when Nietzsche defines it as "one more means of overcoming resistance so as to be

---

20. *Pace* Nehamas's claim that "the view that Christianity and its morality have outlived their usefulness runs through the whole of Nietzsche's later work." Ibid., p. 60. Karl Löwith shares this view of Christianity's utter obsolescence in a Nietzschean polity when he suggests that "the new masters of the earth shall 'replace God' for the unbelieving masses." *From Hegel to Nietzsche*, p. 262. When Ansell-Pearson complains that Nietzsche's political vision is bereft of any account of how his new political organization will be justified to the ruled, he similarly assumes that Nietzsche's pronouncement of the death of God prevents his new elite from using religion to legitimate itself. See *An Introduction to Nietzsche as Political Thinker*, pp. 42–43, 51, 153–158.

able to rule: a bond that unites together ruler and ruled and betrays and hands over to the former consciences of the latter" (ibid.).

Nietzsche thus considers a central question in the history of political thought—how religion can be used to the advantage of the powerful and in the service of the best social order (HAH 472). This becomes especially apparent in a fragment noting that "moralities and religions are the principal means by which one can make whatever one wishes out of man, provided one possesses a superfluity of creative forces and can assert one's will over long periods of time—in the form of legislation, religion and customs" (WP 144). Some of the virtues Christianity promotes in the mass of people could be useful for future rulers. As a "herd religion," it "teaches obedience. . . . Christians are easier to rule than non-Christians" (WP 216). Future rulers might "patronize and applaud" this faith because it fosters in the mass "virtues that make their subjects useful and submissive" (ibid.). Nietzsche is highly cognizant of the fact that

> a doctrine and religion of "love," of *suppression* of self-affirmation, of patience, endurance, helpfulness, of cooperation in word and deed, can be of the highest value within such classes [of decaying and atrophying people] even from the point of view of the rulers: for it suppresses feelings of rivalry, of *ressentiment*, of envy—the all too natural feelings of the underprivileged—it even deifies a life of slavery, subjection, poverty, sickness, and inferiority for them under the ideal of humility and obedience. (WP 373)

As noted in Chapter 2, moreover, Nietzsche believes that the mass of ordinary people need religion—specifically, Christianity—both as a solace for suffering and as a rationale for obedience (GS 347). It can give meaning to their mediocrity by providing servility with "the appearance of a virtue" that is "quite astonishingly beautiful" (HAH 115; cf. WP 216). From Nietzsche's political vantage point, then, Christianity has redeeming features. His call to superior types to acknowledge God's death and to overcome Christian values does not, therefore, preclude Christianity from fulfilling a civic function by inculcating obedience in the masses. Nietzsche outlines the proper role of religion in *Beyond Good and Evil*, arguing, as Hobbes does, that it is strictly for the use of the rulers—they are not to be ruled by it: "It costs dear and terribly when religions hold sway, not as a means of education and breeding in the hands of the philosopher, but in their own right as *sovereign*, when they themselves want to be final ends and not means beside other means" (BGE 62).[21]

The obvious objection to Christianity playing even an instrumental role in a Nietzschean politics of the future is that while it teaches obedience, it also preaches the "equality of souls"—an article of Christian faith Nietzsche repudiates incessantly.[22] Given its premise of fundamental human equality because of equal worth before God, Christianity would seem an unsuitable ideology for the sort of highly stratified and unequal political organization Nietzsche promotes. This emphasis on equality destroys the pathos of distance so essential for the resurgence of nobility.

However, the idea that equality in the eyes of God must be translated into secular equality—into equality before the law and equal rights—is a particular, modern reading of Christianity. While liberal philosophers such as John Locke, Mary Wollstonecraft, and Alexis de Tocqueville grounded their arguments for secular equality in such Christian ideas, not all adherents of Christianity have inferred an imperative to secular equality. In the history of Christian-influenced political thought, it has been argued to the contrary that precisely because all individuals are, as God's creatures, essentially equal, their worldly status is of little or no importance.[23] A form of Christianity could serve as a doctrine legitimating hierarchical rule in a transvalued future—provided that it did not demand some form of secular equality.

21. Ronald Beiner argues cogently that "Nietzsche is entirely faithful to the modern tradition of civil religion as set forth by Machiavelli, Hobbes and Rousseau." Beiner, "George Grant, Nietzsche, and the Problem of a Post-Christian Theism," in *George Grant and the Subversion of Modernity*, ed. Arthur Davis (Toronto: University of Toronto Press, 1996), p. 126.

22. Passages where Nietzsche associates Christianity with the doctrine of human equality include BGE 62, 202, 219; GM III, 14; TI IX, 37; A 43, 46, 57; and WP 684 and 898.

23. See St. Augustine's *City of God*, XIX, 12, 15 and Luther's "On Secular Authority" in *Luther and Calvin on Secular Authority*, ed. and trans. Harro Höpf (Cambridge: Cambridge University Press, 1991). The writings of Sir Robert Filmer (d. 1653) constitute another example of the marriage of Christian faith and belief in social and political hierarchy. See Filmer, *Patriarcha and Other Writings*, ed. Johann P. Sommerville (Cambridge: Cambridge University Press, 1991).

Thus despite his many virulent attacks on Christianity and its legacies for modern Europe, Nietzsche does not insist that it be jettisoned. Christianity could have a place in a transvalued future, but a much more chastened and circumscribed one than it currently occupies: "The ideas of the herd should rule in the herd—but not reach out beyond it; the leaders of the herd require a fundamentally different valuation for their own actions" (WP 287). Rulers need not believe in the truth-claims of a lying religion that they grant to the all-too-human.

Plato's Perfect State

The structure of Nietzsche's envisioned political order can be described as two concentric circles, with an inner circle of higher human beings surrounded by a much larger circle representing a majority population that is both subordinate to the ruling minority and instrumental for its continued flourishing.[24] It is important to note that Nietzsche's main interest is in fact in the inner circle. However important the subjugation of the majority may be to the sustenance of elite activity, the "main consideration" is "not to see the task of the higher species in leading the lower . . . , but the lower as a base upon which [the] higher species performs its *own* tasks—upon which alone it can stand" (WP 901). Nietzsche envisages and tries to inspire "not merely a master race whose sole task is to rule, but a race with its own sphere of life, with an excess of strength for beauty, bravery, culture, manners to the highest peak of the spirit, an affirming race that may grant itself every great luxury" (WP 898).

If, however, Nietzsche's vision is that of a "master race" with "its own sphere of life," how could he also countenance its political rule over inferiors? The answer becomes clearer when the parallel between Nietzsche and Plato on this question is considered. Plato declared in *The Republic* that if the finest human beings refused to rule

24. This section takes issue with Bernard Williams's suggestion that Nietzsche has "no coherent set of opinions" about how politics ought to be organized in the modern world. *Shame and Necessity* (Berkeley: University of California Press, 1993), pp. 10–11.

their inferiors they would be ruled by them, a sentiment Nietzsche evinces when he observes "with anguish and contempt the politics of present-day Europe, which is, under all circumstances, also working at the web of the future of *all* men" (WP 367). Since the politics of herd society has a corrosive effect on human excellence, oppressing those of potentially great talent and stature, the latter should create a politics more in keeping with their needs.

In light of Nietzsche's vilification of Socrates and his identification of Platonic metaphysics with the "slave revolt" in morals it may seem strange to argue for the resemblance of Nietzsche's imagined political order to Plato's ideal *polis*. As others have noted, however, Nietzsche's view of Socrates/Plato is not entirely negative.[25] His greatest difficulty with Plato relates to the latter's notion of the Forms, which is rooted in a metaphysical realist framework that, as we first noted in Chapter 1, Nietzsche resolutely rejects. As far as Plato's politics are concerned, however, their unapologetic elitism and authoritarianism are heartily embraced.[26]

One element of *The Republic* to which Nietzsche is particularly drawn is the notion of a martial class of "guardians" whose function is to insulate the inner circle of nobles from the majority plebeian class.[27] This is especially apparent in *The AntiChrist*, where he evokes the prospect of a "predominantly spiritual type" [*die vorwiegend Geistigen*] directing a "predominantly muscular and temperamental type" that in turn would relieve the former of "everything *coarse* in the work of ruling" [*alles "Grobe" in der Arbeit des Herrschaft*] (A 57). Nietzsche's suggestion that the management of "mediocre types" be delegated to an intermediary buffer class can be explained by his belief that the close proximity of the higher to the lower would be noxious for the former.

---

25. See, for example, Nehamas, *Nietzsche: Life as Literature*, pp. 24–34, and Berkowitz, *Nietzsche: The Ethics of an Immoralist*, p. 45.

26. As early as the 1872 essay "The Greek State," Nietzsche makes admiring comments about "Plato's perfect state" [*Der vollkommne Staat Platos*]. See "Der griechische Staat," *Werke: Kritische Gesamtausgabe*, ed. Georgio Colli and Mazzino Montinari, 30 vols. (Berlin: de Gruyter, 1967–197⁰) III, 2:258–271, and his discussion of Plato in the essay "Schopenhauer as Educator" in the collection *Untimely Meditations* (SE 8).

27. *The Republic* III, 412c–421c.

A higher human type in close quarters with the herd, as we noted in Chapter 3, is always in danger of being "sucked dry" by the parasitical majority. Hence the imperative of maintaining a form of apartheid between master and slave types. A "master race" at its highest level of development simply cannot remain preoccupied with the mundane tasks involved in ruling over inferiors. In this context Nietzsche refers approvingly to the Indian caste system, singling out the Brahmins as an admirably disciplined order that "have themselves the power of nominating their kings for the people, while keeping and feeling themselves aside and outside as men of higher and more than kingly tasks" (BGE 61; cf. TI VII, 3).

This division of labor between different types of political rule—between the self-rule of higher-order peers and the rule over inferiors—also recalls Aristotelian political philosophy. Aristotle, we recall, associates the best type of rule with a politics conducted among free, self-governing men and contrasts it with the despotic rule over slaves or slavelike persons, who, for whatever reason (innate deficiencies, economic deprivation, etc.), cannot govern themselves.[28] Nietzsche similarly deems the kind of rule "over select disciples or brothers" to be best and "most refined," whereas the direction of the larger community of unequals is said to require a cruder form of rule, "the *necessary* dirt of all politics" [*dem "notwendigen" Schmutz alles Politik-Machens*] (BGE 61).

Nietzsche believes that this "dirty" type of rule over inferiors should be structured by "the entire administration of law [*Recht*]" which would serve as a crucial tool in the efforts of the rulers to subdue the mob's "reactive feelings" (GM II, 11). As it was in the aristocratic societies of antiquity, so it should be in the future: rulers must use "the institution of law" [*die Aufrichtung des Gesetzes*] "to impose measures and bounds upon the excesses of the reactive pathos and to compel it to come to terms" (ibid.). This, he proffers, is entirely consistent with the claims of justice, for wherever it "is practiced and

28. "All the different kinds of rule are not, as some affirm, the same as each other. For there is one rule exercised over subjects who are by nature free, another over subjects who are by nature slaves." Aristotle, *The Politics*, I, 7, 1255b16–17. Cf. 1253 a20–24; 1160a10–b32; 1295b18–22; 1324b31–35.

maintained one sees a stronger power seeking a means of putting an end to the senseless raging of *ressentiment* among the weaker powers that stand under it" (ibid.).

The just political order is therefore one in which the vast majority is regulated by stringent legal codes. This is as it should be, for law is an instrument in the power struggle among social forces and is one of the most valuable tools in the hands of the artist-tyrant: "Law-giving moralities are the principal means of fashioning man according to the pleasure of a creative and profound will, provided that such an artist's will of the first rank has the power in its hands and can make its creative will prevail through long periods of time, in the form of laws, religions and customs" (WP 957).

The Political Agon

While countenancing the use of law for the purpose of disciplining the majority, Nietzsche is highly critical of liberal democracies for their insistence that systems of law must apply to and constrain everyone—even the strongest and most vital. Especially galling to him is the notion that everyone is a bearer of natural, inalienable rights and thus deserving of respect.[29] The universal application of such egalitarianism is "*hostile to life*, an agent of the dissolution and destruction of man" because it works to the advantage of the morbidly weak, those who have conspired together to secure rights in order to enjoy "security, safety, comfort and an easier life for all" (GM II, 11; BGE 44). In Nietzsche's view, the complementary notions of "equal rights" and "the rule of law" have been employed historically by the inferior as devices for controlling the strong: "One speaks of "equal rights"—. . . as long as one has not yet gained superiority one wants to prevent one's competitors from growing in power" (WP 86; cf. WP 80). The weak have always had an interest

29. In arguing thus, I draw upon Ruth Abbey's paper, "In a Similar Voice: Nietzsche on Rights," presented to the Annual Meeting of the American Political Science Association, Chicago, August 1995.

in perpetuating the idea that rights are fixed—"a sacred, immutable state of affairs" (WS 39)—rather than fluid, contingent manifestations of power.[30]

In light of his view, expressed in *Beyond Good and Evil*, *The Genealogy*, and *Zarathustra*, that struggle, domination, injury, violence, and appropriation are inescapable features of existence, one can see why Nietzsche prefers to look upon all rights as provisional "conquests" of the strong (WP 120).[31] In his imagined political order, higher human beings are "beyond the law" [*Jenseits des Rechts*] in the sense that their negotiations and struggles with others are not artificially constrained by an independent juridical system of rights and entitlements (GM II, 10).[32] On the contrary, everything is based on merit and remains perpetually open to negotiation, contestation, and struggle. Instead of equal rights for all, Nietzsche proposes a vision of a minority inner circle composed of those who are "equal-in-rights" [*Gleichberechtigen*] in virtue of sheer ability (BGE 265). This is the meaning of the Nietzschean *agon*.

The *agon* thus plays as central a role in Nietzschean politics as it does in his understanding of friendship. In an early essay entitled "Homer's Contest" (1872), he argues that the institutionalized competitions of the Greek *agon* provided a constructive outlet for the potentially destructive wills of competitors, thereby preserving Greek community life and fostering its high culture. Casting his eyes to the future, Nietzsche wishes to foster a space of contest and rivalry with a similar function. "Who can command, who can obey—*that is experimented here!*" (Z III, 12.25). The experimentation must be constant and never-ending, for one of the basic characteristics of Nietzsche's higher individuals is their burning desire to rule. "The best shall rule," proclaims Zarathustra, "the best *wants* to rule! And where it is taught differently, there—the best is *lacking*" (Z III, 12, 21).

30. This view, also on offer in D 112 and HAH 93, casts doubt on Warren's contention that in his middle period Nietzsche looked favorably on "political cultures that include equal rights." Warren, *Nietzsche and Political Thought*, p. 72.

31. See BGE 259; GM II, 11; and Z III, 12, 10.

32. Detwiler notes Nietzsche's "repudiation of all legalistic approaches to political thought" in his *Nietzsche and the Politics of Aristocratic Radicalism*, p. 192.

Whereas all variants of slave morality hypocritically discourage and disparage the desire for rule, Nietzsche's *agon* tosses all hypocrisy aside in favor of an open and honest "lust for power" [*Herrschsucht*] (Z III, 10, 2). When evinced by the loftiest of men, such a desire scarcely warrants the appellation "lust": "Lust for power: but who shall call it *lust*, when the height longs to stoop down after power! Truly, there is no sickness and lust in such a longing and descent!" (ibid.). The open clash of competing wills to power in the aristocratic inner circle is, for Nietzsche, a thing of beauty.

Whatever tentative, provisional stability there is in this agonistic inner circle is the result not of any notion of "social contract" but rather of the relative equality or equilibrium of strength and virtue that leads to a guarded sense of mutual respect and recognition.[33] Like the nobles of antiquity, Nietzsche imagines his higher types constraining themselves through "custom, respect, usage, gratitude, and even more by mutual suspicion and jealousy" as well as with "consideration, self-control, delicacy, loyalty, pride, and friendship" (GM I, 11; cf. GM II, 2). In a sociopolitical context of relative equality, noble types would quite naturally "exchange . . . honors and rights" and consider it "good manners" [*guten Sitten*] to refrain "from mutual injury, mutual violence, mutual exploitation" (BGE 265; BGE 259). Given the agonistic nature of this community of rivals, however, any social peace would be tentative and temporary, repeatedly giving way to challenges and contests of an unspecified nature.

With respect to this inner circle, then, Nietzsche proposes replacing the juridical state and its allegedly small-minded rules and regulations with a self-policing community of outstanding individuals. Impartial legal codes would be replaced by the self-governing instincts of those who design their own punishments for breaking promises and other infractions. Zarathustra evokes this Rousseauian scenario of a self-policing citizen-legislator when he claims that "when he [the living creature] commands himself . . . also must he

33. See GM II, 17. Zarathustra similarly decries as "soft-hearted" the view that society is a contract (Z III, 12, 25). Contractarianism is the likely target when he claims elsewhere that the demand for "oaths instead of looks and hands" reveals a contemptibly "timid mistrustfulness" (Z III, 10, 2).

make amends for his commanding. He must become judge and avenger and victim of his own law" (Z II, 12).[34]

This state of affairs, we should recall, applies only to the inner circle. What of the mass of ordinary people, subjected to the laws of an elite that itself is exempt from the rule of law in the conventional sense? In the final chapter we turn to the lot of the majority in a Nietzschean polity. Would the noble sensibility of their betters be enough to save them from oppression?

34. In his middle period Nietzsche advances a similar picture of a transgressor who "calls himself to account and publicly dictates his own punishment, in the proud feeling that he is thus honoring the law which he himself has made, that by punishing himself he is exercising his power, the power of the lawgiver" (D 187; cf. D 437). Ansell-Pearson perceives the Rousseauian nature of this passage in his *Nietzsche contra Rousseau: A Study of Nietzsche's Moral and Political Thought* (Cambridge: Cambridge University Press, 1991), p. 215.

_s e v e n_   **The Evil of the Strong**

Noblesse Oblige

As we have just seen, Nietzsche rejects the view that the mass of ordinary human beings have inalienable rights and legal recourse against their betters. In his ideal polity there is no right "that is not supported by the power of enforcement" (WP 120). Whereas noble types may well have obligations toward themselves and their peers, they owe nothing at all to the majority and have complete license to act toward them as they think best (GM II, 2; WP 943). There is no such thing as committing acts of "justice" or "injustice" toward the many-too-many, for "justice can be hoped for

. . . only *inter pares* [among equals]" (WP 943; GM I, 11; cf. WP 926). Against this background it is hard to avoid imaging a scenario in which lesser types are trampled on by their superiors.

Those inclined to dismiss such a scenario often try to deflect concern by pointing to Nietzsche's repudiation of overt, malicious cruelty.[1] Their case seems strong at first glance, for Nietzsche does evince an undeniable repugnance for the idea of lording it over an inferior. As early as *Daybreak*, he writes that it is only the "evil of the weak" [*das Böse der Schwäche*] that "*wants* to harm others and to see the signs of the suffering it has caused" (D 371). From the standpoint of nobility, the idea of gratuitous cruelty toward those clearly inferior in strength is abhorrent: "An easy prey is something contemptible for proud natures" (GS 13). Only vulgar pretenders to virtue take advantage of their positions of power to "scratch out the eyes of their enemies with their virtue"; in Zarathustra's words, they "raise themselves only in order to lower others" (Z II, 5). Elsewhere Zarathustra teaches us to "mistrust all in whom the urge to punish is strong" (Z II, 7). He identifies the effort to inflict pain and suffering with bitter resentment and deems it a form of "despotism" [*Gewalt-Herrischen*] that is the antithesis of nobility (Z III, 12, 11).

Clearly, the flaunting of one's superior position through malicious torment of the abjectly vulnerable would be in the worst possible taste. We have already seen, moreover, that Nietzsche is more inclined to counsel disengagement from vulgarity than active engagement with it. Being "prickly toward small things," in Zarathustra's view, is but "the wisdom of a hedgehog" (Z III, 5, 2).

When contact with inferiors is unavoidable, a measured politeness is sometimes recommended. Zarathustra claims to exemplify such politeness "towards every small vexation," and Nietzsche insists

1. Alexander Nehamas, for example, argues that "Nietzsche's 'immoralism' is not the crude praise of selfishness and cruelty with which it is often confused." *Nietzsche: Life as Literature* (Cambridge: Harvard University Press, 1985), p. 167; cf. p. 216. In a passage that wonderfully encapsulates a core assumption of the popular "progressive" reading of Nietzsche, Alan White invites us to be "as charitable to Nietzsche as to Aristotle: let us grant that those who are most noble, admirable and self-affirming will not attempt to exploit others." *Within Nietzsche's Labyrinth* (New York: Routledge, 1990), p. 130. Bonnie Honig cites this passage approvingly in "The Politics of Agonism," *Political Theory* 21, 3 (August 1993): 533.

in his own voice that his "nature" directs him to be "mild and benevolent towards everyone" and "full of consideration for the basest
people" (ibid.; EH XIII, 4; EH II, 10). The noble type also reveals
his magnanimity by restraining all signs of annoyance at the *canaille*
and maintaining a lofty forbearance. "There is often more bravery in
containing oneself and passing by," suggests Zarathustra, "*in order* to
spare oneself for a worthier enemy!" (Z III, 12, 21; cf. GS 276).

There is a distinct echo of ancient moral philosophy in this stress
on moderation and forbearance in one's interactions with inferiors.
Aristotle also speaks of how the *megalopsuchos* believes that "an attempt to be impressive among inferiors is as vulgar as a display of
strength against the weak."[2] And when Nietzsche praises mercy
[*Gnade*] as the "privilege of the most powerful man," he seems to
evoke the memory of Seneca's influential tract for the young emperor Nero, "On Mercy" (GM II, 10). Like Seneca, Nietzsche believes that the gentleness with which an exceptional human being
handles those under his power is a duty (A 57). But whereas Seneca
(and Aristotle) crucially speak of the duty of princes towards their
charges,[3] the more radically elitist Nietzsche insists that higher types
cannot be accountable to inferiors in any way. They are bound only
by duties to themselves, to their own sense of good taste, and to
those equal in power and stature.[4]

Nietzsche assures us that in a new order under the control of well-
bred, high-spirited types with natures that "are the antithesis of the
vicious and unbridled," complete confidence can be invested in their
tact, judgment, and good taste (WP 871). They can be trusted not to
abuse their absolute freedom, for they possess a "dominating spiritu-
ality" that "put[s] a check on an unrestrained and irritable pride or a
wanton sensuality" (GM III, 8). Their disciplined selves evince a hatred of *laisser aller*, of "blind indulgence of an affect," which is con-

2. Aristotle, *Nicomachean Ethics*, 1124b22–23.

3. In "On Mercy," 14.1, Seneca likens the duties of the prince to those of "good
parents," which evokes the notion of strong emotional and ethical bonds. *Seneca:
Moral and Political Essays*, ed. and trans. John M. Cooper and J. F. Procopé (Cambridge: Cambridge University Press, 1995), p. 146.

4. Peter Berkowitz similarly contends that the Nietzschean nobleman's politeness
toward inferiors is rooted in "considerations of enlightened self-interest." *Nietzsche:
The Ethics of an Immoralist* (Cambridge: Harvard University Press, 1995), p. 120.

demned as "the cause of the greatest evils" (BGE 188; WP 928). Nietzsche explains that although the noble self is "a tremendous multiplicity," full of passionate intensity and creative impulse, it is "nonetheless the opposite of chaos" and is tightly bound in a disciplined manner (EH II, 9). In the language of his early essay *The Birth of Tragedy*, the exceptional man's protean substratum of Dionysian energy is given form and order by an Apollonian discipline.

Yet despite this stress on self-discipline and aristocratic disdain for malicious cruelty, the mass of ordinary people in a Nietzschean polity might still have reason for grave concern about their personal safety. The violence that could well befall them would have less to do with malicious cruelty than with thoughtless, destructive behavior issuing from the self-absorbed higher type's creative experimentation.

Violence and the Second Innocence

As noted in the previous chapter, Nietzsche suggests that the potentially violent drives of the exceptional men in his aristocratic *agon* are, for the most part, tightly controlled in order to maintain a sense of mutual respect and tenuous order. *The Genealogy* reveals, however, that the "constraints and conventions" of an agonistic society of equals create a great psychological tension which cries out for sporadic release. This is illustrated in *The Genealogy*'s first essay, which depicts the ancient warriors' need for brief periods of respite from the *agon*'s self-imposed rigor, periods in which their "hidden core" [*verborgenen Grund*] would be allowed to "erupt" (GM I, 11). Temporarily liberated from the constraining discipline of their peers, these innocent, high-spirited men found themselves in a state of nature–like "wilderness" and set about purging their inner tension by metamorphosing into "triumphant monsters" [*frohlockende Ungeheuer*] bent on a "disgusting procession of murder, arson, rape, and torture" (ibid.). Thus purged, they rejoined the *agon* "exhilarated and undisturbed of soul," as if their violent savagery "were no more than a students' prank" (ibid.).

A sympathetic account of this unleashing of murderous destruction during periods of respite also appears in *Ecce Homo*'s brief, idiosyncratic comments on evil in the Bible. There it is suggested that the serpent in the garden of Eden is none other than God "recuperat[ing] from being God" (EH X, 2). The Almighty, we are informed, "had made everything too beautiful. . . . The Devil is merely the idleness of God on that seventh day" (ibid.). Having created a perfect world that seemed to require no further improvement, the divine creative will, unable to discharge its strength in further creation, turned its instincts toward destruction and mischief-making.[5]

Although the era of the "blond beast" is gone forever, Nietzsche appears intent on encouraging something like a modern analogue to his beast of prey–like "innocent conscience" [*die Unschuld des Raubtier-Gewissens*] (GM I, 11). Such an analogue is suggested in *The Genealogy*'s second essay, where Nietzsche evokes the prospect of a postreligious, noble "second innocence" [*zweiter Unschuld*] (GM II, 20). Only when the Christian legacy of guilt and self-abnegation is purged will the modern type be free, as Nietzsche claims elsewhere, to innocently, joyfully "do things that would convict a lesser man of vice and immoderation" (WP 871).

In Nietzsche's view, there is simply no comparison between this sort of instinctive need to purge creative tension and the violence unleashed by a malicious, vulgar character who enjoys lording it over the weak and defenseless. While the latter is clearly in bad taste, the former—described in a felicitous middle-period passage as the "evil of the strong" [*das Böse der Stärke*]—is positively life-affirming (D 371). Nietzsche considers it an innocent form of cruelty because (in his view) the higher type simply cannot do otherwise. As a concatenation of drives and instincts, a product of forces beyond his conscious control, the exceptional man is "a piece of fate" (TI VI, 8; cf. TI V, 6).

In light of this strong streak of fatalism one must qualify the previous chapter's claim that Nietzsche associates nobility with responsibility. Whereas he hopes to galvanize his higher men into feeling responsible for raising the species as a whole, he also wishes to dissuade them from feeling responsible in any way to ostensibly inferior

5. Cf. Bruce Detwiler, *Nietzsche and the Politics of Aristocratic Radicalism* (Chicago: University of Chicago Press, 1990), p. 167.

human beings. Indeed, in his account the path to species improvement entails a willful disregard of any accountability to the majority.

To berate innocent nobles for their lack of consideration or remorse would betray an adherence to the same slave morality that attempts to engender shame and bad conscience in noble types for their essentially healthy instincts and inclinations. As Nietzsche claims in *The Gay Science*, the feeling of remorse [*die Reue*] when "something goes wrong" as a result of one's actions is appropriate only for servile types who "have received orders and . . . have to reckon with a beating when his lordship is not satisfied with the result" (GS 41). In place of shame, guilt, and vacillating self-doubt, Zarathustra prefers his sort of men to be "shameless" [*Schamlosen*] and impervious to attacks of conscience (Z II, 4).[6] Once purged of all guilt and mendacious systems of belief, noble souls are expected to affirm unconditionally their every instinct; they implicitly understand that "all instincts are holy" and "follow [their] own senses [*Sinne*] to the end" (Z I, 22, 2; Z II, 2). A "complete automatism of instinct," after all, is "the precondition for any kind of mastery, any kind of perfection in the art of living" (A 57; cf. BGE 287).

Apart from the destructive venting of built-up tension, Nietzsche evokes a complementary scenario just as likely to perturb the safety of the many: the prospect of "collateral damage" caused by the creative activity of those obsessively self-absorbed and oblivious to anything but the task at hand. As I argued in the previous chapter, one of Nietzsche's favorite images of his new sort of political actor is that of the creative sculptor hammering away at the "formless" material that is modern humankind. Absorbed in his work, the sculptor does not care if, in the midst of his creative rage, stone fragments are sent flying in all directions: "What is that to me?" asks Zarathustra, as fragments fly from the blows of his "raging hammer" (Z II, 2; cf. EH IX, 8).[7] And if the fragments strike unfortunate innocents who happen to be in their path? Nietzsche's likely answer is found in the *Nachlass:* "One must learn to sacrifice *many* and to take one's cause seriously

6. "From what one *hears* of it, a pang of conscience [*Gewissensbiß*] does not seem to me anything respectable. I should not like to leave an act in the lurch *afterwards*" (EH II, 1).

7. Eric Blondel interestingly discusses other forms of hammer imagery in Nietzsche's work—e.g., the hammers that "sound out idols" and reveal them as hollow in

enough not to spare men" (WP 982). Any suffering produced as a by-product of creative activity is of little consequence compared to the grandeur of the artist's *oeuvre*.[8]

The possibility of widespread havoc that could be wreaked innocently is also evoked in the course of Zarathustra's descriptions of the "overflowing" nature of the highest sort and of the need for sudden releases of the flow. Virtue has "its origin and beginning" in the "surging" of a heart "broad and full like a river" that is both "a blessing and a danger to those who live nearby" (Z I, 22, 1). Further on, the metaphor of the surging river is complemented by that of a raging storm: Zarathustra's "happiness and freedom," we are told, come "like a storm" that may be mistaken by his "enemies" for a great evil (Z II, 1). In part IV, moreover, we learn that the "laughing storm" that is Zarathustra's free-spirited nature has a tendency to "blow dust" in the eyes of "the dim-sighted and ulcerated" (Z IV, 13, 20). Once again, aggression toward an inconsequential plebeian element is shrugged off as the inevitable, ancillary product of the inner workings of creativity.

Sublimation of Cruelty?

That Nietzsche even countenances such innocent cruelty in a transvalued future is resisted by those who argue that Nietzschean self-

---

the foreword to *Twilight of the Idols*. Holding an unreservedly benign view of Nietzsche, he insists that "the least important use assigned by Nietzsche to the hammer is that of the destruction of mass." Blondel, *Nietzsche, the Body, and Culture: Philosophy as Philological Genealogy*, trans. Sean Hand (Stanford: Stanford University Press, 1991), p. 106. For a similar attempt at deflecting attention away from Nietzsche's more violent hammer imagery, see Laurence Lampert, *Nietzsche and Modern Times: A Study of Bacon, Descartes, and Nietzsche* (New Haven: Yale University Press, 1993), pp. 401–402.

8. Nietzsche's exceptional men bear a striking resemblance to Hegel's "world-historical individuals" in this respect. In his lectures on the philosophy of history, Hegel describes how "so great a figure" who "commits himself unreservedly to one purpose alone" must "necessarily trample on many an innocent flower, crushing much that gets in his way." *Introduction to the Philosophy of History*, trans. Leo Rauch (Indianapolis: Hackett, 1988), p. 35. This parallel, of course, has its limits: unlike Nietzsche's higher human beings, Hegel's world-historical individuals are unwitting servants of the unfolding *Geist*. My thanks to Brian Walker and Ruth Abbey for calling my attention to the parallel.

overcoming involves the sublimation of the cruel, savage impulses of primitive humanity. Kaufmann, for example, suggests that Nietzsche approves of the transformation of overt violence toward others into a "spiritualized" cruelty toward oneself.[9] Nietzsche's comments in *Beyond Good and Evil* and elsewhere on the sublimation and "spiritualization" [*Vergeistigung*] of cruelty as preconditions for modern "high culture" are said to illustrate his abhorrence of anything like the oppression found in ancient warrior societies. Nietzsche's brand of cruelty, concludes Kaufmann, is concerned exclusively with "the individual's attitude toward himself" and involves "man's conquest of his impulses, the triumph of reason and—in one word—self-overcoming."[10]

It would be a mistake, however, to assume that a description of a historical process implies an endorsement of it. When we recall Nietzsche's assertion that a "sweetening and spiritualization" [*Versüßung und Vergeistigung*] is "virtually inseparable" from an "extreme poverty of blood and muscle," it would seem at least possible that the author of *Ecce Homo* is not nearly as enamored with modernity's sublimations as recent commentators would have us believe (EH I, 1). Nietzsche does indeed associate the sublimation and interiorization of cruelty with the rise of "high culture" in Europe, if by "culture" we mean the development and increasing sophistication of the arts and letters, and science and technology. But he never considered *this* high culture to be "high" in the sense of noble or lofty; on the contrary, it is often referred to depreciatingly as *Zivilisation* and compared unfavorably with an idealized realm of *Kultur*, that is, a truly noble sphere of human achievement. Nietzsche imagines himself to be clearing the path for a true cultural revitalization in this second sense of the term: "Only after me are there again hopes, tasks, prescribable paths of culture [*vorzuschreibende Wege der Kultur*]" (EH XII, 2).[11]

---

9. Walter Kaufmann, *Nietzsche: Philosopher, Psychologist, AntiChrist*, 4th ed. (Princeton: Princeton University Press, 1974), p. 228.

10. Ibid., p. 246. Similar views are expressed in Richard Schacht, *Nietzsche* (London: Routledge and Kegan Paul, 1983), pp. 276, 331, and Nehamas, *Nietzsche: Life as Literature*, pp. 217–218.

11. Blondel notes that for Nietzsche, "*Kultur* and *Zivilisation* are opposites from the point of view of values: the former implies the 'noble' values of an intellectual or

While it is certainly true that Nietzsche dismissed as nostalgic nonsense the prospect of a return to the unreconstructed "blond beast" of antiquity, part of his pedagogical-therapeutic project involves urging his imagined readers to throw off the unmanly "taming" of their instincts perpetrated by those civilized purveyors of "intolerance against the boldest and most spiritual natures" (WP 121).[12] In *The Genealogy* we are told that although the "thirst for cruelty" [*Lust an der Grausamkeit*] of yesteryear remains with us moderns, it lingers only in a debased form under the weight of centuries of feminizing spiritualization and sublimation (GM II, 6). Previously, one openly and honestly took pleasure in seeing cruelty inflicted upon others: "Without cruelty there is no festival: thus the longest and most ancient part of human history teaches" (ibid.). In modern times, by contrast, our pleasure in cruelty perversely requires "a certain sublimation and subtilization [*Sublimierung und Subtilisierung*], that is to say it has to appear translated into the imaginative and psychical and adorned with . . . innocent names" (GM II, 7). Hence the tartuffery of a modern culture that has tamed the animal "man" in part by convincing him to repudiate his still intense love of cruelty (GM II, 6; GM II, 7).[13]

The Inhuman and the Superhuman

Nietzsche believes that the human species as a whole will advance only when its most perfect exemplars conduct themselves in accordance with "Dionysian pessimism" and unconditionally embrace an

---

spiritual end, while the latter is linked to the pejorative appreciation of realizations considered 'simply' material." *Nietzsche, the Body, and Culture*, p. 42.

12. The association of *Zivilisation* with the domestication of higher natures is further highlighted in WP 871: "Struggling 'civilization' (taming) needs every kind of irons and torture to maintain itself against terribleness and beast-of-prey natures."

13. Schacht seems to acknowledge Nietzsche's view of the deleterious effects of "sublimation" on the will to power when he notes that Nietzsche deems it "a form of 'sickness' in relation to the 'healthy animality' of a kind of life governed by an undisrupted, smoothly functioning and comprehensive instinct-structure." *Nietzsche*, p. 277; cf. pp. 389, 434. But he hastens to add that Nietzsche "is far from supposing that the latter is inherently preferable to it" (p. 277).

eternal, "terrible" truth: the inescapably violent, cruel nature of life (GS 370). Speaking admiringly of the ancient Greek tragedians for their recognition of "everything terrible, evil, cryptic, destructive and deadly underlying existence," Nietzsche lauds their tragedies for laying bare the fearfulness of reality (BT Preface 4; cf. EH XIV, 4). Philosophers in later, Hellenistic Greece are taken to task for having turned away from this important lesson and thus for precipitating their culture's decline (BT Preface 1). A society that turns its back on this hard truth, that sublimates and spiritualizes the cruelty implicit in existence and embraces an "optimistic, superficial [oberflächlicher], . . . logical interpretation of the world" is already in decline and doomed to go under at the hands of rival cultures still honest and courageous enough to embrace the truth (BT Preface 4; cf. BGE 257). Nietzsche, for his part, does not want his kindred spirits to make the mistake of the Hellenistic Greeks. "Terribleness is part of greatness" [Zur Größe gehört die Furchtbarkeit], he intones in his notebooks, "let us not deceive ourselves" (WP 1028).

Once in touch with their deepest inclinations and instincts, Nietzsche's higher men will come face to face with primordial evil and violence within themselves. It is no accident that the exceptional man's exploration of his inner "depths" is described repeatedly as an encounter with an inner core of dreadfulness and evil. "Evil [das Böse]," claims Zarathustra, "is a man's best strength. . . . The most evil is necessary for the Superman's best" (Z IV, 13, 5). The same point is made in part III, where Zarathustra declares that "the wickedest in man is necessary for the best in him . . . [A]ll that is most wicked [Böseste] in him is his best strength and the hardest stone for the highest creator" (Z III, 13, 2; cf. Z I, 19). Part of what it means to attain the heights of normative-spiritual development is to discover an especially hard truth: that growing "better" also means growing "wickeder," that "man is beast and superbeast; the higher man is inhuman [Unmensch] and superhuman [Übermensch]: these belong together" (Z III, 13, 2; WP 1027; cf. GM I, 16). The Genealogy speaks similarly of the "unstable equilibrium between 'animal and angel'" within all "well constituted, joyful mortals" (GM III, 2).

The "pale criminal" of the first part of Zarathustra is presented as a cautionary example of someone who had initially made this discovery—who took the initially courageous step of exploring and reveling in his noble, beastly side—but whose indoctrination in slave morality led him in the end to recoil and take flight from it. In a liberating, all-too-fleeting moment of mad blood-lust, the pale criminal committed an act of violence; his soul "wanted blood, not booty: he thirsted for the joy of the knife [*Glück des Messers*]!" (Z I, 6). In the immediate wake of the liberating act, however, the criminal's "simple mind," slavishly caught up in the dictates of plebeian morality and not wanting "to be ashamed of his madness," drew him back from his joyous reveling. "'What is the good of blood?'" he asks himself, suddenly taking a small-minded, utilitarian view of his action. "'Will you not at least commit a theft too? Take a revenge?'" (ibid.). Unable to imagine how the joyously performed act of violence could stand on its own, as a monument of passionate, innocent self-expression, the criminal then performs a base action—he steals—in a pathetic attempt to "justify" his violence.

Nietzsche's point seems to be that only one of refined sensibility and good breeding, fully in touch with his dark side, could see that the initial murderous attack is self-justifying. But for those of (or infected by) the herd, this deed could only make sense by being married to a vulgar act that ensures some sort of material "payoff." The pale criminal is thus a "heap of diseases" not because of his terrible, violent crime but because of a "simple-mindedness" unequal to his deed (ibid.).

Nietzsche longs for a society in which creative men no longer leave their actions in the lurch like the pale criminal. His free-spirited man joyfully embraces his "madness" and understands the "method" behind it (Z I, 7). Affirming one's dark side frees one from all vestiges of bad conscience and allows the healthy impulses free rein, whatever the destructive consequences. Only this type of society, moreover, would benefit the species as a whole, for "everything evil, dreadful, tyrannical, beast of prey and serpent in man [*alles Böse, Furchtbare, Tyrannische, Raubtier- und Schlangenhafte am Menschen*] serves to enhance the species 'man' [*zur Erhöhung der Spezies "Mensch" dient*]" (BGE 44).

Further on in *Beyond Good and Evil* Nietzsche becomes even more specific, noting that "certain strong and dangerous drives, such as enterprisingness, foolhardiness, revengefulness, craft, rapacity, [and] ambition," while today calumniated and stigmatized by mainstream morality, must be allowed full expression (BGE 201). In particular circumstances, as Zarathustra readily suggests, life-affirming *Jasagen* may require killing and stealing: "Is there not in all life itself—stealing and killing?" [*Ist in allem Leben selber nicht—Rauben und Totschlagen*] (Z III, 12, 10). To claim the contrary, warns Zarathustra, to place any universalistic legal or moral constraints on the actions of the highest sort, is to preach "a sermon of death" that contradicts and opposes all life (ibid.; cf.. GS 19).[14] In "the general economy of the whole," the unleashing of such potential destructiveness would be a far better thing than the maintenance of a safe and prudent humanitarianism: "The fearfulness of reality (in the affects, in the desires, in the will to power) are to an incalculable degree more necessary than any form of petty happiness, so-called 'goodness'; since the latter is conditioned by falsity of instinct one must even be cautious about granting it a place at all" (EH XIV, 4).

Nietzsche could not help but profess a grudging admiration for the audacity of an ascetic moral project that sublimates healthy drives and turns the psychic inner life of man into a "torture chamber" (GM II, 16). As I argued in Chapter 1, however, this grudging profession of respect for otherworldly asceticism hardly amounts to strong support. Nietzsche gestures toward the possibility of a cultural order that both permits and endorses outward forms of aggression with an openness and innocence of conscience that would outrage modern liberal democrats. And he would see their outrage as a sign that he was on the right track.

Against Pity

Although Nietzsche wants his higher men to maintain an empathetic connection with their kindred spirits, he calls upon them to resist the slide from empathy toward a softening, feminizing commiseration.

14. Passages such as these create difficulties for those who, like William Connolly, assume only "fools" think that the Nietzschean conception of nobility could sanction murder. Connolly, review of *Within Nietzsche's Labyrinth* by Alan White, *Political Theory* 29, 4 (November 1992): 705.

His disparaging treatment of pity can be explained partly by his view of the deleterious consequences that expressions of pity have for a friend's spiritual development (see Chapter 4). To pity a friend is to both insult and mollycoddle him: mollycoddle, because the comforting gestures of the pitier invariably encourage the pitied to become reconciled to his weakness rather than overcome it; insult, because the very act of pitying presumes that the object of pity is vulnerable to misfortune, when in fact a truly noble type is capable of surmounting and mastering all fortune.

But this is only one side of Nietzsche's critique of pity. If commiseration is an inappropriate expression of empathy for one's equals, it is also seen as ill-advised toward inferiors. Wherein lies the danger of a higher human being showing pity for an inferior?

Nussbaum has reminded us how pity can serve to reconfirm and reinforce the view that both pitier and pitied are tied together by the bonds of their common humanity.[15] In pitying other human beings for misfortunes befalling them through no fault of their own, we acknowledge the fact of our own vulnerability—the fact that we could just as easily have fallen prey to a similar misfortune. Pity, in other words, "contains a thought experiment in which one puts oneself in the other person's place, and indeed reasons that this place might in fact be, or become, one's own."[16]

Nietzsche is all too aware of these cognitive and affective linkages and is deeply concerned that any pity for the weak and inferior would generate bonds of solidarity and commonality that would undermine the psychological distance and feeling of superiority he wishes to foster. In *Ecce Homo*, he candidly reveals that his "reproach against those who practice pity is that shame, reverence [*die Ehrfurcht*], a delicate feeling for distance [*das Zartgefühl vor Distanzen*] easily elude them" (EH I, 4). To pity the sufferings of the herd would be tantamount to forming an affective bond with them, leading the exceptional man down a slippery slope toward a disastrous identification of his vocation with the servicing of their needs and interests. As we have seen,

15. Martha Nussbaum, "Pity and Mercy: Nietzsche's Stoicism," in *Nietzsche, Genealogy, Morality*, ed. Richard Schacht (Berkeley: University of California Press, 1994), pp. 139–167.
16. Ibid., p. 157.

Nietzsche sees the free spirit's vocation as lying elsewhere, in a form of self-indulgence that is said to lead to the flourishing of the species as a whole. Hence the need to combat anything that would tear the noble type away from himself and those of his kind.

By relegating the vast majority of the human species to an inferior plane of existence, Nietzsche constructs a lofty imaginative space that remains impervious to the suffering of the many. Zarathustra's "mind and longing" "go [only] out to the few," to "the protracted, the remote things" (Z IV, 13, 6). As for the petty travails of the weak, his attitude is haughty and dismissive: "What are your many, little, brief miseries to me!" (ibid.). In light of his inability or unwillingness to recognize the common humanity he shares with these sufferers, Zarathustra reacts predictably. Indeed, the psychology that undergirds his arrogant imperviousness was outlined over a century earlier by Rousseau:

> Why are kings without pity for their subjects? Because they count on never being mere men. Why are the rich so hard towards the poor? It is because they have no fear of becoming poor. Why does the nobility have so great a contempt for the people? It is because a noble will never be a commoner.[17]

Because the talented men of Nietzsche's new order are taught to revel in their difference and superiority and to understand the eternal nature of the rank order, the likelihood of their ever feeling compassion for the majority is remote indeed. It would appear that those designated as *canaille* must make do with nothing more than Nietzsche's condescending promise of "gentleness" toward them. (*Bien entendu*, this is a promise the nobleman makes only to himself; it can always be overridden when the need for venting creative tension is felt.)

The pledge of a gentle stance toward the majority becomes even more tenuous in light of the naked contempt that Nietzsche's exceptional humans are expected to hold toward their inferiors. In and of themselves, "the great majority of men have no right to existence [*ohne Recht zum Dasein*]" (WP 872). Their right to exist is "a thou-

17. Jean-Jacques Rousseau, *Emile, or On Education*, trans. Allan Bloom (New York: Basic Books, 1979), p. 224. Nussbaum puts this passage to good use in "Pity and Mercy: Nietzsche's Stoicism," p. 144.

sand times" smaller than that of their noble betters, who embody the hope for the future perfectibility of humankind (GM III, 14).[18] This unbridled and shameless contempt undergirds Nietzsche's conviction that the mass of ordinary humans should be spared the rigors of the *agon*. Under the presumption that there is no "honest" [*rechtschaffenen*] duel between unequals, he declares that "where one despises [*verachtet*] one *cannot* wage war" (EH I, 7).

In marked contrast to his occasional tendency in the mid- to late 1870s to speak of "the human, all too human," the foibles of human beings as such, the mature Nietzsche deems the less-than-human majority to be unworthy opponents. In a particularly graphic reference to those whom he calls "teachers of submission," Zarathustra declares that "wherever there is anything small and sick and scabby, there they crawl like lice; and only my disgust [*mein Ekel*] stops me from cracking them" (Z III, 5, 3). In his eyes, the champions of slave morality who have been honored hitherto do not count "as belonging to mankind at all—to me they are the refuse of mankind [*Ausschuß der Menschheit*], abortive offspring of sickness and vengeful instincts" (EH II, 10).[19]

Retrieving the Fear of Man

Nietzsche claims that an open expression of fear and trembling at the sight of his omnipotent caste of self-aggrandizers would be an encouraging sign of social progress—a sign that reverence and respect for the human species had been reinstated on a wide scale. A passage from the

18. Cf. the third of Nietzsche's early (1874) "untimely meditations," "Schopenhauer as Educator": "The question is this: how can your life, the individual life, receive the highest value, the deepest significance? How can it be least squandered? Certainly only by your living for the good of the rarest and most valuable exemplars [*seltensten und wertvollsten Exemplare*], and not for the good of the majority, that is to say those who, taken individually, are the least valuable [*wertlosesten*] exemplars" (SE 6).

19. Like many recent Nietzsche scholars, Schacht chooses to "pass over Nietzsche's rhetorical excesses" because he believes that "dwelling upon them gets in the way of coming to terms with the substance of his philosophical thought." *Nietzsche*, p. xv. *Pace* Schacht, my view is that Nietzsche's "rhetorical excesses" shed important light on his basic politico-ethical stance and thus should be subjected to critical scrutiny.

middle period suggests that fear "has promoted knowledge of men more than love has" (D 309). Whereas love often leads us to erect false images of our beloved, visceral terror concentrates the mind and obliges us, for prudential reasons, "to divine who the other is, what he can do, what he wants" (ibid.). When the majority are in abject terror of the strong, in other words, the eternal truth of rank order is more likely to remain foremost in their minds. Zarathustra similarly comments on the desirability of plebeian fear: because the souls of the inferior—the "good and just"—are "so unfamiliar with what is great," it is a very good sign indeed if the higher man appears "fearful" [*furchtbar*] in their eyes (Z II, 21). If, on the contrary, the majority felt perfectly safe in his presence, something would be terribly wrong.

Indeed, in Nietzsche's view something *has* gone terribly wrong in modern Europe, where fear has been replaced with comfort, security, and the maxim "love thy neighbor." Lamentably, many "naïve peoples and men" have succumbed to "the pleasing effect produced by the 'good man' [*gute Mensch*] (—he arouses no fear [*er erweckt keine Furcht*], he permits one to relax, he gives what one is able to take)" (WP 386). The cultivation of the "good man" is but the flip side of the active persecution of the fearful, predator-type man, whose near extinction has resulted in a "diminution and leveling of European man" that Nietzsche claims is "*our* greatest danger" (GM I, 12). "Together with the fear of man," he insists, "we have also lost our love of him, our reverence for him, our hopes for him, even the will to him" (ibid.; cf. D 551; BGE 201).

Nietzsche believes that a social order dedicated to human greatness must involve a recovery of the healthy fear of one's betters. For him, the choice is clear: "Who would not a hundred times sooner fear where one can also admire than *not* fear but be permanently condemned to the repellent sight of the ill-constituted, dwarfed, atrophied, and poisoned?" (GM I, 11; cf. WP 91, 386). Zarathustra echoes this sentiment, declaring that he "would rather have noise and thunder and storm-curses than this cautious, uncertain feline repose . . . and uncertain, hesitating passing clouds" (Z III, 4). Elsewhere he insists that "petty thoughts" are far worse than cruelty: "Truly, better even to have done wickedly than to have thought pettily!" (Z II, 3).

Conclusion:

The Perils of Agonistic Politics

Compared with his often detailed critique of modern social, political, and cultural institutions and practices and his genealogical explanations of how they came to exemplify the qualities he despises, Nietzsche's sketch of what an agonistic politics of the future would look like is just that: a sketch. Exactly what his high-spirited warriors would fight over and what form their struggles would take are left undetermined. While this may seem to leave him open to the same criticism of emptiness leveled at a more recent philosophical champion of the *agon*, Hannah Arendt,[1] Nietzsche might respond that his task is not to prescribe in precise detail how his new philosopher-rulers should exercise power. Providing a de-

1. Hanna Pitkin, "Justice: On Relating Private and Public," *Political Theory* 9 (1981): 327–352.

tailed blueprint for political action would, in his view, be tantamount to showing disrespect for the agency of his free spirits.

However, even considering this steadfast refusal to provide firm, prescriptive rules for future conduct, the broad outlines of a Nietzschean agonistic politics are nevertheless clear. Nietzsche believes that a castelike society, offering unparalleled freedom and unending competitive challenges to the finest of men, is essential for revivifying the creative capacities of the species. Political action aimed at instituting the new order would put a stop to the centuries-old effort of "public opinion" to condition the finest specimens of humanity to serve the interests of the mediocre majority. Living in a sphere untainted by the close proximity of ordinary human beings, Nietzsche's high-spirited aristocrats would devote themselves to artistic-political achievement in an intensely competitive *agon*. Constrained only by a sense of respect for and gratitude toward their peers and focused on the contests and challenges at hand, they think nothing of using the mass as fodder for their creative enterprises. They also accept with equanimity the prospect of widespread destruction and loss of life that occur as a by-product of their innocent experimentation.

This model is pervaded with unresolved tensions. It is unclear, for example, how the long-term institutional stability so prized by Nietzsche could become a reality in light of his refusal to countenance any brake on the experimentation of his highest men beyond the restraints imposed by powerful rivals. In his unwillingness to consider the idea that a stable social and political order requires even the finest specimens of humanity to submit to a more systematic regime of discipline, Nietzsche compares unfavorably to Max Weber, his great successor in German social and political thought. Although Weber expressed some rather Nietzschean reservations about bureaucratic routinization—the process whereby the achievements of charismatic, innovative leaders are transformed into stable institutional forms—he at least took this phenomenon seriously and accepted (albeit unenthusiastically) the prospect of a tradeoff. Nietzsche cannot bring himself to do this; his aristocratic radicalism runs too deep. As a result, his avowed interest in a durable sociopolitical order is compromised. Another source of tension in Nietzsche's writing, as we have seen, is the lack of fit between his insistence upon the dependency of higher types on others (both friends/enemies and inferiors) for full human flourishing and his occasional evocation of a form of self-sufficiency incompatible with any form of sociability or dependency.[2]

Despite these difficulties, many contemporary philosophers and political theorists have been quick to reclaim the Nietzschean *agon* for egalitarian political purposes. Despite Nietzsche's repeated insistence that a natural hierarchy of human types is one of the unalterable "hard truths" of existence, they assure us that his aristocratic radicalism is but a readily detachable module in a broader, subversive philosophical project that could be pressed into service for radically democratic ends. His unmasking of the dishonesty, hypocrisy, and *ressentiment* of ruling classes and his insistence on the primacy of the political, of struggle and contestation, are seen as useful tropes for those interested in celebrating the fact of pluralism, diversity, and difference and—more specifically—championing the interests of the marginalized and disadvantaged.[3] Nietzsche's transfer into the camp of radical democracy, as already noted, is often expedited by collapsing his work into that of Foucault, whose well-known call for nonconformism and resistance to oppressive "normalization" render talk of the *agon* much more palatable for democratic sensibilities.

I remain skeptical, however, about recent theoretical efforts to reconcile a radical Nietzschean *agon* with egalitarian political aspira-

2. Those who take Nietzsche to be a forerunner of postmodern philosophy may well be tempted to dismiss such concerns for consistency by pointing to his alleged deconstruction of such "logocentric" categories. This view is difficult to reconcile with Nietzsche's belief that the *"fundamental will* of knowledge" of his ideal philosopher impels him to "demand. . . greater and greater precision." Philosophers of his sort demand consistency: they have "no right to *isolated* acts of any kind"; all of their "values," "yeas and nays," "ifs and buts . . . [are] evidence of *one* will, *one* health, *one* soil, *one* sun" (GM Preface 2).

3. Nietzsche is not the only radically antidemocratic modern thinker whose work has been deemed helpfully subversive by radical democrats. Mark Lilla has recently written of a similar attraction of opposites in the curious left-wing admiration for the Nazi-sympathizing constitutionalist Carl Schmidt. "In the view of some European leftists, Schmitt was a radical (if right-wing) democrat whose brutal realism can help us today to rediscover 'the political' . . . [H]is unabashed defense of the friend-enemy distinction is said to remind us that politics is, above all, struggle." See Lilla, "The Enemy of Liberalism," *New York Review of Books*, May 15, 1997, p. 42; cf. p. 39.

tions. The notion of unending struggle or competition has an undeniable appeal, of course, in particular, circumscribed fields of endeavor. Open-ended struggle does indeed have a salutary effect in many fields, from political philosophy to figure skating. The perpetual contestability of one's achievements and victories guards against complacency and keeps one on one's toes. Moreover, rough-and-tumble political struggle among and between individuals and groups will always remain an integral component of any democratic politics worthy of the name.

It is one thing to acknowledge the necessity of these circumscribed forms of struggle; it is quite another, however, to follow Nietzsche in celebrating a universalization of struggle, to posit perpetual contestation as a normative goal in itself. Those who do so in theory would have us believe that its actualization in practice would improve our democracy. The unending, unbounded nature of agonistic struggle, in this view, would guard against any imposition of a stultifying, permanent hierarchy. But is such a vision, once fully and consistently worked out, truly inimical to all forms of domination? Could it not conceivably lead to a debunking of key liberal-democratic verities—such as our notions of universal suffrage, equal respect, and human rights—even as it resists the establishment of a *permanent* structure of hierarchy?

Postmodern theorists, as good democrats, rightly (and thankfully) shrink from such imaginings. But their adherence to the contemporary democratic consensus reveals a crucial disjuncture between their bold rhetoric of unbounded struggle and their more constrained substantive politics. The theoretical call for a politics constituted by an "endless subversion of codes" is routinely belied by a humane, liberal-democratic willingness to attenuate the demands of one's will in the face of the wants and needs of others.[4] Political philosophers of previous ages were less reluctant to make sense of this willingness theoretically; John Stuart Mill, for example, claims that the moral su-

4. The phrase in quotation marks comes from Dana R. Villa, "Postmodernism and the Public Sphere," *American Political Science Review* 83, 3 (September 1992): 719. I should note that in this article Villa draws upon Foucault and Arendt, rather than upon Nietzsche, in his depiction of a postmodern politics.

periority of modern civilization lies in its successful inculcation of disciplined restraint—what he calls the "social principle"—in those of "strong bodies or minds."[5]

Postmodern political thinkers balk at this language, preferring a politics that resists all forms of discipline and "normalization." Millian talk of social discipline, in this view, is but a Trojan horse that carries within it a subtle, insidious form of domination and repression. And the fact that Mill evokes the need for discipline and civilization in order to justify the British imperialism of his time seems to strengthen the argument.

I am concerned, however, that a key insight is being lost when we dismiss Mill's views *in toto* because of his ideological implication in the nineteenth-century imperialist enterprise. Postmodern democratic theorists can make blithe assumptions about the benignity of a politics of struggle because they take for granted the (admittedly tenuous) moral and legal achievements of modern civilization.[6] Fragile though they are, they remain achievements; although it has become unfashionable to say so in contemporary political theory, it seems to me that one of liberal democracy's great historical achievements has been the establishment of institutional barriers that prevent the slide into the type of radically politicized competitive space for which

5. See "On Liberty," chapter 3, in John Stuart Mill, *On Liberty and Other Essays*, ed. John Gray (New York: Oxford University Press, 1991), p. 67. Mill, of course, was concerned that modern democratic societies were succeeding all too well in their constraint of individuality and spontaneity, and struggled to outline a vision of the political that would combine the necessity of disciplined restraint with the encouragement of forms of human excellence that would not endanger the public safety. Nietzsche, who in WP 30 dismisses Mill as a "flathead," was disdainful of *any* endorsement—however qualified—of modern civilization's "taming" of strong individuality.

6. See, for example, William Connolly's picture of a "politics of disturbance" in which "friends, lovers, and adversaries" restrain themselves in the end "through mutual appreciation of the problematical bases from which they proceed." Connolly, *The Ethos of Pluralization* (Minneapolis: University of Minnesota Press, 1995), p. 29. If this picture of self-restraint through radical self-doubt is at all attractive, it is due, to my mind, to a preexistent, taken-for-granted achievement of civilization. (I am thinking of something like Mill's social principle.) I argue this at greater length in "Agonism and Modernity" (paper presented at the annual meeting of the American Political Science Association, Boston, September 1998).

Nietzsche yearns. At their very best—sadly, an all-too-rare condition—liberal democracies provide protection and means of self-
betterment for society's most vulnerable members.[7]

Nietzsche is certainly correct in pointing out that the entrench-
ment of notions of universal and equal rights in liberal democracies
serves to inhibit the strong and aggressive. But if we subscribe to
some version of the egalitarian ideal,[8] should we not embrace what
Nietzsche decried about modern liberal democracies, namely that
they treat rights as something very different from the booty of
victors?

Competing Conceptions of the *Agon*

As I suggested above, it would be a grave mistake to denigrate the
role of contestation in liberal-democratic politics altogether. A
regime that takes individual and group rights seriously must include
an *agon* of sorts—although not of the Nietzschean variety. Once we
turn to the Western philosophical tradition in search of an ideal of
political contestation more in line with liberal-democratic sensibilities, Aristotle appears to be of much greater help than Nietzsche.
Seeing the former as an agonistic thinker of any sort has until recently been difficult in light of the popular "communitarian" association of Aristotle with communal harmony and shared understand-
ings. Fortunately, Aristotle has been wrenched out of his confining
role in the "liberal vs. communitarian" debates of the 1980s by those

7. Among the many contemporary political theorists who criticize the inability or
unwillingness of our governments to make good on these commitments are those who
argue that a truly just political order must make room for forms of political expression
not readily suited for agonistic competition—for example, the more tentative, concil-
iatory, and consensual forms that are often associated with the feminine. See, for example, Iris Marion Young, "Communication and the Other: Beyond Deliberative
Democracy," in *Democracy and Difference: Contesting the Boundaries of the Political*, ed.
Seyla Benhabib (Princeton: Princeton University Press, 1996), pp. 120–135.

8. Just why we subscribe to it is no idle question. As I argue below, a confrontation
with Nietzsche can provoke us into usefully articulating what all too often is considered self-evident: why we adhere to views about the equal moral worth of all human
beings.

who rightly highlight his clear-eyed countenance of perpetual political conflict in even the most stable regimes.[9] But what is it about Aristotelian agonism that makes it more promising to liberal-democratic eyes than the Nietzschean variety? Did not Aristotle also possess an aristocratic sensibility and build heavy elitist assumptions and a suspicion of democracy into his political models?

The aristocratic tastes and gestures of the Aristotelian *megalopsuchos* are undeniable, as is Aristotle's tendency to insist, like Nietzsche, that the perceptions and intuitions of the man of virtue should be looked upon as a yardstick.[10] However, the *megalopsuchos* is distinct from the Nietzschean *Übermensch* in one key respect: the former is not granted the absolute discretionary power that Nietzsche's exceptional man demands as his right. Even the best of us, argues Aristotle, can have our judgment distorted by personal interest and passion: "Desire is a wild beast, and passion perverts the minds of rulers, even when they are the best of men."[11] Hence the need for law, which, as a mechanism denuded of passion and particular attachments, ensures the constancy and stability required for the maintenance of public order. By declaring the rule of law to be "preferable to that of any individual,"[12] Aristotle tempers the *agon* in a manner unacceptable to the self-policing hubristic man of Nietzsche's fantasies.

At one point Aristotle does seem to toy with the prospect of spiritual and moral perfectibility when he imagines the discovery of an individual who is as far above other citizens in virtue as the gods are above mortals. Such a divine being, he concedes, should be exempt from all law and given absolute power.[13] Aristotle's skepticism is evident, however, in his conclusion that "since this is unattainable, and kings have no marked superiority over their subjects," all should submit to the law.[14] "In our own day," he observes, "men are more upon

9. See especially Bernard Yack, *The Problems of a Political Animal: Community, Justice, and Conflict in Aristotelian Political Thought* (Berkeley: University of California Press, 1993).
10. See, for example, Aristotle, *Nicomachean Ethics*, 1166a12–13; 1176a17–19.
11. Aristotle, *The Politics*, 1287a32.
12. Ibid., 1287a20.
13. Ibid., 1284a3–15; cf. 1332b15–20.
14. Ibid., 1332b22–30.

an equality, and no one is so immeasurably superior to others" as to warrant blanket exemption from the laws.[15]

Aristotle's refusal to seriously countenance the prospect of human perfectibility also leads him to suggest that the best *polis* would allow less talented citizens some share of political power. Whereas an all-powerful individual "is liable to be overcome by anger or by some other passion" and have his judgment perverted, the *demos* is "less easily corrupted" and can thus serve as a safeguard to good order.[16] Although as individuals "they may be worse judges than those who have special knowledge, as a body they are as good or better," provided, of course, they have not been "utterly degraded" by poverty, disease, and/or oppression.[17]

Nietzsche, by contrast, is much more inclined to maintain a lofty contempt for the less resourceful, insisting on their degradation as a self-evident fact and scornfully dismissing the poor taste of Aristotle's suggestion that the artist-legislator might have something to learn from those subject to his laws.[18] Nietzsche's artist-legislator, unlike Aristotle's, is an artist-tyrant who can accept challenges to his authority only from a select circle of peers. Whereas Nietzsche insists that respect for the dignity of humankind requires showing profound *disrespect* for the needs and wishes of the vast majority,[19] Aristotle maintains that there is something worthy of respect and admiration even in the lowliest. The talented and the less able, who can sustain a political friendship of shared interest in the Aristotelian *polis*, can experience only contempt and fear for each other in the community envisioned by Nietzsche.

15. Ibid., 1313a6–9.
16. Ibid., 1286a32–35.
17. Ibid., 1282a15–17.
18. "There are some arts whose products are not judged of solely, or best, by the artists themselves, namely those arts whose products are recognized even by those who do not possess the art; for example, the knowledge of the house is not limited to the builder only; the user, or, in other words, the master, of the house will actually be a better judge than the builder, just as the pilot will judge better of a rudder than the carpenter, and the guest will judge better of a feast than the cook." Ibid., 1282a17–25.
19. "The weak and ill-constituted shall perish [*zu Grunde gehn*]: first principle of *our* philanthropy ['*unsrer*' *Menschenliebe*]" (A 2).

Nietzsche's Importance for Liberal Democracy

If, as partisans of liberal democracy, we reject Nietzschean agonism in favor of the Aristotelian variety, what are we to make of Nietzsche's legacy? Are we to return to the pre–Walter Kaufmann era, when Nietzsche was banished from all respectable academic discourse? Some have suggested this might be for the best; Alasdair MacIntyre, for example, considers the Nietzschean *Übermensch* better suited for a bestiary than for serious philosophical scrutiny.[20] Friends of democratic equality might be better advised, however, to attend seriously to his message. The point is not to "discredit" Nietzsche but rather to invite democracy's friends to face the depth of his challenge head-on with a reasoned and effective defense of democratic ideals.

Like other keen nineteenth-century European observers of modern Western civilization, Nietzsche feared that the post-Christian, liberal, and democratic emphasis on equality and rights was eroding the sociopolitical conditions for the flourishing of human greatness. He, no less than J. S. Mill and Alexis de Tocqueville, uncovered the penchant of "democratic man" for the "pitiable comforts" associated with a life dominated by the narrow pursuit and accumulation of material goods.[21] All of these thinkers warned of the "leveling" of modern culture as democratic majorities lose their traditional deference and, through prurient, suffocating attention and envy, chase those still capable of grand achievement to the margins.

In many ways a thinker such as Tocqueville is more palatable for the egalitarian-minded, largely because his worries are balanced by a genuine admiration for democratic virtues and the hope that countervailing factors (especially religious belief) would check its narrow materialism and sustain some element of transcendent striving in the democratic populace. Perhaps Nietzsche's continuing ability to disconcert lies in his uncompromising rejection of all Tocquevillian calls for countervailing measures. We must choose, he insists, be-

20. Alasdair Macintyre, *After Virtue: A Study in Moral Theory* (Notre Dame: University of Notre Dame Press, 1984), p. 22.

21. See Alexis de Tocqueville, *Democracy in America*, vol. 1, Part 1, chaps. 3, 5; vol. 2, part 2, chaps. 1, 14 and part 4, chaps. 6, 7.

tween democratic equality and cultural entropy on the one hand and inequality and heightened levels of human flourishing on the other.

Contemporary political philosophy has "responded" to this Nietzschean claim with either silence or obfuscation. Many egalitarian-minded philosophers and political theorists—I am thinking especially of partisans of liberalism in the Anglo-American academy—consider talk of such a choice both distasteful and dangerous. Hence the insistence that all such "perfectionist" talk be marginalized, that is, barred from political debate and relegated to a private sphere of aesthetic self-expression. In order to join in respectable political discussion, we are told, we must already be part of the "overlapping consensus" that accepts certain beliefs—for example, in the equal moral worth of all human beings, and in the importance of concern for the weak—as givens. To try to articulate and defend publicly the assumptions behind these beliefs would be divisive and futile, because (they claim) such efforts invariably introduce metaphysical and/or religious values that may not be to everyone's liking in a modern pluralistic society. To ensure maximum inclusiveness, they conclude, public debate must simply accept equality as a given and move on to matters of procedural justice and rights adjudication.[22] Citizens whose lives exemplify particular conceptions of human flourishing and who complain that the public commitment to equal treatment undermines these conceptions must not expect the political order to accommodate their concerns in any way.

One self-declared "postmodern liberal," Richard Rorty, echoes this view, claiming that the optimal arrangement for those who share the "moral intuitions" of Western liberal democracies involves a politics that excludes public debate over basic values and a private life given over to expressivist and perfectionist urges.[23] Although Rorty invokes Nietzsche as an inspiration for the "private," expressivist component of this convenient arrangement, he ignores Nietzsche's

22. Both John Rawls and Jürgen Habermas typify this attitude.

23. Richard Rorty, "The Priority of Democracy to Philosophy," in *Objectivity, Relativism, and Truth* (Cambridge: Cambridge University Press, 1991). See also his *Contingency, Irony, and Solidarity* (Cambridge: Cambridge University Press, 1989).

own profound skepticism about such easy compartmentalization. As we have seen in Chapter 3, Nietzsche casts doubt on the very possibility of a satisfying and admirable form of "private" expression in the face of an ambient political culture that discourages innovation. Much like modern feminists, he wants to unmask as spurious the conventional lines between the personal and the political, insisting that self-overcoming at the individual level can succeed only with a radical revitalization of culture.[24] (Unlike modern feminists, of course, he insists that such revitalization entails a forceful public reassertion of antiegalitarian and masculinist values.)

We would do well to question the wisdom of the popular decision to ignore Nietzsche's charges. By taking the belief in equality simply as a given in debates about justice, by encouraging inarticulacy over such paramount questions as "why equality?" and "equality of what?," political philosophy abandons rigorous argument in favor of pious wishes and good faith. It is sometimes asserted that liberal democracies have no need of a reasoned defense because antidemocratic visions of a Nietzschean sort are increasingly marginalized in the West. But even if we grant the accuracy of this sociological claim, the assumption that democratization eliminates the need for reasoned justification is tendentious. In a recent response to Rorty, Stephen Mulhall and Adam Swift put the matter cogently:

> It may well be that the ethical and political vocabularies of Nietzsche and Loyola are losing their grip on Western culture as a whole; but any individual who regards this development as a good thing and wants to speed it up, must do so by revealing the poverty, ugliness and irrelevance of these vocabularies *in argument*, not by declaring that development to have been completed

---

24. Daniel W. Conway rightly notes Nietzsche's unequivocal insistence that "'healthy' self-creation is never strictly private" because it always involves "a Dionysian element of excess or superfluity" that could not abide being artificially restricted to a private sphere. *Nietzsche and the Political* (London: Routledge, 1997), p. 129. Keith Ansell-Pearson makes a similar point in *An Introduction to Nietzsche as Political Thinker* (Cambridge: Cambridge University Press, 1994), pp. 170–172.

already. However devoutly to be wished this consummation may be, it will not be brought about by wishing alone.[25]

So long as political theorists and philosophers dismiss Nietzsche's radical aristocratism as uninteresting and trivial, his serious charges against democracy will remain unanswered.[26]

25. Stephen Mulhall and Adam Swift, *Liberals and Communitarians* (Oxford: Blackwell, 1992), p. 247 (emphasis added).

26. In arguing thus I draw upon Ruth Abbey and Fredrick Appel, "Domesticating Nietzsche: A Response to Mark Warren," *Political Theory* 27:1 (February 1999).

Index

Mara, Gerald, 8, 118
Mill, John Stuart, 8, 162–63, 167
Moderation, 45–47
Modernity, 1, 38, 101, 122–25,
    150–51, 163–64; and industrialism,
    130–32
Morality, 11; master, 6, 43; slave, 2, 6,
    37–52, 129
Mulhall, Stephen, 169–70

Napoleon, 38, 102, 120, 126
Nature, 19, 32–38
Nehamas, Alexander, 10, 13, 16, 28,
    57–58, 73, 119, 121, 127, 132–33,
    137, 144, 150
Nietzsche, Elisabeth Föster-, 9, 76,
    104, 114
Nietzsche, Friedrich: antipolitical
    interpretations of, 12–13,
    117–19; against nostalgia, 6,
    56–58; as pedagogue, 12, 59–61;
    postmodern readings of, 3–5, 9–10,
    161–63
Nihilism, 20, 53, 69, 130
Nussbaum, Martha, 55, 78, 80, 82,
    90–91, 119, 155–56

Owen, David, 4–5

Perspectivism, 5, 28
Pippin, Robert, 14, 76, 85
Pitkin, Hanna, 159
Pity, 91–93, 154–57
Plato, 14–15, 46, 56, 136; and the theory
    of Forms, 18, 137
Pletsch, Carl, 61, 112
Politics: agonistic, 4, 6–7, 140–41, 146,
    159–62; as art, 119–23, 148–49

Racism, 9, 111–12
Rangordnung. See Rank order
Rank order, 6, 23–30, 49, 65, 122, 126,
    128, 156, 158
Rawls, John, 168
Reason, 22, 25, 55–56

Renaut, Alain, 10, 12
Ressentiment, 40, 139; and revenge,
    43, 69
Romanticism, 19, 33–34
Rorty, Richard, 4, 10, 168–69
Rosen, Stanley, 12
Rousseau, Jean-Jacques, 100, 124; on
    pity, 156
Ruling, 32, 127–32, 140

Sadler, Ted, 13
Schacht, Richard, 12–13, 45, 57, 82,
    150–51, 157
Schmidt, Carl, 161
Schutte, Ophelia, 11
Science, 16, 22–23, 36; positivist notions
    of, 17–18, 20
Selfishness, 14, 64–65, 125
Sen, Amartya, 7
Seneca, 145
Socrates, 47, 55–56, 78–79, 110
Solitude, 13–14, 81–83; pernicious
    effects of, 84–85; and suffering,
    70–73
Solomon, Robert, 25, 126
Stern, J. P., 12
Stoicism, 13, 66–67, 78–80
Strong, Tracy B., 5, 10, 24, 57, 82, 106,
    111, 121, 132
Swift, Adam, 169–70

Taste, 26–27, 59, 144–47; ethical
    significance of, 27–28
Taylor, Charles, 3, 12, 35, 57
Thiele, Leslie Paul, 13, 17, 119
Thus Spoke Zarathustra: irony in, 14;
    Nietzsche's assessment of, 104; the
    "pale criminal" in, 152–53
Tocqueville, Alexis de, 135, 167
Transcendence: earthly, 19, 62
Truth, 11, 18–19, 22, 24–28, 30,
    36, 152

Vanity, 40–41
Villa, Dana R., 162

Virtue, 13, 21, 32, 34, 39–41, 101, 105,
149; of the herd, 64, 82, 92, 94, 129;
and nature, 32–35; woman's, 97–98.
See also Courage; Duty; Moderation

Walker, Brian, 149
Warren, Mark, 4, 82, 107, 128, 140
Weber, Max, 20, 160
White, Alan, 5, 144, 154

Williams, Bernard, 11, 32, 57, 80,
125, 136
Will to power, 27, 30–32, 35–36, 43,
49, 101, 119, 127, 154
Women, 93–102

Yack, Bernard, 5, 33, 37, 165
Young, Iris Marion, 164
Young, Julian, 120